CHICANAS/LATINAS
IN AMERICAN THEATRE

CHICANAS/LATINAS
IN AMERICAN THEATRE
A HISTORY OF PERFORMANCE

Elizabeth C. Ramírez

INDIANA UNIVERSITY PRESS
Bloomington and Indianapolis

This project has received funding from the NEH Summer Research Program Special Initiative (1994), the NEH Travel to Collections grants program, the University of Oregon Center for the Study of Women in Society (1997), the University of Oregon Summer Research Award (1995) and Junior Professorship Dean's Award from the College of Arts and Sciences, University of Oregon (1994, 1995, 1996), and the University of Arizona Quincentenary and College of Fine Arts Dean's Award (1992). A portion of Chapter 2 is forthcoming in Lilliana Mansor and Alicia Arrizón, eds., *Latinas on Stage: Criticism and Practice* (Berkeley, Calif.: Third Woman Press), and a portion of Chapter 5 appeared in "Chicanas/Latinas in Performance on the American Stage: Current Trends and Practices," *Journal of Dramatic Theory and Criticism* 13, no. 1 (Fall 1998): 133–141.

This book is a publication of

Indiana University Press
601 North Morton Street
Bloomington, IN 47404-3797 USA

http://www.indiana.edu/~iupress

Telephone orders 800-842-6796
Fax orders 812-855-7931
Orders by e-mail iuporder@indiana.edu

The paper used in this publication meets the minimum requirements of American National Standard for Information Sciences—Permanence of Paper for Printed Library Materials, ANSI Z39.48-1984.

Manufactured in the United States of America

Library of Congress Cataloging-in-Publication Data

Ramírez, Elizabeth C., date
    Chicanas/Latinas in American theatre : a history of performance / Elizabeth C. Ramírez.
        p.   cm.
    Includes bibliographical references and index.
    ISBN 0-253-33714-3 (cl) — ISBN 0-253-21371-1 (pa)
    1. Hispanic American theater—History—20th century. 2. Women in the theater—United States. 3. Hispanic American drama (Spanish) 4. American drama—Hispanic American authors.   I. Title.

PN2270.H57 R36 2000
792'.082'0973—dc21
                                                                                00-029578

1 2 3 4 5   05 04 03 02 01 00

For my parents,

MARGARITA CANTÚ
and
PEDRO FUENTES RAMÍREZ,

who have valued performance for as long as I can remember;

for MY FAMILY,

and especially mi ángel de la guardia, my older sister,

THERESA RAMÍREZ CASIANO,

who along with my mother read page after page of my manuscript at a time when my myasthenia gravis prevented me from lifting my eyelids or holding up my arms.

CONTENTS

ACKNOWLEDGMENTS

In memory of Ruben Sierra, to whom I am indebted for leading me to the U.C.L.A. recruiter when he knew that I wished to pursue graduate studies in performance, and for his reviews of my manuscript. I have been privileged to work with historians who have generously encouraged me to expand the scope of historical inquiry in all of my work to include the Chicana/Chicano experience.

At U.C.L.A., Juan Gómez-Quiñones was among the first Chicano historians to urge me to pursue the special contributions of Chicanas and Chicanos. Ricardo Romo served early on as an important role model when he was working so hard to complete his doctoral studies in history at a time when the exclusion of Chicanas and Chicanos in that field was the norm. Jorge Huerta planted an important seed in me that led to my study of "Necessary Theatre" of Chicanas/Chicanos in performance. From the first moment I spoke with him in a telephone interview when I was seeking a thesis topic, he spent countless hours sharing his expertise with me as he encouraged my growing interest in the history of Chicanas/Chicanos in theatre history and world drama. He shared ideas about curriculum and how to get started when I founded and directed the Chicano Theatre Program at California State University, Sacramento, a program which remains ongoing. He introduced me to TENAZ and CLETA when I asked to serve as the historian for Chicana/Chicano teatros. Both Jorge and his wife, Ginger, sustained me through memorable moments in my life, and I will always be indebted to them for both their personal and professional support, which remains constant. Since the 1970s, Juan, Ricardo, and Jorge have influenced and inspired me to continue my pursuits in historical studies, scholarly research, and teaching in higher education as well as administration.

Luis Valdez has been instrumental in providing me with access to his original playtexts, materials, and special practical experience in training and teaching Chicana/Chicano theatre. Luis and his wife, Lupe, have always been profoundly generous about sharing their work and in finding a way to help me educate others about the Chicana/Chicano experience. I have witnessed firsthand the wide-ranging impact that Luis has had in the annals of theatrical history, and I remain eternally grateful for his willingness to share his vast knowledge, his expertise, and the true genius of his art with me and others.

It was also through Luis Valdez and El Teatro Campesino that Oscar G. Brockett found a special place for me and my work, because of his keen interest in Chicana/Chicano theatre. Among all of those historians to whom I am indebted, none has been more significant than Oscar Brockett. Brock has been a mentor, a colleague, and a friend who has challenged me far beyond any expectations I may have had for my goals in theatre and higher education. In his view, if he could write an entire history of theatre, unquestionably I could write one on Latinas and Latinos in the United States, and his attention to scholarship on the vast multicultural richness that constitutes theatrical history led me down the path of the subject of my research and professional work in dramaturgy with a focus on new plays by playwrights of color.

Additionally, since my days as a doctoral student at The University of Texas at Austin, Jack Brokaw has believed that I could further the research he began in professional Spanish-language theatre, and he generously extended a helping hand to aid me in pursuing that field to its fullest extent. I am thankful for his guidance; along with David Nancarrow, Jack always envisioned that I would produce the work as well.

During my time at the University of Arizona, my colleagues Dianne Winslow, Harold Dixon, and Richard Hanson gave me memorable opportunities for collaboration, which served to inform much of my dramaturgical work. Early portions of my research resulted from the very generous support I received from the University of Arizona.

At the University of Oregon, my tenure as Director of Ethnic Studies allowed me to focus on the significant history that underrepresented groups have to offer in higher education. I owe a debt of gratitude to Dean Risa Palm and Dean Joe Stone for their willingness to allow me to broaden the curriculum to include performance in a wide range of ethnic studies, as well as for providing me with various funding resources to allow me to do further research in the field and to attend meetings and conferences where my work could be heard. The Ethnic Studies faculty at the University of Oregon, including Linda Kintz, Forest Pyle, Cheyney Ryan, Sandy Morgan, Garrett Hongo, and Roland Greene, gave me continuing support in my endeavors to build a program and broaden the curriculum. I will always have special memories of the work we shared, with special regard for the many students in the Program that I had the opportunity to teach and mentor, and the guiding light that Quintard Taylor provided for me. President Dave Frohnmayer and Lorraine Davis always maintained an open line of communication that made my work more effective, and the Theatre Arts Department faculty gave me the opportunity to experiment with new courses in dramaturgy and multicultural theatre and performance venues that could inform my research. Robert Barton and Grant McKernie generously offered me their many years of experience in teaching and approaches to performance that I found valuable.

There are special women of color who have been enormously helpful to me, including Milcha Sanchez-Scott, Roberta Uno, Diane Rodríguez, Hortensia and Elvira Colorado, and Tina Cantú Navarro. These women are among the mujeres of the twenty-first century who continue to make important contributions in uncharted courses in performance. I owe a special debt of gratitude to Kathy Perkins, who continues to be so prolific that she provides me with a necessary challenge to continue my work and keep brown faces in the forefront in print.

At St. Philip's College, the oldest historically Black- and Hispanic-serving institution in the United States, I have been assisted by Rita Castro, Pat Williams, Mark Barnes, and Patrick Evans in the Learning Resources Center. Many students, faculty, and staff have been supportive of my work and keen to hear the results at various stages. I am indebted to Mr. and Mrs. Marion and Inez Elizabeth Stringer and their family for the time they have taken to bring me into the community they share with St. Philip's. Dr. Charles Taylor, Dr. Homer M. Hayes, our new president Dr. Angie S. Runhels, Dr. Lanier Byrd, Vice President for Academic Affairs, and Dr. Sandra Mayo, Dean of Arts and Sciences, have shown high regard for my scholarly pursuits at a time when the arts are more often ignored than supported in higher education, and I am indebted to them for their encouragement to continue my work. In Dr. Mayo I have found the ideal role model of a woman of color in theatre who faces every challenge with a smile and accomplishes her goals in a positive and worthwhile manner, serving students, the College, and the community.

Dr. Jackson and the Neurology Department at The University of Texas Health Science Center and the Muscular Dystrophy Association have given me the remarkable gift of allowing me to believe that I can accomplish impossible feats as a patient with myasthenia gravis, and helped see me through a near-fatal crisis during the time that this book was being shaped. I am proud to say that I am one of "Jerry's Kids."

My sister Patricia Ramírez-Long and her son, Guillermo, and my brother Mario and his wife, Yolanda, and daughters, Sonya and Marisa, have borne the times of toil and stress I have undergone in working on this book. Both my brothers, Pedro and Mario, have given me years and years of assistance in photography, and I am pleased to be able to include some of their work here. Most especially, I wish to thank my older sister, Theresa, and my mother for the countless hours they spent at my hospital bedside reading aloud to me so that I could continue my work, as well as the patience of my father in finding a way to see me through the hardship. I will always be especially appreciative of the ideal guidance and nurturing that I have received from Theresa; she and her husband, Dr. Victor L. Casiano, saw me through the difficulties of my disability, and they have encouraged me to share some very special time with their daughters. Catherine and Elizabeth Ramírez Casiano have given me countless hours of research assistance for many, many years. Catherine and Elizabeth served as interns in the Ethnic Studies Program at the University of Oregon during the time I chaired the Program, and both assisted me in research during the time I was a Fellow at the American Repertory Theatre and while I was teaching at Harvard University when my research was in its early stages.

I am indebted to Joan Catapano, Assistant Director and Senior Sponsoring Editor at Indiana University Press, for her efforts to strengthen Chicana/Chicano Studies through a growing body of work in performance. I also gratefully acknowledge the generous help and assistance of Jane Lyle, Managing Editor, and copy editor Kate Babbitt, whose expertise in women's studies, along with a keen eye and helpful suggestions, was invaluable.

During many years of working with the Special Collections at the Benson Library at The University of Texas, Austin, Dr. Laura Gutiérrez-Witt has been extraordinarily helpful, and I express my deep appreciation to her and her staff. One of my most cherished informants, Sra. María Luisa Villalongín de Santos, offered inspiration and encouragement, insight and information that I will always treasure, and I remain indebted to her and her son, Dr. Frank Santos, Jr., D.D.S.

Note regarding the use of accents in Spanish terms: Accents have been omitted when these markings have not been used by authors in print, and in quotations and other printed matter in which accents were not used.

INTRODUCTION
AN OVERVIEW OF CHICANA/CHICANO/LATINA/
LATINO DRAMA ON THE AMERICAN STAGE

Latinas/Latinos are the fastest-growing traditionally underrepresented population group in the United States today. The term Latina/Latino applies to those descendants of Latin American parents born and/or living in the United States. In earlier decades (primarily during the Nixon administration) there was a concerted effort to combine all Spanish-speaking groups in the United States into one, designating the term "Hispanic" for this massive population. Although it is perhaps the most rejected term by the groups studied here, "Hispanic" does serve to represent the more conservative, traditional segment of the Spanish-speaking population of the early decades of this century. On the whole, despite continual discussion and debate, "Latino" remains the most widely used term to designate the large population of women and men in the United States descended from Spanish-speaking groups. The Spanish language is a common link among those of this cultural background, yet some speak it fluently or have learned it in school while others have no familiarity with it at all. Although numerous distinct ethnic groups exist under this ancestry, the largest of these are comprised of Chicanas/Chicanos (or Mexican Americans), Puerto Ricans, and Cuban Americans.[1]

Chicanas/Chicanos constitute the largest particular ethnic group in the Southwest. The presence of Mexicans in the Southwest from the turn of the century through the 1920s serves as the basis of Chicana/Chicano communities that continue to this day. The very long history and deep roots of these communities in the United States have produced a particular set of cultural norms. Although some important sociological and political histories of this group have emerged in recent years and have brought about a better understanding of the contributions Chicanas/Chicanos have made to American and world history, many of this group's societal and cultural contributions still remain sadly neglected. In theatrical history, scholars have only begun to investigate these contributions and to make information available in English. Clearly, further research is needed in order to comprehend the vast richness of this particular tradition (see Romo 1977; Montejano 1987; Takaki 1993).

SOCIAL, HISTORICAL, IDEOLOGICAL, AND CULTURAL PERSPECTIVES ON CHICANA/LATINA DRAMA AND THEATRE

Chicanas have played a significant role in the history of their people. However, the place of Chicanas/Latinas is still being defined. The crucial roles women played in Chicana/Latina history must be traced, beginning in the pre-conquest period (before 1519) through the conquest period (1519 to the fall of México-Tenochtitlán in 1521), the post-colonial period (México gained independence from Spain in 1821), and into the modern era. Various studies have pointed out that traditional histories of the U.S. West have largely ignored women, and only in the past decade or so has a new generation of historians begun to "create a multicultural history of women in the West," making women a significant part of that history (Schlissel, Ruíz, and Monk 1988, 2).

It is necessary to situate Chicanas historically. As Schlissel, Ruíz, and Monk point out, "The cultural and historical shaping of gender, the political and legal construction of sexuality and the family, the meaning of language and landscape, the evolution of value systems and of family support systems and interactive cultural contacts" continue to provide directions for scholarship (342). The significance of Chicanas in American history remains neglected in many chronicles about important socio-political events in relations between Mexico and America. While Chicana/Chicano and Latina/Latino history is certainly vast, it is time for us to think about how we can broaden the scope of historical inquiry to enable us to include rather than exclude these women. This detailed study of performative activity provides an element of women's history and expands the scope of inquiry.

Chicanas/Latinas have helped to create a rich theatrical heritage, and an investigation of distinct contributions by such women can provide us with important discoveries about the vital role they have played in American history. Through an examination of extant theatrical playtexts, performance chronicles, and other available documentation of pertinent information, this study attempts to understand the participation of Chicanas/Latinas in the shaping of an important history, one which most notably surfaces during critical moments of political crisis to help create a cultural history of that people.

The pre-conquest period reveals only scant information about women serving critical roles. In Mesoamerica, now known to us as Central America, that narrow strip of land connecting the North American and South American continents, Mayan Indians developed the western hemisphere's first great civilization in this southern tip of North America. In the southern region of México, the Toltecs also developed a civilization, and in about A.D. 600 both the Maya and Toltec tribes joined forces in México to build another great civilization which subsequently spread to Central America and was ultimately destroyed by the Spaniards during their invasion in the 1500s.

Chicanitas in local Chicana/Chicano barrio park (young girls in the neighborhood) for Cinco de Mayo celebration, Sacramento, California, 1975.
Photo by Mario C. Ramírez.

While traces of a sort of matriarchal societal formation in Mesoamerica still
exist, the available information fails to illuminate any formal empowerment of
women within this structure. By the time of the colonial period, patriarchal
dominance was clearly evident. The changing population was now comprised
of Indian, Spanish, or mixed Indian and Spanish ancestry. Through the period
of conquest, women were restricted to recognizable domestic parameters and
were excluded from battle and positions of supremacy. The conquest brought
further subjugation to both Indian women and men when European males
assumed positions of power. European women were treated as commodities,
either as adornments for men or as assets for trade. Fortunately, historians are
beginning to investigate whether any women in this period of crisis and change,
either Indian or European, did, in fact, have an impact politically or socially.
Yet chronicles do not yet provide the kind of evidence which surfaces in subsequent periods of Mexican and Chicana/Chicano history to be able to corroborate the positioning of women (Gómez-Quiñones, "Questions within Wom-
en's Historiography," 88; Zoraida Vasquez, 375–398).

The history that has been written to date relegates women to substatus
roles that stemmed largely from the influence of the Church in the post-con-
quest era. Catholic ideology restricted women's roles to the extent that adherence to conventional behavior obliterated women's liberties rather than allowing their expression. Their position in society was determined by their moral

conduct and demeanor. The cultural values placed on women during the colonial period shaped them for what have become traditional roles, namely childbearing and performing household duties. Early marriage for both Indian and European women, which was customary during this period, thus relegated them almost exclusively to home life.

Perhaps the most serious hindrance for women was the lack of education, but the most obvious exclusion of women was in the arena of political activity. Juan Gómez-Quiñones notes that "from the time of Mesoamerican civilization to the settlements in the Southwest, Mexican women constituted an essential part of society, yet they remained unrecognized and were discriminated against because of their gender, their class if laborers, and ethnicity if Indian, mestiza or mulatta" (Gómez-Quiñones, "Questions within Women's Historiography," 89). Situating women in this way significantly deterred their ability to have a public presence in this period.

Through the seventeenth and eighteenth centuries, women became more prominent both politically and economically, however, and isolated instances of some important women can now be chronicled (Castañeda García 1990, 101–112; Gómez-Quiñones 1982, 8; Gómez-Quiñones, "Questions within Women's Historiography," 89; Orozco 1993, 680–681; Pablos 1999, xiii–144). In performance history, Sor Juana Inés de la Cruz (1651–1691) is important as the first known woman playwright in the New World. Her plays were performed and published. In *Women Singing in the Snow,* Tey Diana Rebolledo notes this seventeenth-century nun's desire to learn and her inclusion in the artistic and intellectual community of México. Although she made important contributions to Mexican theatre history, this playwright will not be discussed here since she has been studied at some length elsewhere and because performative traditions more directly associated with those occurring in American history had already begun to take shape and require our attention (see M. Gonzáles 1990, 237–253; Rebolledo 1995, 58–62; Case 1988, 41–42; Franco 1989, xv, 23–54). In the nineteenth century women had an opportunity to participate in political life during México's revolt for independence against Spain. Their participation, which is celebrated in the United States today on September 16th as the highpoint of Hispanic Heritage Month, began with the *Grito de Dolores* (the cry of Dolores): "¡Viva la Independencia! ¡Viva América! ¡Muera el mal gobierno!" and "¡Viva Nuestra Madre Santísima de Guadalupe!" (Long live independence! Long live America! Down with bad government! and Long live our Holy Mother of Guadalupe [the Virgen de Guadalupe]!). These cries were issued by Father Miguel Hidalgo y Costilla in the town of Dolores on September 16, 1810, which began a revolt that lasted through 1821, when Spain was finally forced to concede México's independence. Women were also involved to some extent in México's war with the United States (1845–1848) and battle against France (1862–1867), services to their country that they performed with great courage (Acuña 1988, 31–33; Castañeda 1990,

213–236; Chipman and Joseph 1999, 250–277; Dysart 1976, 366; Franco 1989, 79–101; Gómez-Quiñones, "Questions within Women's Historiography," 90; M. González 1990, 239–253; *La Independencia de México* 24, 38, 40–41; Orozco 1993, 680–681; Salas 1990, xi–35. See also Rebolledo 1993 and 1995).

But perhaps their most prominent involvement centers on their increasing participation across the northern provinces and into the United States (see Alatorre 1961; Soto 1990; Cantú 1996, 8–10; Funes and Tuñon 1990, 336–357; Orozco 1993, 680–682; R. Ruíz 1980, 243; Salas 1990, 36–66). By the time of the Mexican Revolution, which began in 1910, Mexican women/ Chicanas were not only succeeding in maintaining a political identity for themselves, but they were making their indelible mark in political advancement as well (Acuña 1988, 169–171; *Así fue la Revolución Mexicana* 898; Orozco 1993, 680–681; Pérez 1990, 459–482; Soto, "The Women's Movement," 483–491; Zoraida Vasquez 1990, 377–398). The ways in which these women have functioned as essential participants in United States history has increasingly drawn the attention of scholars (see DuBois and Ruíz 1990; Alarcón, et al. 1993; Córdova, et al. 1996; Del Castillo 1990; Franco 1990, xvii, 79–152; Orozco 1993). We are just beginning to understand the vital role of Mexican women/Chicanas in this presence. As Barbara A. Driscoll has pointed out: "The historical and cultural legacy of Chicanas, or Mexican women living in the United States, like that of all Americans of Mexican descent, transcends American society and its geopolitical boundary with Mexico" (Driscoll 1986, 136–137; Veyna 1986, 120–133). To this group we must also add the even broader national and international Latina links (Castañeda 1993, 93; Villegas 1994, 306–320). While many aspects of the historical contributions of women may be studied, the examination here focuses on their participation in theatrical performance, whereby we can discover the critical contributions they made in terms of cultural, social, and political arenas.

PATTERNS AND TRENDS

We know that during the nineteenth century, and even earlier, the Spanish-language professional acting companies that arrived in the United States from México formed a lasting tradition. This theatrical heritage stemmed from a long history of both amateur and professional Spanish-language activity that originated in Spain (see Shergold 1967). Few scholars have noted that the golden age of Spanish drama, the highly productive years between 1580 and 1680 when Spanish theatre flourished, coincides with the entry of Spain into the New World. When the conquistadores arrived in New Spain they also brought their interest in dramatic literature. More significantly, the conquistadores also gave the first dramatic performances on American soil.

Although chronicled in the first volume of G. C. D. Odell's *Annals of the*

New York Stage, Spain's unique contribution to American theatre and its impact on the New World is rarely mentioned by theatre historians. Scholars are just beginning to investigate the rich performance heritage of indigenous Americans since before the conquest, from the Mayan and Aztec to the Chicana/Chicano oral traditions. Clearly, this unique theatrical heritage has made a major mark in theatre history, but we must continue to broaden the scope of this historical inquiry.

My research for a history of Mexican American professional theatre in Texas revealed a distinct tradition of dramatic acting companies that lasted a long time in that state—from 1875 to 1935. Further research on this particular activity now reveals significant contributions by women to this tradition that have yet to be chronicled in English. During the Mexican Revolution, a period in which significant structural, demographic, and behavioral changes in U.S. society occurred, the role of women in the Spanish-speaking theatre took on new and significant proportions (see Ramírez 1990, 1993). Migration of rural Mexicans to urban centers in the United States brought changes in lifestyles and individual behavior that were "profound," as Romo points out, influencing "traditional customs, formal organization, sex roles and marriage, role of women in the labor force, and attitudes toward urban life" (Romo 1997, 196; Acuña 1988, 151, 161, 168–170, 221–226; Montejano 1987).

Eventually, the Great Depression struck the thriving theatrical activity of professional dramatic companies in the United States. Mexican American resident stock companies were among the first casualties. Spanish-language vaudeville, motion pictures imported from México, and local Spanish-language radio replaced theatrical entertainment. Amateur productions, however, both religious and secular, continued the tradition of theatrical fare in Spanish and by Latinas/Latinos and helped preserve the values of Mexican Americans. The decline in stock-company activity lasted through the late 1930s and the period of World War II.

The historical antecedents of Latinas/Latinos in the United States provided the roots of theatrical expression, but this heritage had remained dormant for several years before Luis Valdez reawakened it on the contemporary stage in the 1960s. The success of Luis Valdez and El Teatro Campesino gave rise to a whole generation of Chicana/Chicano theatre groups. Several significant groups emerged, yet in contrast to its appeal to a broad spectrum of the community during the early years of the century, Latina/Latino theatrical activity of this period addressed a small portion of the Spanish-speaking population. The groups were largely organized around amateur performers, as was El Teatro Campesino in its early stages. Jorge Huerta points out that "until the early 1980s Chicano theatre in this country could only be found in the Chicano communities that had spawned their own *teatros,* playwrights, directors, and actors" (Huerta 1994, 37). Plays about the Chicana/Chicano experience were not produced by mainstream theatre companies, "either out of apathy, or, perhaps, because they assumed that much of that theatre was being expressed in Spanish," adds Huerta (38).

Huerta credits two critical and financial successes for mainstream interest in Chicana/Chicano/Latina/Latino writing. The New York Public Theatre's production of Miguel Piñero's *Short Eyes* in 1974 and the Center Theatre Group's co-production of Luis Valdez's *Zoot Suit* in Los Angeles in 1978 and subsequent production on Broadway in 1979 brought greater attention to this new voice, thus allowing a movement from alternative to mainstream theatre. Works by Chicanas/Latinas began in the late 1970s and emerged as a distinctive voice through the 1980s. Women soon became prominent participants in the *teatro* movement, shaping their roles in all aspects of production. Chicanas/Latinas began to explore serious issues about gender and sexuality within their own community. Making their mark as playwrights, directors, actors, producers, or behind the scenes, as well as influencing and nurturing audiences, women in performance offer a long-standing history worth examining. Contemporary Latina/Latino theatre now represents a wide range of backgrounds, including Chicana/Chicano, Cuban, Puerto Rican, and twenty other Latina/Latino backgrounds, and the women in this history have been a significant force.

CHICANAS/LATINAS
IN AMERICAN THEATRE

1

HOMELAND/SIN FRONTERAS TO BORDERLANDS
The Theatre

PRE-COLUMBIAN BEGINNINGS

The pre-Columbian Mexican performance tradition is filled with public performances of religious origin, yet examining performative activity allows us to extend that list to include a wide variety of events. Formal wedding feasts, elaborate dinners, tournaments, and other activities make this a rich period in indigenous performance.

Studies of theatrical presentations of indigenous peoples center largely around religious rituals in which performers are either exclusively male or those in which male performers dominate in the performance. Miguel León-Portilla's *Pre-Columbian Literatures of Mexico* provides important resources and textual examples of celebrations but only tantalizing references to the role of women in these events. Generally the roles for women were those of young girls, not roles drawn from the extensive pantheon of gods. Women might appear in these dramatic events when their actions support the manifestation of great men or gods, such as in the case of women dying in childbirth, "because they bore a man in combat, a prisoner in the womb" (León-Portilla 1969, 33), or when relating the legends of the greatest gods.

The myth of Quetzalcóatl in the Náhuatl language relates that during the age of the Fifth Sun, which began in Teotihuacán, the gods decided to establish a new race of humans on earth. The restoration of man was entrusted to this god:

> He gathered up the precious bones.
> The bones of the man were together on one side
> and the bones of the woman together on the other side
> and Quetzalcóatl took them
> and made a bundle. . . .
> The precious bones were scattered . . .
> Quetzalcóatl bled his male organ on them. (37, 39)

Besides being responsible for the continuation of a great race, this god is also lauded for innumerable feats and achievements, including "wisdom of the su-

preme divinity, restorer of men and discoverer of maize" as well as serving as a
"priest, the inventor of the arts, and the great spiritual leader of the Toltecs"
(40). Yet in this account the roles of women hardly signify.

The birth and early deeds of Huitzilopóchtli, the legendary tribal god and
young warrior, are also chronicled. The poem that describes his miraculous
conception when a ball of fine feathers entered the womb of his mother, the
goddess Coatlicue, emphasizes the role of the powerful son who must rescue
his mother. Even the sister, Coyolxauhqui, a single female voice among 400
male siblings, demands Coatlicue's death:

> She was mother of the four hundred gods of the south
> . . . one day,
> when Coatlicue was sweeping,
> there fell on her some plumage,
> a ball of fine feathers.
> Immediately Coatlicue picked them up
> and put them in her bosom.
> When she finished sweeping,
> she looked for the feathers
> she had put in her bosom,
> but she found nothing there.
> At that moment Coatlicue was with child. . . .
>
> The four hundred gods of the south,
> seeing their mother was with child,
> were very annoyed. . . .
>
> And their sister Coyolxauhqui
> said to them:
> "My brothers, she has dishonored us,
> we must kill our mother. . . ."
>
> But her son Huitzilopóchtli, in her womb,
> comforted her . . . he destroyed them. . . .
>
> he never had any father. (42–48)

Coatlicue not only stands accused of dishonoring an already dysfunctional family in a household completely out of her control, but she is also portrayed as
morally beneath contempt in bearing a son without a father. Further, because
she is placed in a domestic setting, one of the most important female goddesses
in Aztec mythology is thus relegated to a shallow figure incapable of rising
above the image of a naive and senseless woman requiring comfort and protection.

Other subjects in which women were engaged in these texts of pre-Hispan-
ic Náhuatl theatre include the "Song of the Harlots" in which, as León-Portilla
tells us, "the characters are mostly women" (112). There are two "gladdeners,"

or women of pleasure. The mother of one of these women appears along with two "more or less reformed" gladdeners and a young man. Although the text is described as "light poetry," León-Portilla points out that despite surviving as fragments, we can glimpse the "richness and uniqueness of native American drama" through these original forms of expression. Through these few remaining fragments, the "truly dramatic dialogue in these texts" reveals fascinating qualities of sadness, remorse, and mixed feelings about continuing a dissolute life, as well as motherly concerns and a wide range of suffering, complications in love, and a mother's peaceful happiness.

Many texts of a historical nature also include women. In one legend of Quetzalcóatl, cultural hero of the period, we discover his birth by magic very much along the lines of an immaculate conception by his mother Chimalman:

> It is said that his mother
> was called Chimalman.
> And thus it is told
> how Quetzalcóatl was placed
> in the womb of his mother:
> she swallowed a precious stone. . . .

When Quetzalcóatl then began his work as ruler and priest of the Toltecs, the myth told of the great priest's discovery of the supreme mystery of divinity, whereby he invoked both

> Someone who was deified,
> in the innermost of heaven:
> She of the starry skirt.
> He who makes things shine;
> Lady of our flesh, Lord of our flesh;
> She who supports the earth,
> He who covers it with cotton. . . .

indicating that the duality inherent in the nature of his existence was comprised of both male and female counterparts.

León-Portilla notes that many examples of Náhuatl didactic prose—such as royal proclamations and discourses on solemn occasions like birth, marriage, and death and the advice of parents to their children—are found in various collections of colloquy by elders (135). In general, young virgins are captives who are often counseled by their fathers or elder wise men and must be taken care of and comforted. In one myth the young girl is a Mexican captive princess (130–131).

Numerous accounts of entire crowds or times when the community was wholly celebratory at certain events indicate that women were participants in at least some presentations. Fray Diego de Durán writes in his chronicles about the Náhuatl schools for dance and relates instances of some dances where some women take part also. Men and women pretend to be drunk, carrying cups and pitchers in their hands, as if they were drinking; all this pretending gives great pleasure and relaxation to the people of the city; they are delighted by a thousand different kinds of games invented by those in the schools for dances and by farces and interludes and songs of much mirth. (107)

However, performers were presumably males who took on the role of women when such roles were called for, as in the case of the only extant and still performed Maya-Quiche dance-drama, *Rabinal Achí* (*The Warrior of Rabinal;* the entire text of *Rabinal Achí,* translated by Richard E. Leinaweaver, is in *Latin American Review* 1 [Spring 1969], 3–53). *Rabinal Achí* tells of the capture, investigation, and ultimate sacrifice of the Warrior of Quiche, an enemy of the people of Rabinal, in the Guatemala region. Through dialogue between two central characters and some interjected dialogue from other characters, a captive warrior is confronted with his transgressions against his captors and ultimately joins in communion with the cosmos through his death. The princess, "mother of the small green birds," has no speaking part (although she dances with the prisoner). Other non-speaking characters include a number of men and women slaves, eagle and tiger knights, and people of the village. Besides appearing as slaves, women probably also appeared as members of the village populace. Obviously, the princess is a commodity in order to ensure the prosperity and rejuvenation of the village through this connection with the townspeople and their universe. The use of the princess fulfills one of many honors and privileges expected for someone of the captive warrior's rank as a lord, and dancing with the young girl is the result of custom. The princess is expected to take part in the ritual accompanying the sacrificial death of the captive warrior, and she serves the important role of helping to ensure continued security and longevity for the entire village by her participation.

After the conquest, the earlier plays vanished and in their place religious plays began to appear. The new Christian faith brought a new form of drama with different plots and themes. Christmas performances and allegorical plays featuring religious themes, or *pastorelas,* and dramatizations of the Spanish conquest became the new fare. Miguel León-Portilla tells us that at times Spanish plays were translated and adapted to indigenous languages, such as in the case of *El gran teatro del mundo* (*The Great Theatre of the World,* c. 1645), Calderón de la Barca's allegorical poem which was translated into Náhuatl (León-Portilla 1969, 103).

PASTORELAS AND FOLK AND POPULAR THEATRE IN THE SOUTHWEST

Perhaps the longest and most widely known tradition of Spanish-language performance is the *pastorela,* the folk drama of the Southwest. It has been traced back to the sixteenth century; the first recorded mention of a dramatic presentation after the conquest indicates that a version of the Christmas play, *Los pastores* (*The Shepherds*), was performed in Spanish for the soldiers in 1526 (Jones 1966, 460). It is difficult to trace an exact version, but this play is quite similar to *The Second Shepherds' Play* found in the English medieval repertory. In his extensive study, *Los Pastores: History and Performance in the Mexican Shepherd's Play of South Texas,* Richard R. Flores tells us that the *pastorela* underwent several significant changes during the Mexican colonial period.

Essentially, the drama revolves around a group of shepherds who are visited by the Archangel Michael, who announces the birth of the Messiah. The shepherds decide to travel to Bethlehem to visit the new king. Along their journey, they encounter a hermit who also decides to go along. Upon hearing the news, a band of devils also follows, with the intention of thwarting their trip. The archangel comes to their aid, and the culmination is a visit to the manger with Mary and Joseph and the Christ child.

The *pastorela* stems from at least two forms of religious drama developed in Spain, the *auto sacramentales* and *coloquios*. Typical comic figures of the Devil and Vice appear, as well as numerous stock characters such as shepherds. Flores points out that "a striking characteristic of the Spanish religious dramas that appeared at the end of the fifteenth century was their use of popular and festive humor." Despite their religious origins, "these autos and coloquios now focused on the activities and pranks of the shepherds, and if religious elements were maintained, they were overshadowed by the ludic antics of these characters" (Flores 1995, 40).

In the only two female roles, we have contrasting figures: the pure and almost silent Mary, and Gila, the female shepherd. Gila primarily functions as a cook, preparing dinner while the hermit prays, and complaining throughout. She is positioned as temptress to the men as someone they may gain in marriage, to the relief of her lazy father, who wishes to be rid of all responsibilities. More harmfully, she functions as a threat to the hermit's virginity, and when in some performances she is asked by her father to dance for the others, this centering adds to the subjugated female role the qualities of menace, temptation, and harmful spectacle to the larger group of men surrounding her.

Mary Austin records an old woman of ninety in Monterrey, México, who remembered playing the part of Gila when she was twelve years old in the house of the Spanish governor of California. In the English version, this character typifies a dominant, scolding, and dishonest figure who tempts her husband to steal a sheep. However, the young age of this actor reminds us that performers were generally involved in a family event or enterprise, and that parental and familial presence and guidance were common. Austin notes that the parts were handed down in families just as were the stage properties and the stage business (Austin 1933, 602).

In 1533 a Náhuatl version of *El juicio final* (*The Last Judgment*) was produced by the friars. This Spanish *auto sacramental* (religious play associated with the Feast of Corpus Christi, a festival after Easter in honor of the Real Presence of Christ in the Blessed Sacrament and a holy day of obligation in countries other than the United States) draws from both medieval mystery and morality play forms, with humans, allegorical figures, and religious figures. The didactic drama tells the story of the downfall of a prostitute, Lucía, who chooses a wayward life instead of the Church, which leads to her eternal damnation in Hell. As was typical on the medieval Spanish stage, this play uses spectacle for heightened effect. The climactic scene of this play shows Lucía's torture amidst flames and serpents as she laments her sinful past. Pyrotechnics and frightful devils effectively served to terrorize the natives to the point of conversion to Christianity, although Jorge Huerta makes an interesting point that "the use of serpents as symbols of punishment and death was probably somewhat confusing to the Mexica [Aztecs]" since Aztec ideology viewed the serpent as life and Quetzalcóatl, their savior, was represented by the "Feathered Serpent" (Huerta 1982, 190). With the Church represented as mother, and with devils in the garb of Aztec priests, the didactic intention of the play to disengage believers from indigenous ideology served the Spanish missionaries well (Corbató 1949; Ravicz 1970, 141–157; Huerta 1982, 190).

In 1539 the Spaniards presented *El sacrificio de Isaac* (*The Sacrifice of Isaac*), translated into Náhuatl for the Tlaxcalan celebration.[1] In this early colonial religious drama God has instructed Abraham, a noble figure and great warrior-type, to kill his dutiful young son. The role of Sarah, the mother, shows a figure fretting over her aged husband if he should die, leaving no one to properly instruct their young son, Isaac:

> I weep because of my precious son, Isaac, the splendor and light of my soul—he who is truly my first-born and of my own blood and complexion. What if I gave him my milk, what if I nurtured him with my own milk? Now we see by his countenance that he is already grown. Who will be able to say to us that perhaps we have merit because of our son if perhaps he will be of some service to Him [God]. . . .
>
> Perhaps he will not follow His [God's] law, as He has ordained us His creatures to do! If you should die tomorrow or soon afterwards, who will there be to teach him? Who will make him see the honorable life which has carried others to heaven? (Here she weeps.) . . . My soul weeps because my milk, my own milk, will be lost in vain. Truly it would have been better had I never conceived, never given birth! (Ravicz 1970, 83–98)

Although only a few scant fragments of text are designated for her, we witness her total lack of self-respect and her complete inability to provide spiritual, moral, and ethical guidance as she points out her husband's strengths over her own weaknesses. Sarah views herself as so completely incapable of nurturing and sustaining her son that it would have been better not to have borne him at all.

In *The Merchant,* a Náhuatl manuscript dated from the sixteenth century, we have an essentially non-liturgical and secular playtext. It has more women's parts than most plays of this time period. We witness one woman who suffers at the hands of the rich merchant as she addresses the town's mayor:

> My lord, I have come here to tell you that six months ago my husband died. He had left money in the care of the merchant for the help of his soul, as well as the other wealth and property which he willed to me and my children. Now he [the merchant] does not admit having my house and my cultivated fields. He has taken possession of them and is keeping them for himself. For this reason I humbly bow before you; I beg you to order him to present himself before you to give an accounting of his trust. I have nothing with which to bring up my children,—these poor servants of yours present here. For the sake of our Savior and his beloved Mother, I earnestly beseech you to do this for me! (99–118)

Despite her powerful plea, a will is produced and she is proved false. But the merchant eventually suffers a terrible demise, essentially proving that the rich merchant is still held accountable for his wrongdoings. Left with children to care for and a household to run, this woman's invocation of the Savior and his Mother seems to guarantee that she will eventually be protected. She has little to lose in attempting to make a case for herself against two powerful men in her society, but only her religious faith can intervene in order to bring justice in the end. Thus, even secular playtexts hinted strongly at the didacticism evident in the religious drama of the time.

The Spaniards continued their move northward as they proceeded to colonize new lands. Because of Juan de Oñate's expedition into New Mexico, we have documentation of the performance of the first European play in what is now the United States on April 30, 1598 (Odell 1927, 2). By the banks of the Rio Grande somewhere near the present site of El Paso the Oñate party stopped to witness the performance of a play written by Captain Farfán, one of the members of the expedition. According to Gaspar Pérez de Villagra's epic poem of the *Historia de la Nueva México* (*History of New Mexico*), the soldiers performed the play. Three months later, at what is now Santa Fe, New Mexico, they performed the second play produced in the region, *Los moros y los cristianos* (*The Moors and the Christians*). Although we know little else of these particular performances, clearly there was a strong interest in dramatic performance; yet women's roles in these productions are virtually lacking, and women themselves seem to have been absent from the stage.[2]

Other religious plays also appeared, and through the titles we can gather that whether women actually appeared on the stage or not, something not unusual in Spanish theatre at least, their roles were generally those of virgin, prostitute, or temptress. We know that *autos* about Adam and Eve and the passion of the Lord during Holy Week existed. One popular religious play is the *Four Apparitions of Our Lady of Guadaloupe* [*sic*], based on real events (Austin

La Virgen de Guadalupe (Our Lady of Guadalupe) image in
contemporary artwork by Enedina Vásquez, San Antonio, Texas
(c. 1997) in the private collection of Dr. and Mrs. Victor and
Theresa Casiano.
Photo by Pedro C. Ramírez.

1990, 603). In this story the appearance of the Virgin is as an Indian maiden
who sends the poor Juan Diego to the archbishop with a demand that a chapel
be erected on the place of her appearance and in her honor. While she is a
commanding figure, she must still prove her case to the archbishop and does so
with a gift of roses that miraculously appear in the arid and desolate land along
with the transference of her image on Diego's cloak. Austin refers to the Virgin's part as one of the three "genuinely good acting parts" in the piece.[3]

The dance of La Matachina is related to performances for the Virgin of
Guadalupe. Once the Virgin's appearance was recognized by the Church, the
native Indian bishops produced this dance in honor of "Our Lady." This ballad
dance shows the progress from Indian pageantry to Christianity. Largely performed by men (although Norma Cantú documents women participating in
the Laredo, Texas group), the dance depicts *la mujer perversa,* a perverse woman's search for the true cross. Austin's description of the female role is that of
the bride who represents the soul which is to be won over to Christianity.
Thus, the female figure is represented as tempted by the deviltry of "El Toro"
and by lusts of the flesh before she is converted with the help of the dominant
male Church figures (Cantú 1995, 60–61; Austin 1990, 603). Clearly, an integration of both Indian and Spanish traditions is evident in religious performative activity, and its practice has managed to survive and evolve up to today
(see Herrera-Sobek 1995 and Cantú 1995).

In addition to ongoing religious folk drama, secular plays also appeared in
the Southwest. Secular folk plays appeared during the latter part of the eigh-

teenth century and during the nineteenth century. Two examples, *Los coman-ches* (*The Comanches*) and *Los tejanos* (*The Texans*), show the aggressive colo-nizers as dominant conquerors; women are virtually absent in either female roles or as a stage presence.[4] Their social and political status is clearly evident in these accounts, in which men are instrumental in warfare and determining his-tory. *Los comanches,* written after 1777 and before 1800, dramatized the Span-ish defeat of the Comanches around 1777–1779 and was performed on horse-back, glorifying the Spaniards and denigrating the Indians. *Los tejanos,* possibly written between 1841 and 1846, portrays the New Mexican defeat of a Texan expedition to New Mexico in 1841. Male roles are central and emphasize pa-triotism; women's roles are omitted.

This amateur theatrical tradition soon made its way beyond the South-west. The long tradition of Mexican and Central American Indian amateur performative activity eventually evolved into theatre and performance practices that became pervasive in Mexican and Southwestern culture. Eventually, traces would be found in the Midwest and farther afield. In Florida, long traditions stemming from pre-Columbian and colonial periods through the period of the influx of Cubans also informed amateur performance, and in New York, Puerto Rican traditions would also make their mark. In each of these areas amateur performance was kept alive despite Anglo American domination, assimilation, and the melting of the Chicana/Chicano/Latina/Latino into the American social and cultural mainstream. Resistance to mainstream hegemony included the retention of Mexicano cultural patterns that encompassed region, race, religion, and language (Rosenbaum 1981, 8–10), and amateur theatrical activ-ity held strong. Even the periodic mass repatriations of Mexicans and contin-uous border conflicts and hostilities could not halt the survival, preservation, and adaptation of performance traditions for this group in the United States (140), and these traditions remain with us to this day. This amateur tradition coincided with another tradition—professional theatre, which also made its distinctive mark. Although not as long-lived, professional theatre enjoyed its own success, which led to well-established patterns of theatrical practice.[5]

The earliest reference to Spanish-language professional theatre dates from 1789 in California, yet it was not until the mid-1800s that we have firm evi-dence of its existence. Professional Mexican theatre companies touring in north-ern México prior to its ceding to the United States had become resident com-panies in Los Angeles and San Francisco as early as the 1860s, and by the turn of the twentieth century, touring from México and Spain had been established along the border. Accounts of theatrical activity in Texas, New Mexico, and Arizona and from southern California to San Francisco reveal a major move-ment in professional theatrical activity that lasted for a long time. During the Mexican Revolution, the greater influx of Mexicans brought an even greater demand for such entertainment. Soon Spanish-language theatrical activity in the United States led to the formation of resident companies, producing the first native performers and playwrights, and creating cultural centers that remain with us today. Spanish centers of theatrical activity also arose on the opposite side of the country, in New York and Florida. In this tradition, women would soon make their mark.

PROFESSIONAL THEATRE FROM THE TURN OF THE CENTURY THROUGH THE 1930s

Several studies dealing with Spanish-language theatrical activities in the United States before 1900 show that they were an important and vibrant part of the cultural life that was developing in the country. While the Anglo American theatre was dominated by the large touring companies from the East Coast and abroad, which generally gave only short-run performances, the Mexican American community had resident professional theatre on a regular basis. Professional acting companies from México established a lasting tradition in the United States, stemming from a long tradition of both amateur and professional Spanish-language activity originating in Spain.

My book *Footlights across the Border* details professional Mexican American theatre in Texas from its beginnings in 1875 to its demise in 1935. This study provides examples of the kind of professional activity typical in the United States. In addition to performances by members of an amateur theatre, professional companies from México appeared regularly. The cultural development and taste of Mexican Americans are evident through detailed analyses of representative plays produced by the dramatic companies. Three types of companies appeared between 1875 and 1935—touring, resident, and combination "star" companies—each with distinct organization, operations, and contributions. The theatre, through its language and cultural themes, created a cohesive force for Mexican Americans that supported their identification with the mother country and provided an experience in which the entire family could participate (Ramírez 1990).

LATINAS AND MEXICAN AMERICAN WOMEN ON THE TEXAS STAGE, 1875–1930s: FEMALE ACTORS, ACTOR-MANAGERS, AND VARIETY PERFORMERS

Both Latinas and Mexican American female actors played a major role on the American stage although the former, coming from Spain, Latin America, and farther afield, did not remain permanently in the United States, as did the latter. The term "Latina" is used here for women of Latin American, Spanish, and/or Mexican ancestry, while "Mexican American" refers to people of Mexican ancestry who were born in or lived in the United States. During the period under discussion here, "Mexican American" is used instead of the term "Chicana," which connotes the political awareness or consciousness that is manifested from the 1960s on.

Reviews of performances reveal the value the critics placed on the plays

Antonia Pineda de Hernández
(c. before 1911).
Villalongín Collection, Benson Latin American
Collection, University of Texas at Austin. Photo by
Pedro C. Ramírez.

themselves. The scant attention given to production elements in newspaper reviews and in accounts of performances indicates the significance of the content of the plays. Accounts of the performances emphasized the plays, especially their didactic and moralistic merits. However, it was the performers themselves who were generally noted for their ability to convey the full meaning of the plays. The performers not only acquainted audiences with traditional and innovative drama, but they also often set standards in language, customs, manners, and fashion. Thus, before turning to examples of the dramas produced during this time, we may first glimpse those actors who were able to bring these works to life on the American stage.

The first quarter of the twentieth century brought a great many Spanish-language actors to the United States.[6] The most numerous accounts of a female actor performing prior to 1900 are about Antonia Pineda de Hernández (b. ?; d. c. 1927). At the age of eighteen this Mexican female actor married Encarnación Hernández, whom she met when he was performing with a company in Colima, México. Hernández trained Antonia as an actor, and she eventually became the leading actor of the company that Encarnación organized, the Compañía Hernández. Upon her husband's death around 1888, Sra. Hernández assumed responsibility of company management, which she continued until her retirement in 1904, when Carlos Villalongín, her son-in-law, took over. She also continued as leading female actor for Carlos Villalongín. Her children included one son, Luis, who acted with the company, and two daughters, Herlinda and Concepción, who became actors in the Hernández-Villalongín Company and later in the Compañía Villalongín. Herlinda, who generally performed in various second-line parts, married Villalongín, and Concepción assumed the leading role when she could fill the part and as her mother took fewer or smaller roles before eventually retiring.

Antonia Pineda de Hernández was best known for her roles in romantic tragedies and melodramas. Her last known performance was as the leading female actor in *La campa de la mudaña* (*The Camp of the Wandering Woman*) for a benefit at Beethoven Hall in San Antonio in 1917. The peak of Hernández's career was before 1900 (Ramírez 1993a).

From the extant early accounts we can gather some facts about both audiences and performers from 1875 to 1900. Appropriate behavior was the responsibility of both audience and performers at theatrical events since members of the Mexican (and sometimes Euroamerican) upper class attended as well as families. The fare had to be suitable for everyone—families were the heart of the audience and the family was the basis for the organization and operation of the acting company.

The theatre provided an important social gathering place and there was a desire to retain it as such for several reasons. The theatre became a cohesive force in the Mexican American community, a factor most profoundly shown through the Church's willingness to sponsor or participate in such activity. The theatre provided a wide variety of fare for the varied audience members and it catered to an unusually wide spectrum of community tastes and values (Ramírez 1990, 17–18).

The twentieth century brought many more performers and performances to the United States. The tastes and demands of the Mexican American community influenced the policy and practice of the acting troupes, which soon proliferated. Three female actors stand out as particularly powerful figures on the Mexican American stage in Texas: Magdalena Solórzano, Margarita Fernández, and Concepción Hernández. Since these three women performed in more or less the same style, it is possible to select one as representative (Ramírez 1986).

Concepción Hernández[7] is an excellent example of the type of leading female actor commonly found in the Mexican touring companies that appeared in the United States. She is also important because she represents the type of female actor that remained in Texas after immigration to continue the theatrical tradition through the resident company. Her early career was based primarily in Nuevo León, a province in northern México, although she made infrequent tours in the southwestern United States—in 1900 the troupe was invited to perform in San Antonio, Houston, Victoria, and Dallas, Texas. In 1911 the company had agreed to perform at the Teatro Aurora in San Antonio for an

Concepción Hernández, leading
female actor with the Compañía
Villalongín. Daughter of
Encarnación and Antonia Pineda
de Hernández (c. 1920).
Villalongín Collection, Benson Latin
American Collection, University of
Texas at Austin.
Photo by Pedro C. Ramírez.

extended run. However, the Mexican Revolution made the Compañía Villalongín decide to remain permanently.

Srta. Hernández's training began in childhood, and she grew into the parts
she played. She eventually became the leading lady of the company. Among her
principal roles were Marta in *Tierra baja* (*The Lowlands*), *María Antonieta, La
Llorona* (*The Weeping Woman*), and Doña Ines in *Don Juan Tenorio*. Her skills
most often noted by newspaper critics were her intelligence, ability to comprehend her parts, and ability to present a well-studied role with clear diction. Her
principal strength, however, was a unique vocal range. A vivid description remains of her most memorable role, that of Marta in *Tierra baja,* in a newspaper
review of the performance of February 20, 1910. She is said to have been
"truly inspired" and to have "painted with vivid colors all the sufferings" of
Marta, "that sublime disgraced martyr." Carlos Villalongín included the review of this performance, which took place in Matamoros, México, in his memoirs.[8] This review is important because it provides an account of one of the
Compañía Villalongín's productions known to have been presented in San Antonio once the company took up permanent residence there.

This Spanish play by Ángel Guimerá was written before 1900 and translated from the Catalán by José Echegaray, one of the most popular dramatists
of the Mexican and American Spanish-language stages. Written in three acts,
the plot of this melodrama revolves around Marta, an orphaned young woman
who must be sold by her mother because of their extreme poverty. Brought up

Broadside announcing performance of *Tierra baja,* place and date unknown but known to be prior to arrival of the Compañía Villalongín to San Antonio (before 1911) while still in México. Villalongín Collection, Benson Latin American Collection, University of Texas at Austin. Photo by Pedro C. Ramírez.

Drawing found in the promptbook of *María Antonieta* (1907). Promptbook No. 56 in the Villalongín Collection, Benson Latin American Collection, University of Texas at Austin. Photo by Pedro C. Ramírez.

by Sebastián, a wealthy landowner who has secretly been having sexual relations with her, Marta is soon to be married off in order to stop scandalous gossip about this inappropriate behavior by her guardian. Sebastián selects Manelich, a common, good-hearted backwoodsman who lives on Sebastián's property. Manelich has never seen a woman and immediately falls in love with Marta. Manelich's goodness and kindness make Marta, in turn, fall in love with him. When Sebastián attempts to reclaim Marta, Manelich fights back. Justifiably killing Sebastián, Marta and Manelich flee the lowlands in search of hope and promise awaiting them in the highlands. While the poor strive to own their own land and seek freedom in life, they must fight their oppressor for liberation. The highlands represent the nearest hope for happiness on earth, and it seems they can attain the freedom they seek at the end.

In the role of Marta, Concepción Hernández exemplified an ideal performer. Her most outstanding feature was her powerful and wide-ranging voice, which she used with great skill in conveying emotion:

> Her potent voice ranged from the ferocious roar of injured dignity to soft, dove-like billing and cooing, sweet and harmonious as a murmur of breezes from the fjords, when for the first time she felt the palpitation inside her chest of the sweet sensations of true love. . . . All the inflections of her throat imprint a stamp of truth to the different sensations of hate, indignation, dignity, contempt, passion and tenderness with which the difficult role of Marta is filled; in all of those transitions this singular artist knew how to triumph, receiving for it merited ovations.

Of all the other actors it was reported in the review that they "in general, made a conscious secondary performance to that of the two principal figures of the drama," Concepción Hernández as Marta and Carlos Villalongín as Manelich.[9]

The manners of the period required that the declamatory actor perform in moral and instructive dramas suitable for the entire family. The fact that Concepción Hernández was performing in a family enterprise, always accompanied by her mother, sisters, and other relatives, probably enhanced the image of wholesome entertainment that the Compañía Villalongín provided. She received many tokens of admiration and friendship, some of which are found in the Carlos Villalongín Dramatic Company Collection at the Benson Latin American Collection at The University of Texas at Austin—cards and photographs from admirers, generally wishing her successful benefit performances.

The contributions by touring companies are several. The companies sustained the public's interest in full-length dramas that were primarily serious in nature, which they combined with comic afterpieces to make an evening both full and diverse. These groups also maintained an audience for theatre, produced plays never before seen in Texas, and produced original native dramas. Above all, these dramatic companies were able to establish a reconnection between Mexican Americans and México. Rather than isolating themselves in the United States, the Spanish-speaking communities were able to continue cultural relations with México. Evidence also shows that the audiences included Anglo Americans and Italian Americans as well (Ramírez 1990, 62).

The turmoil of the Mexican Revolution convinced Carlos Villalongín, his family, and some other actors—though they had expected to return to Coahuila, where the company held temporary residency—that they could not return. The revolution enabled the tradition of Spanish-language dramatic entertainment to continue on the American stage through resident companies. Although we will spend more time examining the period of political strife in northern México and analyze its impact on theatre history in the United States, for the moment its significance in forcing actors to remain in the United States must be underscored. This extensive period of political uncertainty ensured the permanent establishment of professional theatrical activity. Concepción Hernández was one of the first leading actors to remain on a permanent basis, and her training of others meant that theatrical practice of the highest caliber became firmly entrenched. Her niece, María Luisa Villalongín, was her apprentice, taking the ingenue parts until she replaced Concepción upon her retirement.[10]

Although the resident stock company was rather short-lived and was eventually undermined by the extended engagements of the touring star combinations, the former contributed greatly to the success of the latter in four important ways. First, as theatre managers saw the need to build a thriving, successful business, they increased the promotion of that business. Second, with this type of company we see the rise of the first native Mexican American female actors, since the children born to company members tended to remain within the United States and continue in their parents' profession. Third, the companies performed native Mexican American drama, which rose from the demand by the permanent companies for new plays. Fourth, and most significant, since these troupes provided dramatic entertainment on a regular basis as they firmly established an audience for such activity, the resident companies made the theatre a permanent part of the culture and the community (76).

Resident companies contributed to their own demise by accommodating combination companies, which guaranteed audiences and theatres in which to perform. Combination companies, that is, companies traveling with a star and full company, were less frequently seen on the Mexican American stage than other kinds of companies; nevertheless, they had a considerable impact on the practice and policies of the others. Combination companies generally featured female stars, and usually arrived from the Mexican stage, although some Spanish companies also appeared when traveling either through México or Florida. The largest centers of Spanish-language theatre were Los Angeles, San Antonio, New York, and Tampa. A glimpse at the Compañía Virginia Fábregas can serve to show the tremendous impact that this type of company made in the United States.

Virginia Fábregas probably best represents the "modern" actor, although there are other examples, such as Mercedes Navarro, Rosita Arriaga, and María Guerrero, the major Spanish female actor of the modern period, who appeared in San Antonio in 1927 on her way to the San Francisco stage and canceled that engagement upon discovery of a very vibrant Texas stage.[11] Many of these female actors were significant for their new styles of acting and introduction of new roles. Although none resided permanently in Texas or the United States, their contributions were important.

The Compañía Virginia Fábregas was the first combination company to perform in Texas. The star of that company may have appeared in Texas or near the border in 1899. This company, composed of thirty members of Spanish and Mexican origin, had been formed in Spain and arrived in México with Luis Martínez Tovar as the leading man to Fábregas's leading female parts. This notable troupe introduced the practice of giving consecutive performances of a single play featuring "stars," a practice new to the Mexican American stage. The company began a tour of Texas in December 1917 with a female star and a male star in five plays that both stars had made famous. The combination companies also performed in larger theatres generally not available to Spanish-language acting companies. The Compañía Virginia Fábregas performed in Laredo at the Royal Opera House (and later at the Teatro Strand), in El Paso at the Texas Grand Theatre, and in San Antonio at Beethoven Hall. María Guerrero performed at the Municipal Auditorium in San Antonio. These theatres were outside the Mexican American communities and typically had non-Spanish-speaking audiences. Thus, combination companies made a major contribution by broadening the audiences of Spanish-language entertainment.

Virginia Fábregas as leading female actor
(*primera actríz*), México, 1902. From Manuel
Mañon, *Historia del Teatro Principal de México* 242.
Photo by Pedro C. Ramírez.

No individual star had a greater influence than Virginia Fábregas on both the Mexican stage and the Mexican American stage in Texas and Los Angeles. Mexican American male and female actors often drew directly from her company's organization and practice. According to Rodolfo Usigli, "She is the first actress with vision, not of what the theatre was then [in the last decade of the nineteenth century] but of what it would be later, and consequently, she is the first modern actress of Mexico" (Usigli 1975, 110). Probably her most outstanding attribute was her ability to convey emotion in a thoroughly natural and believable manner.[12]

Fábregas's performance in *La Mujer X* (*Madame X*) was internationally acclaimed, and her portrayal of Angélica in *La Hija del Rey* (*The Daughter of the King*) played a significant role in the revival of romanticism in México. She later turned with much enthusiasm to plays by modern dramatists, believing that presenting drama with universal appeal, capable of reaching the widest possible audience, was the greatest accomplishment of any performer. Fábregas constantly sought to provide "a new repertory, new stage spectacle, and new actors" for her public. She was said to "possess the unique ability among leading actors of sensing the need of updating the repertory with the latest works of world theatre" (*La Prensa*, May 2, 1928, 6, 9). Through her Spanish-language performances, she was the first to introduce San Antonio Spanish-speaking audiences to important modern works, and she set the standard of performance by which other combination companies were judged. When Jacinto Benavente appeared briefly in San Antonio en route from New York to México, Fábregas performed in a tribute to him with one of his works, *Rosas de otoño* (*Roses of Autumn*). Fábregas was the first to present Pirandello in San Antonio with *All for the Best,* produced in 1926 at the Teatro Nacional. She also presented two of Oscar Wilde's plays, *A Woman of No Importance* and *Lady Windemere's Fan,* in 1926 at the Nacional (see Ramírez 1990 for a more in-depth study of Fábregas and her company).[13]

As combination companies displaced resident companies, the touring stock companies were forced to perform in the smaller Spanish-speaking communities. In Texas they extended their tours to cities that were becoming accessible by train, automobile, and truck. However, as smoothly as tours may have generally gone, difficulties soon began to occur. In 1917, the Compañía Virginia Fábregas performed in Laredo without problems and with success and had already made arrangements for performances in San Antonio followed by appearances in El Paso. With subseason tickets already sold, and advertisements already printed in local newspapers, the company could not meet its agreements. One of the company members encountered immigration problems in Laredo and could not go to San Antonio as scheduled. It required word from Washington to straighten matters out, but money had by that time been returned for a sold-out engagement, and a rescheduled performance drew fewer patrons than expected.

Immigration problems occurred in part due to the First World War. By 1917 and 1918 World War I caused a mass repatriation of Mexican Americans to México, especially since México was experiencing a more stable political and economic climate and improved conditions seemed evident. Unfortunately, although the Mexican Constitution of 1917 had offered a sense of hope, the promises were short-lived. By the 1920s immigration problems had increased, and border crossing had become more difficult. By 1930 it was no longer a matter of course for Mexican companies to cross the border. The arrangements for doing so included for each person: (1) a fee of $1.00 or more, (2) a visa, (3) a letter from the contracting manager on the United States side of the border, and (4) proof of citizenship and legal residence. Difficulties eventually became insurmountable for the traveling troupes. The appearance of such companies became more and more infrequent. By the mid-1930s the demise of the Spanish-language dramatic companies was evident. Their history on the American stage was long-lived, however, and the combination companies had made their own unique contribution to the annals of theatre history.

The arrival of Spanish-language combination companies influenced the practice and performance of the other types of dramatic troupes on the Mexican American stage. These newer companies introduced new plays, and the public compared the performances of well-known male and female actors to those of the older companies that toured year after year, and they preferred the "stars." Also, touring stock companies could not offer productions as elaborate as those of the combinations because of the cost of scenery, costumes, and properties among other expenses.

Both combination and the large touring companies included female and male actors who remained in Texas to found worthwhile ventures by organizing their own companies or joining others already touring the state. As combination companies displaced the touring stock and resident companies, theatres became larger to meet the demands of a growing public and the touring stock companies were forced to perform in the smaller Texas Spanish-speaking communities. Gradually the touring companies began to include cities not previously visited but which were becoming accessible by new forms of transportation. In 1918, the Compañía María del Carmen Martínez appeared at the Teatro Washington in Brownsville and in 1919 the company of Manuel Cotera began one of its many tours through southwest Texas. In 1926 the Compañía Azteca made a very successful tour through Hebbronville, Benavides, and San Diego which began in June and by August had traveled through Mercedes, Pharr, and Mission, Texas. Both the Cotera and Azteca companies were responsible for many female actors permanently settling in the region. The small valley towns which had not been on the touring routes earlier became regular stops for many companies. Rio Grande City and all the small valley towns between that city and Brownsville were part of the new theatrical circuit for

Comic actors Mariano and Herminia Villalongín, brother and sister
of Carlos Villalongín (c. 1900–1920).
Villalongín Collection, Benson Latin American Collection, University
of Texas at Austin. Photo by Pedro C. Ramírez.

Child female actor,
María Luisa Villalongín, daughter
of Carlos Villalongín, San
Antonio, Texas (1917 or 1918).
In *Los granujos,* comic afterpiece.
Villalongín Collection, Benson Latin
American Collection, University of
Texas at Austin. Photo by Pedro C.
Ramírez.

Postcard from female actor
Concepción L. de Delgado to
Antonia Pineda de Hernández and
Encarnación Hernández, whom she
named as sponsors for her benefit
performance.
Tlaltnango, México (May 26, 1886).
Villalongín Collection, Benson Latin
American Collection,
University of Texas at Austin.
Photo by Pedro C. Ramírez.

Spanish-language troupes, and the growing use of railroads led to routes into Arizona, New Mexico, and California, although direct routes to both the East and West Coasts were also established by water. But probably the greatest contribution of the combination companies was that they broadened the audiences of Spanish-language entertainment as they appeared in theatres outside of the immediate Mexican American community (Ramírez 1990, 88–90).

In addition to professional dramatic female actors, individual female performers and performances made important contributions to American theatre. Beatriz Escalona Pérez (1903–1979), best known as "La Chata" Noloesca, was a well-known Mexican American comedienne. Born in San Antonio, Texas, on August 20, 1903, the daughter of Mexican parents from Galeana, Nuevo León, México, "La Chata" was raised in San Antonio but spent much of her childhood in Monterrey, Nuevo León, with relatives. By the age of ten she was already drawn to the theatre through frequent visits to the Teatro Independencia in Monterrey. Indeed, she was so entranced by theatrical entertainment that she sold bouquets to earn admission. In San Antonio she worked part-time as an usher at the Teatro Zaragoza. At the time, the Teatro Zaragoza, located in the heart of the Mexican American community, was a showcase for entertainment in Spanish. By age sixteen Beatriz had moved up to a position in the box office at the new Teatro Nacional. While working at the Nacional, she met a Cuban-born performer, José Areu, who was a member of the variety company Los Hermanos Areu. He invited her to travel with the company. Beatriz left San Antonio and studied singing and acting with the Areus. She made her first performance at the Teatro Colón in El Paso at the age of eighteen. At Areu's suggestion, she took the stage name Noloesca, an approximate anagram of her last name. She married Areu. Her first and only child, Belia (who later also became a successful performer), was born in Mexico City on October 31, 1921 (see Smith and Ramírez 1996).

Noloesca toured throughout México and the southwestern United States with Los Hermanos Areu. She performed in a variety of popular genres: *risque bataclan* numbers (similar to burlesque), dramatic plays and comic sketches, and traditional and humorous Mexican songs. Although Noloesca had originally aspired to be a glamorous *vedette* (chorus girl), she discovered that she had a special gift for comedy and was encouraged by the Areus to develop her talent. She increasingly specialized in comic roles.

In 1930 she left the company, ended her marriage, and formed her own variety company, Atracciones Noloesca. Between 1930 and 1936 she managed and acted with her company and periodically contracted to perform with other companies. Most notably, she worked with Mexican entertainer Eusebio Pirrín, who was otherwise known by his stage name Don Catarino. Noloesca met and married her second husband, José de la Torre, who was employed with the immigration service in Tijuana. Torre became her comic partner. In 1936 she returned to San Antonio, where she performed at the Teatro Nacional, which had become the center of Spanish-language cultural activity in that city.

Probably in the late 1920s and early 1930s Noloesca developed the popular comic figure she maintained throughout the remainder of her career. She called the character "La Chata," an affectionate nickname that meant "button-nosed." She modeled the character on Mexican and Mexican American maids. Trademarks of La Chata were a brightly printed, flounced cotton dress, perky little pigtails tied with big bows, and chunky men's shoes with boldly striped socks. Through her costume, gestures, and verbal wit, Beatriz invented a character that was simultaneously innocent and savvy, sweet and strong-willed. Typical of the household servant who is always smarter than her employer, Beatriz invented a character who portrayed the inno-

Dolores Garza, female actor, 36 years old. Sabinas Hidalgo, México (January 25, 1890 or 1896). Villalongín Collection, Benson Latin American Collection, University of Texas at Austin. Photo by Pedro C. Ramírez.

Mounted photo to Carlos Villalongín and wife, Herlinda, from female actors Elvira and Lucinda Yañez, sisters. Ciudad Guerrero, México (February 19, 1900). Villalongín Collection, Benson Latin American Collection, University of Texas at Austin. Photo by Pedro C. Ramírez.

Dolores Gamir, comic female actor, in role of old woman in *La viejecita,* comic afterpiece. Photo postcard sent to Herminia Villalongín (April 28, 1924), San Antonio. Photo printed in Nuevo León, Monterrey, México. Villalongín Collection, Benson Latin American Collection, University of Texas at Austin. Photo by Pedro C. Ramírez.

cence of a child while at the same time showing a mature and capable woman with a sharp verbal wit and sophisticated prowess. The remarkable career of Beatriz "La Chata" Escalona Pérez continued for several decades and will be taken up again. "La Chata" was one of many women who were soon able to reach new territories that were now firmly established by resident companies because of their acclaim and drawing power in communities both inside and outside of Spanish-speaking theatrical centers. Audiences awaited them eagerly, for these female stars represented the best performers and ensured quality performances from the Mexican and Spanish theatres that audience members often read about in the United States.

In many ways similarities are evident between historical patterns of English-language American touring combinations and the Spanish-language companies as these larger groups displaced resident stock companies (Poggi 1968, 28–96). Clearly, the stock companies suffered from the publicity, the introduction of the long run, greater emphasis on new plays, and the encouragement of the star system as local support was withdrawn from them and given to touring productions on both English- and Spanish-language stages (Brockett 1995, 409–410). The westward expansion which had at first been so difficult for the initial companies to establish now witnessed the creation of firm cultural centers in which combination companies could perform. The expansion of the railroad proved lucrative for visiting stars on both stages, taking them farther and farther afield in the United States. However, the factors pulling companies back and forth from one country to another are unique in the Spanish-language theatrical activity occurring in the United States. Often the reasons were political. The political upheavals in México between 1910 and 1921 saw much growth in theatrical activity north of Mexico City. Instability caused by World War I, mass repatriations of Mexicans to México, and increasing immigration problems were also factors. Perhaps the single most significant factor contributing to the longevity of theatrical activity in Spanish on the American stage was the sense of nationalism that it upheld for a people who associated the performances in many ways with their mother country. As Carey McWilliams reminds us, the Rio Grande River does not separate the people on either side, but rather "draws them together" (McWilliams 1968, 61).

Through what we know about the performative activity of women during this period we can understand much about Mexican American culture in the

United States. Women were instrumental in the development of a professional theatre as companies came regularly to the United States from México between 1875 and 1935. The plays produced on this stage reveal the values, beliefs, and aspirations of an emerging Mexican American culture. This theatrical work provided the Mexican American community with a type of entertainment which created cohesion through language, themes, and intense performances intended for the entire family.

Probably the single most significant discovery about the Spanish-language theatre of this period has been that theatrical activity appealed to such a wide spectrum of society that it created a firm cultural focus which continued long after acting troupes disappeared. The Spanish-language stage offered universal themes, idealized sentiments, often spectacular productions, and a full and varied bill of entertainment, all of which helped to bring a broad segment of the community together. The Spanish-language theatre on the American stage reflects a broad exchange between the Mexican and Southwestern communities as well as elsewhere in the United States, influencing the cultural life in the United States for a very long time.

The period between 1910 and 1924 saw much growth in theatrical activity due to continuous political upheaval in México. Clearly if the Mexican Revolution of 1910 had not occurred, Mexican dramatic companies probably would not have come to Texas on such a large scale or remained for such a long time. Such companies left seemingly lucrative businesses in México, and many remained in Texas to found centers of theatrical activity that are still active today. Because this period of revolt impacts so tremendously on the history of the United States, we must now turn to that period for closer scrutiny of Mexican and Mexican American women in the theatrical history of the time.

2 THE CRITICAL ROLE OF
THE MEXICAN REVOLUTION
AND ITS IMPACT ON
THE AMERICAN STAGE

After the signing of the Treaty of Guadalupe Hidalgo in 1848 following México's defeat in the Mexican-American War, Mexicans continued to cross the border at will because the established border was not enforced. Between 1910 and 1924, about one million Mexicans crossed into the United States. As Ricardo Romo points out, it was not until 1910 that the Chicana/Chicano population increased significantly and began concentrating in urban areas, and the greatest influx occurred between 1900 and 1930. This urbanization had a distinct impact on theatre history and culture in the United States. Its effect most notably left an imprint in the larger cities of this region, namely Los Angeles, San Antonio, San Francisco, El Paso, and San Diego, all areas offering economic diversity, proximity to the Mexican border, and opportunities for work (Romo 1977, 183, 185).

THE EFFECTS OF URBANIZATION AND IMMIGRATION
ON MEXICAN WOMEN IN THE UNITED STATES

The period when Chicanas and Chicanos moved to cities in massive numbers in the Southwest coincides with the trend toward the breakdown of the Mexican family. This trend was chronicled in the Spanish-speaking theatre of the time. The demographic change that occurred from 1900 to 1930 has been viewed as one of the most important population shifts in the history of the Southwest. About 1,500,000 Mexicans, a little more than 10 percent of México's population, emigrated to the United States during this period. Statistics show that 94 percent of the Mexican population living in the United States in 1930 arrived after 1900; about 82 percent of this group arrived after 1915. Clearly, the political crisis of the Mexican Revolution greatly affected the population shift within the United States (Romo 1977, 194; U.S. Bureau of the Census 1931, 179).

The state of Texas played a significant role in this shift. Before 1920, improved rail connections from México to Texas allowed a greater number of

Mexicans to settle in Texas than in other states. Several Texas cities were possible points of entry for these emigrants from México, namely Matamoros, Laredo, Eagle Pass, and El Paso. In contrast, in Arizona only Nogales was an entry point. Only 6.5 percent of Mexican immigrants to California migrated there in the first decades of the twentieth century, but 70 percent of Mexican immigrants to Texas crossed the border between 1900 and 1920. By 1920, Mexicans made up the largest foreign-born population in all the large southwestern cities, except for San Francisco, where Asian Americans held that distinction. Because of the proximity of Texas to México and the improvement of railroad transportation from México to the United States, the urbanization in Texas stands out as a significant factor in the development of the portrayal of the Mexican experience on the stage. Most outstanding in this regard is the impact of urbanization on the family and the changing family roles of women.

Economic factors played a crucial role in the destruction of the traditional Mexican family unit. Employment opportunities during the periods of heavy Mexican immigration led many young single males to come to the United States seeking work; many families also arrived (M. García 1994, 72). Yet seasonal work and the high cost of bringing entire families across the border were the primary reasons for growing family displacement and eventual rupture of family units. The farther away the Chicano worker was from the Mexican border, the more infrequent was the presence of the Chicana, as well as the entire family unit. There was a considerable inequity between the number of Mexican women in relation to men in the United States. One of the most extreme examples of this inequity can be seen in the state of Oregon, which had few Mexican communities, where 1,247 Mexican males and 321 Mexican females were recorded in 1930, a ratio of 388.5 males to 100 females. Texas, on the other hand, had perhaps the most equitable ratio in the nation, where there were 105.6 Mexican males for every 100 Mexican females (Romo 1977, 195), but this relative balance in gender presence did not necessarily translate into family units.

Although the ratio of men to women for the state of Texas as a whole was almost one to one, in the urban centers of the state those ratios were less balanced. The work patterns of thousands of Mexican men who lived in Texas but traveled to distant cities and communities outside the state for periods of six months to several years help to explain this imbalance. These men frequently left their wives and children behind when they left the state in search of employment; the ratio of Mexican men to Mexican women in El Paso was 86 to 100 in 1930, while San Antonio had a ratio of 95 to 100. Both of these cities served as depots or clearing houses for Mexican workers, and from 1910 to 1920 they "functioned as the most important recruiting centers for midwestern and southern agricultural interests." The ratio of Mexican males to Mexican females in midwestern cities like Chicago (170/100) and Detroit (179/100) were much higher than they were in Texas urban centers (Romo 1977, 196).

The Chicana/Chicano community's changing composition was reflected in new gender roles, new social settings, and the locations they chose. Factors impacting on change for this group that affected women included "some aspects of traditional customs, formal organization, sex roles and marriage, role of women in the labor force, and attitudes toward urban life" (196). Mario T. García, in his article on "Border Culture," uses the model of Mexican immigrants in El Paso to provide a view into the broader southwestern experience of newcomers to the United States, showing how the group was able to maintain "native customs that helped provide a sense of community" (72). García, citing Ernesto Galarza, who has written extensively on Mexican and Mexican American labor in the United States, notes that cultural change occurred within working-class immigration because working-class immigration brought "no formal institutions to perpetuate its culture" (M. García 1994, 72). García adds: "Cultural continuity as well as cultural change, the two in time developing in a Mexican border culture, can be detected in the family, recreational activities, religion, and voluntary associations" (72). These significant societal changes have been the basis for study in other venues, particularly in relation to sociological and historical contexts within Mexican society in the United States. By expanding this examination of the impact of these changes to include theatrical production we can broaden our understanding of the role of culture in that society (see M. García 1994, 72–81; D. Gutiérrez 1995; Montejano 1987; and Romo 1983). We can learn much by studying performative activity during this period of heavy immigration.

CONTEXTUALIZING WOMEN AS SUBJECTS IN PERFORMANCE DURING THE MEXICAN REVOLUTION

Studies of the Mexican Revolution have not produced a detailed analysis of the cultural, social, historical, and political effects of that event on Chicana/Latina theatrical performers in the United States. "The Great Rebellion"[1] had significant effects on a people who had lived under a dictatorship, had left that oppressive society behind, and had emerged within a democratic society in the United States. This great upheaval, which began in 1910, lasted until 1924. Chicanas participated in a major theatrical movement in the United States during this time. An analysis of their distinct role in this period of upheaval will illuminate the significance of women in this history.

The Mexican and Spanish professional theatrical companies that arrived in the United States through México established a long tradition. The effect of the movement of these groups from a society governed by a dictator to a society governed by democracy can shed light on their theatrical activity. Although no known plays by women are available for this period of the Mexican rebellion, an evaluation of women's unique place within the cultural, social, and political context in which they performed helps us to understand the broader socio-cultural implications of their work.

Extant playtexts that represent this period of great influx of immigration into the United States from México can document the contributions by Chicanas to American theatre by demonstrating the means and methods by which they were contextualized during this period. This documentation can also provide broader insights into the Latina/Latino culture and community. Furthermore, through these playtexts we can gain an understanding of the cultural contributions by Latinas/Latinos to American and world culture. The Latina/Latino plays produced during this period illustrate how cultural values, beliefs, and aspirations of Mexican immigrants changed.

Through two play collections available at the Benson Latin American Collection at The University of Texas at Austin, we can begin to understand how women were placed as subjects for viewing by the immigrant newcomers who were reconstructing former and inventing new behavioral strategies in order to ensure survival in their new home. Mexican American audiences were comprised of a broad spectrum of society that was represented by distinct seating arrangements, indicating the different classes of people who attended. The tastes and demands of the Mexican American community influenced the policy and practice of the acting troupes. By analyzing the drama on the Spanish-language stage, we may discover the major characteristics and trends of Mexican American life, and we may also discover an important aspect of Mexican American theatre in the United States and its place in the culture as well. We know that these plays were performed in Texas, but there is also enough evidence to suggest that they were performed outside that state as well.

THE POLITICAL ROLE OF WOMEN IN PERFORMANCE: *LA LLORONA (THE WEEPING WOMAN) AND LA MUJER ADÚLTERA (THE ADULTEROUS WOMAN)*

In the written drama that appeared on the Mexican American stage during the Mexican Revolution, the part women played was largely constructed and controlled by male dramatists who were rooted in the tradition of romantic tragedy that idealized the past through connections with México as the mother country. The representation of women on this stage reveals how the female body and subject were positioned and used as a tool to shape the culture and as a political weapon to sustain ties with the past, reconnect with the old order, and construct a new community. In the context of this culturally specific political climate, the visual presentation of women on stage highlights definitions of desire and object within the Mexican American community during this time. Jill Dolan asks: "How does a given performance—the dialogue, choice of setting, narrative voice, form, content, casting, acting, blocking—deliver its ideological message? How does it convey its assumptions about its relation to social structures?" (Dolan 1988, 17).

La Llorona, a four-act drama in verse by Francisco Neve (date ?), is known to have been performed in Texas as early as December 22, 1906, and the promptbook was brought to Texas in 1911.[2] The Compañía Hernández-Villalongín was only one among several that produced this work, but we know that this company produced the play often and with great success (Ramírez 1986, 353–358, 449–453). Three of the surviving eyewitnesses who have served as important resources for documenting this period have provided numerous accounts about the popularity of this play, and several supporting documents and reviews can corroborate their claims.[3]

The story of La Llorona, the weeping woman, is an old and well-known tale among Mexican people. José E. Limón views her story as a "critical female legend of Greater Mexico" within the realm of the "female context of performance" (Limón 1990, 413, 417). For this noted scholar of anthropology, there is a marked difference in the performers and performance contexts of this legend in comparison to the other two "official" legends of México, namely, the Virgen de Guadalupe and La Malinche. In this figure, there is an "intense international popularity" (409) of the narrative of this legendary figure whose long-standing "relationship to all of the folk masses of Greater México" is "broader and more global" (419) than the other two symbols. Clarissa Pinkola Estés observes in *Women Who Run with the Wolves* that while some say the tale originated in the early 1500s when the conquistadores invaded the Aztec/Náhuatl peoples of México, the story is in fact far older. In some cases the story is related to that of La Malinche, the native woman translator and lover of the Spanish conqueror Hernán Cortés (Estés 1992, 303; Blea 1992, 27; and see Cypess 1991, 1–239). Maria Gonzalez (this author does not use an accent in her name), in "Love and Conflict: Mexican American Women Writers as Daughters," differs with this view: "Collapsing the actual historical figure of La Malinche or Doña Marina, Cortés's translator and mistress, to La Llorona is not accurate" (Gonzalez 1996, 161). She adds: "The myth of La Llorona is much older than the actual historical figure of La Malinche" (161). Whenever it originated, the story itself has to do with a woman who haunts a river in search of her children (Estés 1992, 303).

The tale bears some similarities to the Medea story of ancient Greek myth. A poor woman bears a rich Spanish nobleman two sons before he announces that he will return to Spain to marry a rich woman chosen by his aristocratic family. Knowing he will take his sons with him, the poor unfortunate and betrayed woman attacks him savagely and, in her crazed state, takes her two sons to the river and throws them in. The children drown, and she expires in her grief. Instead of being allowed directly into heaven, however, she must first find the souls of her children in the river. Thus, the woman is said to roam nearby rivers, haunting them in search of her lost innocents.

Generally when this story is told it is used as a warning for living children to stay away from any nearby river after dark, for rivers are all instilled with a lurking danger in the shape of a woman who audibly weeps for her children. The peril lies in the fact that the weeping woman may mistake any children for her own and take them away instead. Estés includes various modern versions of this tale in her extensive study of the "wild woman" figure, categorizing this kind of tale as a "shiver story," overtly entertaining but meant to cause listeners "to experience a shiver of awareness that leads to thoughtfulness, contemplation, and action" (303).

While the plot of the popular romantic tragedy differs from the folk tale in several ways, various similarities may be found when comparing a playtext to the more traditional interpretations of this story which generally draw instead from storytelling performance narrative. The performance arena of the *La Llorona* playtext clearly targeted Chicanas/Chicanos. José E. Limón points out that although the story is told to both female and male children primarily, generally, women narrate this story (Limón 1990, 417). He stresses that point "because it demonstrates that women control this expressive resource, and it therefore speaks to the greater possibility that it is articulating their own symbolic perceptions of the world" (417). As a result of this "collective experience in which women seem to cooperate in developing a single story line" there may never be a dominant speaker or narrative (418). In this "female to female paradigm of experience," then, "in terms of its symbolism, social context and organizational aesthetics, La Llorona is an important, critical contestative performance in the everyday lives of the ordinary women of Greater Mexico" according to Limón. For our purposes, we will examine the choice to perform this story as an example of how resident companies specifically used performance as a means to address those displaced persons who had left their homeland, for whatever reason.

In the case of this particular legend, performance functions to target the newly arrived Mexican Americans during the Mexican Revolution, using theatre as a political, social, and cultural weapon aimed at a dominant oppressive society through resistance, attempts to recover a lost community, and retention of a forgotten past. The legend encouraged audiences to contemplate the circumstances they now found themselves in, and probably incited political action, whether it was overt or covert, as well. Because the play was performed immediately after the first wave of exiles reached San Antonio, the address to Chicanas/Chicanos through a performative act stands out in its attempts to warn this newly forming marginalized conquered group against invasion, conflict, and impending loss of culture; that is, an attack on their values, beliefs, and aspirations.

Francisco C. Neve's tragedy revolves around Ramiro, the son of "Hernando" Cortés, immediately connecting the story both to the conquest and to the historical figure of Hernán Cortés. Here, Ramiro has a son by Luisa, someone he met following "an orgy born one morning" from somewhere in the "Oriente" or "East," "amidst the vapors of wine" (Neve 16). In his delirium, a light shines upon Luisa, whom he sees as "a kneeling angel of God" (17). While he loves Luisa, the demands from his mother and his status as an *hidalgo* (Spanish nobleman) require that he marry within the nobility. When Luisa discovers that Ramiro plans to take his son from her, she decides to take action. Recognizing that Ramiro has in effect "killed the soul of the mother," so too the "son has died" (112). Portrayed as a victim at the mercy of the colonizer and driven by her desire to keep her son from suffering a similar fate, she has taken her son's life as a means of saving him. Unlike Luisa, who is hanged for her crime, Ramiro suffers no blame from his peers in this tragedy, and we are told he eventually marries Ana. In fact, Ramiro's new Spanish father-in-law was responsible for bringing about Luisa's severe punishment of death by hanging. A dramatic scene comprised of a procession, soldiers, the scaffolding, the ladder to the scaffolding, friars, and a public that tosses blasphemies, insults, and rocks at Luisa leads to the horrible end of this ill-fated woman.

Zavala, an outsider newly arrived in "New Spain" (México), is also stricken with love for Luisa, this "perfection" whom he sees one morning with the sun shining from "el Oriente" (the East), exclaiming that "destiny has brought [them] together" (Neve 22, 23). Although Zavala makes several offers to seek vengeance for Luisa and the injustices against her, she firmly maintains that she will take her own action. However, once she is dead, Zavala takes charge. Through Zavala, Luisa has someone to confront Ramiro. But instead Zavala faces Ramiro's accusation that both of them have victimized Luisa. As terrible as Ramiro's actions were against Luisa, Zavala was at fault for having taken it upon himself to tell Luisa about Ramiro's plan to marry someone else, thus setting in motion the terrible results. As her servants affirm "the tale told in the barrio," the ghost of their mistress with the clothes of her slain child in her right hand walks at the stroke of midnight. Zavala leads Ramiro to see the haunting figure of Luisa lamenting for her lost child. Zavala, who had saved Ramiro's life at the beginning of the story when Ramiro was attacked by robbers, now serves as Ramiro's conscience and seeks retribution for Luisa's sake, forcing Ramiro to confront his deed. In his remorse, Ramiro expires upon hearing the "sorrowful lament" always associated with La Llorona.

Just as Fredric Jameson has suggested, the text can be produced both historically and situation-specifically. Instead of examining "the denunciation of the centered subject and its ideologies," we can study "the subject's historical emergence, its constitution or virtual construction as a mirage," which may also stand as "an objective reality" (Jameson 1991, 153). How was the figure of Luisa, who appeared on the Texas stage during the time of political unrest, presented to the new Mexican populace, who were either exiles or had immigrated because of economic factors? Why is Luisa from the Orient? What representation emerges about her with her association with Ramiro, described by a courtier as "the son of the great Cortés and richest inheritor," but denounced and ridiculed by Zavala as "the inheritor of that valor of the great progenitor that put a world at his feet" (Neve 47, 119)? Why does the avenger come from the colonizer's homeland? Does Zavala represent the new immigrant or merely another manifestation of the colonizer?

Edward Said reminds us that "to say simply that modern Orientalism has been an aspect of both imperialism and colonialism is not to say anything very disputable. Yet it is not enough to say it; it needs to be worked through analytically and historically" (Said 1979, 123). The play was chosen by a male actor-manager for performance before a largely Spanish-speaking audience that was either drawn from a native population that had become U.S. citizens following the annexation and statehood of Texas (and thus were an immigrant population in a land formerly recognized as their own) or a group newly exiled from México because of political strife. In many instances the audiences also included non-Spanish-speakers as well. Just as Said views "the Orient that appears in Orientalism" as a "system of representations framed by a whole set of forces that brought the Orient into Western learning, Western consciousness, and later, Western empire," here Orientalism emerges as a distinct product of political forces and activities that cannot be overlooked (Said 1979, 202–203).

Luisa's Orientalism stands out as difference, as sensuality, as something separate and dangerous and menacing to an entire Spanish race, and ultimately, it causes her to be perceived as someone who can be abused and destroyed but never legitimized. She is positioned as the weak outsider who seems to give power and superiority to Ramiro, who represents the imperial Western European oppressor. Luisa has been displaced as inferior, and only someone else who can understand a similar displacement, like Zavala, who struggles with his own displacement from his homeland, can defend her.

Zavala recognizes that, just as he was drawn to awaken by the brilliant sunshine from *el Oriente,* reputed to be the place of "pleasure of Mexican mornings," so too his "will" had been "subjugated" by something "grand and fierce" in Luisa, drawn to her "like a magnet to steel" (Neve 23–24). Ramiro, in contrast, is always drawn to the power of her love for him and his own desire to own her. But he remains the disreputable *mal hombre,* or evil male, throughout, not only the destructive imperialist but also the conqueror of her very soul. In effect, by this portrayal of Ramiro on the Spanish-language stage, the colonizer symbolically retains dominant force over the weaker, oppressed regions aligned with the Orient or distant passages in which Luisa appears only elusively.

What, then, does this tale tell us about the socio-political and cultural status of Chicanas/Chicanos in the Southwest during the Mexican Revolution? We may view Neve's *La Llorona* as a means of reminding the large number of men leaving México and remaining in the United States about the dire circumstances that could result from disrupting the family. But this view can only be sustained if we allow the role of Luisa to represent the Mexican woman as the outsider, the non-American, the one left behind who may, in the end, take action as a result of a crazed frenzy, capable of totally destroying the family once abandoned.

Ramiro emerges as the villain with regard to two women. He not only disrupts his contractual agreement with Luisa which was made under the eyes of God, but he also disrupts his man-made contract with Ana, which was made through legal marriage in the Church. In contrast to this despicable male figure, the image of woman is constructed as honorable and morally flawless. Both Luisa, from the lower class, and Ana, the woman Ramiro marries from the nobility, are portrayed as absolutely virtuous in character. Although Luisa has obviously sinned in the slaying of her child, it is clear that circumstances led her to an incomprehensible and unavoidable moment of insanity, and she visibly suffers greatly for her wrongdoing. The image of honor is reinforced when Luisa appears as the ghost figure at the end in the emblematic garb of justice, shown here as a woman symbolizing a divine justice that is ultimately avenged as she walks with the bloody clothes of her dead child in her right hand in front of Ramiro.

In contrast to the two wronged women, in the mother of Ramiro we see a cruel and dominant woman. She represents the Euroamerican colonizer, and she demands her son's obedience and loyalty. In sharp contrast to this oppressive mother, as the poor outsider in a conquered land Luisa must suffer despite her goodness and honorable character (as viewed by the lower-class servants and others who know her). Despite the image the male dramatist presents of the cruel mother, he seems to wholeheartedly support the lament that women must suffer at the hands of men. Yet another message seems to be at play here as well. It seems that the audience is also being reminded that leaving one's faraway and thus elusive place of origin will undoubtedly bring suffering, as both Luisa and Zavala and even Ramiro illustrate. Luisa has left the Orient and Zavala his native Spain. Zavala says: "Why did I leave my enchanted land?" Luisa's coming from the East, on the other hand, reminds us of the myth of Quetzalcóatl, in which the long-awaited savior of the Aztecs was expected to return from the East. Unfortunately, when the Aztecs mistook the arrival of Cortés for the return of that long-absent god, they met their demise.

Noticeably missing in this retelling of the La Llorona myth is the use of the river imagery that plays such a significant part in the tale as we hear it even today in the Southwest. That omission may already signify a permanent rupture with México resulting from the delineation of a border between the two countries. But because the Rio Grande River had not become the sort of exclusive barrier it would become in subsequent periods, the river was probably simply not an issue and thus not manifested within this tale.

Rather, the important message more directly targets that large population of men in the audience who were leaving families behind in México, and those already in the United States who more and more frequently neglected to return once they had reached the borderlands of the United States or those who, after settling in the borderlands, left their families behind as they went farther and farther away for jobs.[4] The warning in this drama may more readily revolve around the destructive forces behind their further distancing from the borderlands—the search for work and improved living conditions all too frequently resulted in further loss of family once a worker had moved to a new homeland.

The best chance for families to resist American assimilation was to hold on to the family unit. Mario T. García mentions that "the family represented the most basic cultural institution transferred by Mexican immigrants and was the most resistant barrier to American assimilation" (1994, 72). The strongest message in this particular play may be that if working men chose to enter the United States and leave their families behind in México, then they should do all they could to sustain their family ties in order to avoid a similar fate, regardless of the seemingly overwhelming temptations set before them. These temptations might include other women with more money or women capable of improving their societal status, such as the advantages offered by someone like the figure of Ana in the story. Mexican women in the United States were also being impacted by the forces pushing and pulling traditional family patterns apart. Several studies indicate that wives did accompany working-class men on their journey into the United States in substantial numbers. In these cases, women usually entered the labor force as wage workers. Women entering the job market were going against traditions and customs, and the family unit had to suffer some dramatic losses. With at least some education in the United States, women were even "more productive and efficient" (73), says García, and he points out that greater independence for young Mexican working women also accompanied these changes in lifestyles. Also, they might find themselves being used by Euroamerican men and then abandoned, as in the case of Luisa. The play might even suggest that intermarrying would sever ties with their own families and homeland forever. Faced with the possibility that increasing acculturation could subsume the traditional family environment into American mass culture, this drama could effectively remind viewers about the need for Mexicans in the United States to reconnect to their homeland which was just next door. And many could appreciate the performance simply as one of many cultural activities that brought the community together rather than breaking it apart. Certainly, Mexicans could preserve "many native cultural traditions that aided them in their transition to a new American setting by providing a familiar cultural environment," says García (73), and Mexicans did patronize various forms of entertainment, including theatrical events.[5]

Another message of *La Llorona* ties into religious belief, for a strong adherence to Catholicism is evident throughout the play. The young child is described as being "like an angel of the Spanish Virgin," and Ramiro says he serves his country and "the cross" (Neve 86, 87). There are continual laments to God and to heaven for justice and peace. Zavala tells us that remorse killed Ramiro. Zavala's final appeal for eternal justice coincides with his cry to heaven to have pity on those below and that Ramiro suffer eternal punishment for the crime of victimizing Luisa and for the wrongdoings he has inflicted on others. Traditionally Mexicans were Catholics, and that faith helped to unite both rural and urban Mexicans. It even helped to bring them together in support of traditional ways of doing things (Ruíz 1980, 412–413). But Catholicism became suspect and a growing distrust of the Church came with new ideas from the rebel leadership. It is not surprising then that these performances, situated on the United States side, promoted Catholicism, for active church attendance among Mexicans steadily declined as this population moved farther and farther away from the border (Acuña 1988, 177–178).

Other issues revolve around family duty, defending one's honor, parental pressure, and the dangers of resistance. In all of these matters, Zavala continually offers Luisa a better life far away in his own homeland. Distant Spain provides some political points of reference for some significant events in the New World, such as a rising unrest among Indians. This trend was sharply censured by the aristocracy who appear in the drama, positioning themselves in defense of King Philip II. The Oidor, Ana's father who is a minister newly arrived from Spain, is in charge of sentencing for crimes. He says: *"Hay asonadas provocadas por los indios pero estas no nos inquietan y de ellas mucho reimos"* [There are some rumblings provoked by the Indians, but these do not disturb us and we laugh at them]. Alvarado, one of the noblemen, responds: *"Entre los indios hay criollos con valor y con prestigio"* [Among the Indians there are creoles with valor and prestige], to which the Oidor responds: *"Pues á esos se les ahorca ó se les lleva á presidio, y de ese modo termina la semilla de los discolos"* [Well, those are hanged or they are taken to prison, and in that way the seed of disturbances ends]. When another nobleman praises the governance of the Oidor, the minister responds that he has always been the king's disciple. This type of positioning, defending the nobility in power, probably spoke directly to those exiled former defenders of the dictatorship in México; the drama censures them in its support of the common person over the tyranny of the oppressive *hidalgos* and its defense of the lower classes.

Class issues run throughout the drama: the verse form calls considerable attention to class distinctions, and the overall story also makes specific distinctions of status. Luisa comes from the lower class and speaks in prose with the servants, yet her speech becomes noticeably loftier verse when in the company of Ramiro. Material and class gains for Luisa occur through her relationship with Ramiro, and her servants call attention to the fact that despite now being associated with the upper-crust *hidalgo* or nobleman, she does not fail to care for them and understand the circumstances of their lower level. However, with the upper-class Spaniards, there is a clear distinction, and she is rejected by the mother as beneath her status, and devalued by Ramiro, who subjugates her to the level of a prostitute rather than recognizing her as his equal partner and wife under the eyes of God based on the relationship and vows they had previously taken. It is interesting to note that her inferior bloodlines are never considered as part of the makeup of their child. Ramiro rejects Luisa as an appropriate wife for someone of his status, but he wants the child that she bears him. Although she is worthless to Ramiro both in terms of class and race, his recognition that his race will end with him determines his decision to take the child from Luisa. The entire weight of race and nobility lies in his role as sole descendant of Cortés, and he cannot allow that lineage to end. While her bloodlines may be ignored, his cannot be left behind.

This connection to Cortés continually recalls the mythology of La Malinche as the primary referent to the telling of the conquest. The "weeping woman" story is thus male-centered, positioning women as submissive and mere vessels for the continuation of an entire people. In *Plotting Women: Gender and Representation in Mexico,* Jean Franco describes the figure of La Malinche as "the medium of conquest," and indicates that simply because of "scarcity of documentation," this figure became a "literary function (the 'helper' of the hero story), the medium-translator (traitor) of conquest and the flawed origin (mother) of a nation," that would make her "the symbol of the schizophrenic split between the European and the indigenous" (Franco 1989, xix).

This bifurcation of race centers on nationality. In situating the subject represented by Luisa as someone who has sold out her own race, the audience is reminded of the tragic fatality of intermarriage. Franco reminds us of Octavio Paz's positioning of the "Mexican disease" in *The Labyrinth of Solitude*

> in this ambiguous subjectivity of the sons of the Malinche who were shamed by her rape (conquest) and thus forced to reject the feminine in themselves as the devalued, the passive, the mauled and battered, as *La chingada,* the violated, the one who has been screwed over, fucked, and yet is herself the betrayer. (xix)

La Malinche became Cortés's mistress and interpreter, bore him a son, and continued to serve as interpreter after being exchanged yet again and given in marriage to one of his captains. Similarity ties these two flawed figures, La Malinche and La Llorona, both to Cortés and to his descendants, and now Luisa joins in this long lineage of sell-outs.

Yvonne Yarbro-Bejarano has studied the role of La Malinche as the "site of representation of sexuality for a culture." Yarbro-Bejarano views this figure as a way to shed light on the construction of gender, a figure that presages the subjected female constructs of the Chicano theatre of the 1960s. Through her sexual union with the white conqueror, "the defeat of a people and the destruction of their culture" ensued, producing the "half-breed" or mestizo race.

La Malinche thus becomes the construction of the gender "'woman' as subject, as other, reserving the active subject role for the masculine gender" instead of the feminine (Yarbro-Bejarano 1990, 134–135).

Verena Stolcke pushes the role of La Malinche even further with regard to Latina/Latino representation. In "Invaded Women: Gender, Race, and Class in the Formation of Colonial Society," Stolcke attempts a more far-reaching examination of the ideological dimensions of the conquest beyond the very obvious sexual violence perpetrated on women. Stolcke notes that societal and racial conceptualizations were brought over from the colonizer and disseminated through colonial elites. Societal formation thus indicates the process of certain conceptualizations and their formulation and adaptation to local circumstances with the result that a new hierarchical social order is not only legitimized but also perpetuated. Clearly, these changing values affected women (Stolcke 1994, 274).

If we go back to our "weeping woman" model in this process of formulation, we find that Luisa is rather ambiguous. If this portrayal of a good, honorable, and angelic figure, with "Roman virtue," is positioned to construct a national identity, she also represents a displaced, distanced, and strange woman from the Orient who is not only capable of molding different races into one but is also in the position to destroy them. The legitimacy of the child as the rightful heir is never an issue. Luisa and Ramiro have exchanged vows of marriage in the eyes of God. The practice of exchanging vows with each other rather than in a formal ceremony is found in the Spanish plays of Lope de Vega and Calderón de la Barca, among others. A vow under the eyes of God is just as binding as one taken in a church, and Ramiro is thus already married when he formally weds Ana. In effect, he commits adultery by marrying someone else (Neve 20). Here, the fact that Ramiro has already committed himself to Luisa makes her actions even more monumental and can help us understand why Ramiro's suffering must be so severe at the end: it is necessary to bring justice to a disorderly universe where crimes against women run rampant. Ramiro's punishment must equal his terrible wrongdoings against Luisa —he caused a permanent rupture in his family unit which culminated with the loss of his son.

If Luisa is responsible both for bearing a legitimate heir of Cortés and for destroying that lineage, then her treachery is equal to the most powerful treachery of all, both the conquest and the defeat of México itself. The power her figure wields here lies in the ultimate ability to eradicate an entire nation. If she is further positioned as representative of La Llorona at a time when Mexican women were crossing onto U.S. soil, is she not then a destructive and divisive force among men who is capable of reformulating an entire new nation? As Franco reminds us, citing from Ignacio Ramírez, "It is one of the mysteries of fate that all nations owe their fall and ignominy to a woman" and in this instance, this angel figure, appearing as the almost mythical counterfigure of La Malinche, is capable of ending a lineage (Franco 1989, xviii).

But unlike Ramiro's actions, Luisa's act is a heroic one. She sacrifices her son for the sake of resistance and social justice. She has revolted against a patriarchy deeply entrenched in Spanish/Mexican society and she haunts her surroundings in search of ultimate justice for the crimes committed against her. Only because of her sacrificial act can resolution and recovery occur. Through a bloody sacrifice, she brings about the end of the colonizer, and thus, the end of oppression for an entire people. This mother is faced with the most severe loss possible; her situation is made so dire that this choice is her only option. In one sense, she possesses the superhuman capabilities of a savior-figure in her ability to rescue her son from the fate of absolute colonization and complete loss of homeland he would suffer if he were to be taken from her. By extension, her recourse ultimately represents the only means for saving this society from continual domination from oppressors. But, as Maria Gonzalez tell us:

> While La Malinche has a specific politicized use, La Llorona serves the emotional fear of women because, unlike La Malinche, she is capable of enormous destruction. La Malinche does not have to be feared, just controlled. La Llorona is the uncontrollable. She has come to represent the overwhelmingly dangerous mother who is capable of destroying everything, while La Malinche simply is the failed nurturer, and La Virgen is the perfect nurturer. (1996, 161)

The bloody offering results in a pitiful and devastating end to an entire bloodline, reducing the maligned mother, mistress, and progenitor of the new race to hopeless haunting and searching for her innocent child. Resolution and recovery can occur only upon the ultimate death of the colonizer. When Ramiro expires at the end, Zavala looks to heaven to open its doors and provide consolation and hope for a future of restored order in this society. Thus, the larger discourse in this drama revolves around an even more prominent issue for Mexican men and women who crossed the border into the United States; namely, the fact that a downfall occurs if the family unit is permanently severed by oppressive forces against women, but even more so if the family breakdown occurs because family members leave the homeland for a new, faraway, and dangerous place characterized by a Euroamerican society which demoralizes and devalues their presence. In the play, reconstruction and recovery depended on men paying for their wrongdoings to the satisfaction of the watchful eyes of God. The severity of men's injustices against women can only be fully comprehended when set against the utterly tragic results that could occur when women were made to serve as instruments of conquest and then quickly abandoned and/or displaced when men found themselves in a "changing U.S. capitalist and imperialist system" (Castañeda 1990, 220).

Through a powerful figure like La Llorona, a woman could be taken seriously as the wielder of the strength to fight against patriarchal control. Theatrical representations that showed Mexican women resisting domination in a historical and social setting provided important models to emulate. This male-constructed subject revealed distinct ideas about class, race, and cultural identity within a heterosexual family structure. Struggle against injustice, hardships encountered, anger, victimization, and oppression are all topics that surface within this borderland view of the universe. When that figure was placed in the hands of a powerful female actor, the ability to inform, educate, and influence an audience was tremendous. Studies such as the contemporary work of José David Saldívar on "Border Matters," Sonia Saldívar-Hull on "Feminism on the Border," and Ramón Saldívar's analyses of "Chicano Narratives" can serve to inform this type of dramatic expression in these earlier periods (see J. Saldívar 1991 and 1997; Saldívar-Hull 1991; and R. Saldívar 1990 and 1991). As Ramón Saldívar points out in "Narrative, Ideology, and the Representation of American Literary History," narratives indicate that "language and discourse do affect human life in determining ways, ways that are themselves shaped by social history" (R. Saldívar 1991, 12). Narrative representations allow social formations to persist, and can thus be articulated and analyzed. Saldívar further adds: "Giving rise to questions concerning language itself, the sovereignty of our identity, and the laws that govern our behavior, narratives reveal the heterogenous systems that resist the formation of a unitary base of truth" (12). Thus, it is imperative to reread these narratives in order to expose "the framing limits" of what we might otherwise take for granted.

The politics of culture were tied to borderland spaces and cultural forms that stemmed from a patriarchal order. Topics of dominance and subordination, however, soon gave way to resistance and rejection of the past. As Mexican women's changing position in American society occurred during the first two decades of the twentieth century, the changing nature of society was becoming more and more evident. At the end of the first decade, officially 651,596 Mexican workers and their families lived in the United States, according to Acuña (Acuña 1988, 164), and this count was taken before the harvest season. By 1920, the number of Mexicans in San Antonio had grown to 60,000 out of the city's 161,379 residents (169), and by the end of the decade about 70,000 of the city's 232,542 residents were Mexicanos. During the first decade, San Antonio had become a center for Mexican exiles, with 25,000 arriving in 1913 alone, and in the 1920s religious refugees had joined that exile community. These Mexican refugees were mainly middle and upper class, in contrast to the larger number of Mexicans who worked as laborers (169). Not all Mexican women in San Antonio stayed in the home; 16 percent of Mexican women worked outside the home, as compared to the 17 percent of all women in Texas who entered the waged labor force (170).

Evidence shows that the Mexican family unit living in the United States was changing as early as 1911. In "Studying Chicanas: Bringing Women into the Frame of Chicano Studies," Alma M. García points out that the question of gender inequality must be addressed, since most research has focused on the role of "Chicanas as nurturers of family members within a hostile Anglo society" instead of on women's domesticity and gender inequality (A. García 1986, 23). She adds: "The literature on the Chicano family has produced evidence, both historical and contemporary, to challenge the distorted social science view of the Chicano family and the role of Chicanas within it," but "the issue about the source of female oppression and inequality within the context of the Chicano family has not been fully examined" (23). In "La Familia: The Mexican Immigrant Family, 1900–1930," Mario T. García evaluates the Mexican immigrant family during the period 1900 to 1920, stating:

> If the family unit through its cultural and economic support system was the most essential factor in the ability of Mexican immigrants to adjust to life north of the border, at the same time it represented an oppressive condition for women. Women not only maintained and reproduced male workers through their roles as housewives and mothers, but some also had to labor outside the home to supplement family income and in so doing experience a "double day." (M. García 1980, 129)

While Mexicans generally received lower pay than Anglo Americans, Mexican women were "the lowest-paid and most vulnerable workers" at least in El Paso, based on hearings conducted in 1919 by the Texas Industrial Welfare Commission (Acuña 1988, 167, 168). While Anglo women had access to skilled jobs, large numbers of Mexicanas (Mexican women) were employed by establishments that only offered them unskilled jobs, such as the laundries of El Paso. Anglo women earned on average $16.55 per week; Mexicanas earned on average $8.00 per week. Acuña notes that the hearings also showed that some Mexicanas earned as little as $4.00 to $5.00 per week, and those working in department stores were generally relegated to the rear of the store or the basement; higher-paying jobs on the main floor were reserved for Anglo women (168). When employers attempted to explain these discrepancies, they claimed that Anglo women "outworked *Mexicanas*" and, as Acuña adds: "They hired *Mexicanas* only because they could not employ a sufficient number of 'white' women. . . . After all, the standard of living among Mexicans was much lower than that of whites and so they required less money" (168).[6]

The economic need for Mexican women to work challenged the traditional patriarchal Mexican family structure to some degree. Once Mexican women became wage earners in a capitalist economic system, how did they intersect with American society in terms of race, class and gender? By examining another playtext, we can glimpse diverse topics brought about within this changing society. The family had been "significantly affected by changes in the labor process, particularly wives, mothers and daughters who, though still within an economically low income group" gained "greater personal liberties, through employment, education, contact with other women, access to media, recreation, mechanization of domestic work, and the consumption of various goods and services as the family's income" increased (R. Sánchez 1990, 15). Along with these substantial changes, "acculturation to the dominant ideologies" also occurred, resulting in changes in what was "appropriate for women to do, say, and think" (15).

While it is difficult to determine an accurate picture of family life for Mexicans in Texas during the first two decades of the twentieth century, social change was evident for Mexican American women; industrialization and urbanization forced them to adjust to changed conditions (M. García 1994, 81). These women were now faced with being affected by and finding means of interacting with various social elements, including, as Sánchez lists: "labor struggle, labor stratification, immigration, deportations, racism, lower wages, occupational and residential segregation, low educational attainment, lack of political power, as well as urbanization, industrialization, occupational mobility, social mobility, consumerism and ideological assimilation" (1990, 21). Socialization patterns, sexual freedoms and restrictions, reproductive practices, female roles and functions, and the extent of personal liberties for women in their community were increasingly changing, and these women were impacted in ways that have yet to be fully studied in the context of the social, economic, political, and sexual factors that interconnected and affected them. The earlier "victimization and oppression" examined through the playtext of *La llorona* shows some indication of the results of these conditions, and the evident social change now being experienced by these women, "constantly affecting" them and "changing their social relations and social life" (21), may be scrutinized within the framework of theatrical production.

In the midst of this growing societal change for women, the investigation of the emerging Chicana as subject on the American stage can be informed by examining a playtext as representative of women caught in the midst of social change. *La mujer adúltera* (*The Adulterous Woman*) is a four-act drama with a seven-scene prologue, written by Juan P. Velásquez.[7] This text can shed light on the contextualizing of the Chicana on an even broader scale than the earlier text allowed. The promptbook, dated 1907, includes a listing of the itinerary of a tour taken by the Compañía Villalongín y Guzmán in 1916 (see Ramírez 1986). The tour included unspecified cities in Arizona, as well as Cananea, Sonora, and Nogales (although it is not indicated whether it was Nogales, México, or Nogales, Arizona). This playtext is representative of work which appeared at the peak of the period under discussion.

La mujer adúltera is set in Santillana del Mar in the region of Santander, Spain. This place provided the name the Spanish colonists in New Spain (México) gave to a new military settlement that extended from the northern Mexican region of what is now Tamaulipas to the lower Rio Grande valley on the Texas side from Laredo to the Gulf of México, or "Mexican Sea." Symbolically, then, the site embodies the dichotomy of the conqueror/conquered in the New World. Not only is there the direct connection between Santander, Spain, and the New Santander, that is, México, and subsequently the borderlands, but other links with New Spain also surface.

In this play, Magdalena, described as the "pearl" of her surroundings, comes from the sea, although the place itself is vague and mysterious. Her mother too had been an adulteress. Magdalena had been brought *á estas costas de no sé donde* (to these coasts from I do not know where), an old neighbor woman tells us (Velásquez 13). She was given to Angel's family for them to raise. Pablo, Angel's father, had killed Magdalena's mother's lover upon discovery of her infamy. Pablo had been the sea captain for the man whom Magdalena calls her father, Pedro. Amidst *una tempestad horrorosa* (a horrible tempest) at sea, Pablo slew her mother's lover and threw him into the sea in an effort to save Don Pedro from dishonor (44). Pedro is also the one responsible for sending Angel off to sea to make his fortune. Recognizing Angel's expertise as a mariner, Don Pedro assigns him a fleet for him to make his fortune. During Angel's absence, however, Magdalena also succumbs to disgrace. The imagery of the sea, the dominant imagery throughout the play, thus serves as the source of infamy and loss of honor in many ways.

Characterized as unusually ambitious, with a mind of her own that apparently cannot be contained, Magdalena no sooner marries Angel than a wealthy nobleman, Fernando, proclaims he must have her after seeing an artist's portrait of her. Fernando comes to claim her and she leaves her new husband for a presumably better life. Although Fernando makes many proclamations of love for Magdalena, he never marries her. Always unsettled and haunted by her deception and abandonment of her husband, she is soon confronted with her past. While it had been reported that Angel was lost at sea, he soon reappears. An artist had captured Magdalena with Angel on their wedding day, and Magdalena learns that her portrait has been on exhibit at a highly publicized exposition. She soon learns that Angel is alive, although he confronts her in the guise of someone named Sandoval, saying he must be someone else if she rejects the past.

Magdalena fears discovery of her infamy and dishonorable deed. The elite society in which she now dwells will know she has committed adultery. Upon hearing that the painting has been bought, she realizes that recovery is impossible and she decides to confront her past. Magdalena begs forgiveness, recalling for Angel how God forgave María Magdalena. Angel in turn reminds her that even María Magdalena in the Bible sought peace before she was forgiven by Christ.

Magdalena does seek peace and forgiveness. Upon discovering that her husband is alive, Fernando abruptly abandons her. When she goes to her father for solace, he reveals her mother's infamy. Her father has gone insane from the shock of his daughter's treachery. She then goes to Angel to ask that he forgive Fernando, who robbed her of happiness. She begs Angel not to seek revenge. Angel reveals that Fernando has already died, yet he has forgiven him. Achieving the peace she desires, Magdalena expires, thanking Angel and asking for his pardon even at the end. Angel's final words are that her death coincides with the death of Angel's hope to have her, and Angel asks God to pardon her as he does.

ASSESSMENTS

In both plays examined here, *La Llorona* and *La mujer adúltera,* men have attempted to plot women, but it is significant that in one image the female figure appears as a virtuous victim while in the other she appears as an opportunistic adulteress. In both cases, the women suffer and die without attaining happiness on earth and without final absolution for their sins. The fact that male actor-managers chose to illustrate these two figures on the stage offers us an opportunity to shed light on how gender was manipulated in the Spanish-speaking theatre of the United States to represent the problems and experience of the immigrant Mexican. The fact that neither of these women achieves emancipation does, in fact, intricately bind the figure of woman with the fate of the larger community and with the censuring of behavioral patterns in both men and women as Mexicans became more firmly entrenched on American soil and more and more firmly rejected their ties to their mother country, México.

Perhaps certain modes of resistance in the Mexican population in the United States were impacting on the types of performances presented on the Spanish-language stage. It is at an art exposition that Magdalena is revealed to the world as an adulteress. By publicly displaying a woman who has fallen to the dangers of selfishness and personal gain, turning her back on her family and loved ones, the immediacy of the dangers of urbanization and a changing society directly confronted anyone listening to and viewing the performance who might be guilty of similar pursuits. Walter Benjamin views "expositions" as the origins of the "pleasure industry," which "refined and multiplied the varieties of reactive behavior of the masses" in preparing the masses for adapting to advertisements—"Look, but don't touch"—and "taught [them] to derive pleasure from the spectacle alone" (Buck-Morss 1989, 85). The shops depended "on a public clientele of the well-to-do," and folk-based commodities at these fairs became big business. Millions of visitors might attend, and the range of clientele was even broader if the working classes also attended. These events featured "shrines of industry" and partakers came to view the "wonders that their own class had produced but could not afford to own, or to marvel at machines that would displace them" (86). In effect, "the economic possibility and necessity of a social revolution" was put in front of everyone's eyes, and these working classes could glimpse "the previously unheard of levels of development of the means of production" that had been attained by all civilized countries (87). But these expositions could also show that "the modern development of productive powers, given the anarchy presently reigning in production, must necessarily lead to industrial crises" that could cause destruction in their effects on the workings of the world economy (87).

Within this framework, placing Magdalena in an art exposition, on the one hand, threatens to reveal her adultery to the world, and on the other, provides a figure of a displaced national symbol of progress, that is, someone who has moved from a lower-class position to one of progress achieved only for selfish and personal gain. Through Magdalena the Mexican American audience could glimpse in this drama the results of transforming patriotism into a commodity on display. As a commodity Magdalena became woman who met her downfall at the hands of a dominant male from the colonizing nation; she was uprooted from her homeland and appropriated by the colonizer just as he would destructively acquire any other property.

Was the dramatist attempting to place Magdalena on public display? If the intent was for the masses to derive pleasure from the viewing, was that pleasure intended to be the satisfaction of catching an adulteress in her sinful ways, or was it perhaps simply meant to allow the viewer to glimpse this symbol of tainted womanhood? Or was there a more subversive message intended here, along the lines of how the figure of woman has functioned in the work of men? As Susan Suleiman points out, when emancipatory and anti-patriarchal aspects of women emerge, these new views can surpass the old dichotomies of audiences merely invited to participate in witnessing their downfall and destruction (Suleiman 1990, 140).

The time in which these plays were being performed, namely, 1910 to 1924, coincides with a period of mass struggle and political turmoil on both sides of the border. These years were marked by critical social factors, including, as Ricardo Romo indicates in his list of distinct critical conditions in California alone, "an economic depression, the transition from a commerce and trade economy to one of industry and manufacturing, a large influx of alien population, mainly Mexican, which crowded old communities and established prominent ethnic enclaves, Mexican-U.S. border conflict, labor turmoil, and war-related hysteria," all producing a "situation which promoted strong nativist sentiments" throughout the Southwest (Romo 1983, 89). Nationally, Romo adds, "the years 1910–1921 witnessed the rise of radical labor movements and of extremist organizations espousing racial hatred; the passage of immigration quota laws based on race and nationality; and political repression" (89). Added to all of these conditions, World War I brought "dislocation and instability to the United States in a manner unparalleled since the Civil War" (Romo 1983, 107). Thus, we cannot ignore a context that triggers specific concerns about class consciousness that workers could easily identify.

Jean Franco situates revolution within nationalism and modernization. Franco reminds us that "the constitution of Mexican nationalism was a long process that had its roots in the criollo nationalism before Independence and that received a new impetus with the Mexican Revolution during its earlier segment, that is, 1910–1917, a revolution in which the peasantry played a major role." With the postrevolutionary society came a populist nationalism that tended to obscure the Mexican stage as an instrument of capitalist modernization. In 1917, women were well on their way to attaining the national vote—the issue of women's emancipation was a "part of a major campaign against the obscurantism of the Church, and some revolutionary leaders supported emancipation because they saw women's religious 'fanaticism' as an obstacle to revolutionary ideology" (Franco 1989, xix). Supporters of women's emancipation included men like Venustiano Carranza, the first president of postrevolutionary México. Yet, official ideology would return to the idealized patriarchal family, an ideal featured in the playtexts directly drawn from the Mexican stage that we have examined here. However, while women's voices may have been obscured by the political and societal aspects that dominated the new social order in México, performances in the United States featuring the female as subject did not operate under this stricture. Women in performance were not only seen and heard, but they were also either intentionally positioned or they positioned themselves as voices signifying meaningful borderland performance narratives.

Unquestionably, specific textual references in *La mujer adúltera* indicate that the intent is to provide parallels between the homeland and America. The parallels are unmistakably related to place, situating México in contrast to the borderlands. For example, a missionary arrives from California, giving good news to Magdalena—Angel has been away at sea in Ecuador. The Compañía Villalongín's promptbook indicates their change of the text: instead of having Fernando say that Angel comes from "another world," as the original text specifies, the promptbook shows that Fernando says that Angel comes from "America." This attention to historicity and situating of place centers México; its dominant representation is contrasted with a marginalized "America" as the Other, situated somewhere along the unspecified outer boundaries that mark the site of origin for both Magdalena and Angel, that unknown place at sea. Given the drama's preoccupation with this marginalized woman's exile and homelessness, this type of reworking of place is very significant.

The heavy emphasis on water imagery in this play further calls attention to specificity of place when water functions as such a vital factor in border crossing performance narrative forms. The Rio Grande River in Texas served as the physical manifestation of the border between the United States and México.

This body of water came to signify the site of loss of country, ruptured homeland, and place of racial and class conflict. While La Llorona is destined to a bifurcated/bicultural existence, always walking the borderlands, touching both sides of her ethnicity, distanced from her homeland forever as she is now situated on the United States side through performance, Magdalena, on the other hand, comes from those unknown depths of the sea, functioning as a disrupter of domesticity, homeless and exiled in a land that is not her own. Magdalena has violated the marriage contract and permanently disrupted not only her family but also the extended family that surrounds her. Her actions impact on Angel's parents and their relations in the community, and she causes an even further disjuncture with her father, who is also a friend to her extended family, Angel and his parents. Through Angel's subsequent act as a disrupter of a presumed safe haven of feigned marriage and family that Fernando and Magdalena represent, we in fact find that this drama serves as representative of an ideology that places the family unit as the very core of community—only through its cohesive force can chaos and tragedy be avoided. In both plays we have examined, then, the tragic act firmly separates the family forever.

The use of two playtexts as representative of the status of Mexican American women during the Mexican Revolution also raises questions about gender and the roles that these women undertook as they participated in a changing social arena that was both giving way to new family structures and at the same time attempting to adhere to old traditions. Women entering the work force because of the severe economic conditions they faced caused radical change from the old patriarchal hierarchy. Greater independence for young Mexican working women was inevitable, and eventual changes in their status in family relations resulted. Ramón Saldívar points out that: "Socialist feminist scholarship has shown how under capitalist patriarchy 'the control of wage labor by capital and men's control over women's labor power and sexuality in the home are connected'" (Saldívar 1990, 21). He adds: "The relationship of women to men must be understood in both the labor market and families with the result that the family becomes a primary site of political struggle" (21). The many changing social and economic factors that Mexican women in the United States faced placed them in opposition to traditional cultural values and exposed them to racism, exploitation, and discrimination. The new ideologies they forged to replace the dominant patriarchy of their past and to address new questions of class and race and gender resulted in complex contradictions for Mexican American women. The two playtexts we have investigated and the many other extant promptbooks that represent an important period of professional theatre in Texas must continually be explored in order to better comprehend and, in effect, rewrite the role that these women played in American history. These dramatic narratives that were performed by Mexican women in the United States offer significant representations of American life and reveal how they intersected with society, politics, history, and contemporary events, and, as

Ramón Saldívar asserts, these narratives can take on "critical, political functions and appropriate the historical space of the southwestern borderlands," where they are "positioned between cultures, living on borderlines," reflecting in no uncertain terms the forms and styles of their origins (25).

Through this investigation we have been able to arrive at the many ways that women have been able to perform their new and changing experiences in a new homeland. Until we have playtexts written by women of this period, we will have to continue to explore the performative narratives that these works have to offer in order to better understand the impact that women have had on the social, political, and cultural history during the time of the Mexican Revolution. Nevertheless, we can arrive at several conclusions that may be drawn from this examination of two representative types of plays typically found in the repertories of the Mexican acting companies that appeared and subsequently took up residency in the United States. The dramas of the latter half of the nineteenth century and the early twentieth century include features that were already prevalent in European drama. Emilio Carilla points out that plays by Dumas, Hugo, and Schiller, as well as by all the major Spanish romantic dramatists, were already being presented on the Mexican stage by the time the principal Mexican dramatists Ignacio Rodríguez Galván and Fernando Calderón began writing. Thus, such familiar features as sentimentalism, an abundance of entanglements, frustrated loves, orphans, and abandoned honest women helped to create a Mexican romanticism. In form, the plays ran the gamut from tragedy to melodrama. Fatalism, adverse destiny, and gloom, as well as exaggerated passions, made up the scheme of all the works. Women were exalted, noble sentiments were declared, and male heroes were chivalrous. Nature figured in significantly, with sunshine or gloom, depending on the status of characters' souls. The stories were also shaped by a sense of mystery and shadiness in some characters and by appeals to the sentiments over reason. Language was declamatory, lofty, and emphatic. All tragic romantic dramas produced by these companies were historical in content (Ramírez 1990, 43–44).

Some primary characteristics in Mexican romantic tragedy upheld freedom as the highest ideal and as an exemplar of patriotism and Christianity. Secondary characteristics included individualism through which the ideal of human justice was exalted. Melancholy and sentimentality and a strong sense of pessimism about earthly happiness were dominant. With regard to form, freedom was also of the essence, with a mingling of the comic with the tragic, and humor with pathos. Freedom in language, style, and meter and highly improbable plotlines were also evident (44).

Another type of play that was performed was the serious full-length play. The conclusions that can be drawn from studying these works and the principal female characters in them are that the works provide a reflection of Spanish and Mexican life of the times. The dramatists writing in this genre depict and investigate customs and manners and beliefs of early-twentieth-century life through realistic drama. These works more than others gave important views of a changing society. Also, the ever-popular short comic pieces which generally accompanied full-length plays at a complete evening at the theatre illustrated the audiences' desire for humor, as evidenced by the very great number of such plays still extant. These comic short pieces required minor staging demands and reflected the acceptance of a changing language, regionalism, and kinship with México as the mother country above all of the others. This genre reached the height of its popularity in México during the first quarter of the twentieth century and served as the basis for the later "sketch" and comic routines which brought vaudeville and variety acts into vogue in the 1920s and would later be heard on Spanish-language radio and seen on Spanish-language television, performed by many of the professional performers who had appeared on stage with these works (44).

The themes and ideas found in these works reveal the values, beliefs, and aspirations of the Mexican American audiences, that is, their culture and tastes. The value of using the Spanish language stands out because both Spanish and Mexican settings appear. The use of both historical and contemporary settings indicates the strong sense of nationalism and patriotism desired by the spectators who were witnessing their heritage being enacted on these stages. A strong belief in the family unit combined with a positive portrayal of Catholicism surface, and the serious tone of these issues generally prevails. Above all, the people's desires for freedom, happiness, and a better quality of life contributed to the popularity of many of the plays produced for a very long time.[8]

The period during the Mexican Revolution brought to the American stage a wide range of dramas produced by a large number of companies. Through the performances the audiences became acquainted with the dramas of international acclaim, from the old and established plays to the modern repertory, both building and influencing cultural life in the United States. The Mexican theatre of the time had been viewed as an elite institution; Porfirio Díaz and his regime were its major supporters. Understandably, this venue was among those greatly affected by the demise of the Porfirato. Although in the United States the Mexican American theatre catered to all classes, it was especially familiar to those large numbers of the elite taking asylum in Texas during their exile from México.

Immigrants stood together. They held on to their heritage, language, and traditions in the American theatres they supported and they learned to adapt to their new surroundings and integrate into a new society. The Spanish-language theatre played a highly significant part as an institution which opened its doors to all interested participants, and the American stage gave these new audiences a warm and welcoming reception (45–46).

Mexican American theatre thrived for a long time in Texas. Luis Valdez, the director of El Teatro Campesino, and other Chicano dramatists and performers have looked to pre-Columbian rituals and ceremonies and amateur dramatic traditions as the primary sources from which to draw. But the period of Mexican revolt should also serve as a rich resource for those groups. Contemporary Chicana/Chicano theatre companies, always in search of new plays drawn from their own experience and background, can benefit from going back to the plays and performance tradition which the Mexican Revolution brought to American theatre. By reinterpreting these works for contemporary audiences, these groups can broaden the repertory to reflect important connections to their past just as many resident companies throughout the country have been doing with the classics of world drama and certain ethnic drama for a very long time. More broadly, these works serve to expand the scope of history by including such traditions in the annals of American and world performance history. In the history of Chicana/Chicano/Latina/Latino theatre, despite the lack of plays by women, performance has served as a means of empowerment and an exercise of power through male constructs, especially during the period of the Mexican Revolution. However, not until we can evaluate the distinct voice of female playwrights can we broaden the various aspects of the woman's voice in history. Fortunately, contemporary Chicana/Latina playwrights have emerged so that we can begin to more fully examine their voice as a powerful weapon within a cultural, socio-economic, and political context. Before turning to these playwrights, however, we will first examine the major influences on these female dramatists.

3

BARRIOS, BORDERLANDS, AND MUJERES
From Social Protest to Political Performance

In the first four decades of this century about one-tenth of México's population crossed the northern border, resulting in a large mass migration relative to the size of the Mexican population (Acuña 1988, 188). As David G. Gutiérrez discusses in his important study on the significance and meanings of Mexican immigration, *Walls and Mirrors: Mexican Americans, Mexican Immigrants, and the Politics of Ethnicity,* part of this migration was the result of the "steady increase in the rate of immigration from México," followed by the land displacement they encountered as a result of land policies instituted under Porfirio Díaz, drawing them to the United States where they found a "rapidly diversifying and expanding southwestern economy" (Gutiérrez 1995, 39). The numbers steadily increased through the turn of the century, and the Mexican Revolution increased this stream even more. In 1910 the population of México had reached 15.16 million, and in that year at least 382,002 Mexicans lived in the United States (Acuña 1988, 158). Takaki notes that between 1900 and 1930, the Mexican population in the Southwest grew from an estimated 375,000 to 1,160,000; most of this group were born in México (Takaki 1993, 317). About 25,000 had crossed the border within the first decade, and another 170,000 between 1910 and 1920, with "the greatest surge" occurring during the 1920s, when nearly half a million Mexicans arrived in the United States (317). Gutiérrez points out that "by the 1920s their rate of entry for a short time rivaled the great European migrations of the late nineteenth century. Although immigration and demographic statistics for this era are notoriously inaccurate, most scholars concur that at least one million, and possibly as many as a million and a half Mexican immigrants entered the United States between 1890 and 1929" (Gutiérrez 1995, 40). As a result, the Mexican American population underwent considerable change from the turn of the century onward.[1] Mexicans were first encouraged to cross the border, as Ronald Takaki points out, "because their labor was needed" (Takaki 1993, 317). But despite the demand for their labor, they soon found themselves excluded and discriminated against—socially, economically, and politically. Immigration of this magnitude "tended to exacerbate the many social, economic, and political problems Mexican Americans faced in American society" (D. Gutiérrez 1995, 40). Because they were isolated by "the border of racial segregation," Mexicans in the United States forged together as a community (Takaki 1993, 326).

Held together through an ethnic and cultural identity, a shared common language, and the racism of the dominant society, these communities endured despite intensified Euroamerican nativism, forced repatriation, legal and illegal migration, and a declining job market (Acuña 1988, 235). In the Midwest, railroad labor and seasonal migrant work brought the population of Mexicans in that region to an estimated 58,000 by the late 1920s (175). Barrios, or neighborhoods, generally formed close to places of work. Populations grew in Michigan, Ohio, Indiana, and the surrounding area, and Chicago soon developed into the midwest Mexican capital.

By the beginning of the 1930s, over half of the Mexicans in the United States were found in urban centers, and migration to the cities continued to increase (198). Mexicans clustered in barrios resembling their former Mexican *colonias* (175). Ricardo Romo's extensive study, *History of a Barrio: East Los Angeles*, details the Mexican presence in Los Angeles through the 1930s. Romo notes that "by 1930 Mexicanos had created the largest 'Mexican city' in the United States, a stable and growing community that rivaled in size principal cities of most other states" (Romo 1983, 61). We have already noted the increased urbanization of Mexicans in Texas, and almost 20,000 Mexicans lived in Chicago by the end of the decade (Acuña 1988, 175).

While Mexicans were forging new communities in the United States, wave after wave of Latina/Latino immigrants were also arriving (D. Gutiérrez 1995, 116; Acuña 1988, 200; de Varona 1996, 98). Latina/Latino immigrants have come to the United States from many different cultures and constitute a significant portion of the Spanish-speaking population in this country. Puerto Ricans and Cubans comprise the two other largest Latina/Latino populations after Mexicans. Christopher Columbus's visit to Puerto Rico in 1493 soon led to Spanish settlement of that island. The Spanish population there grew slowly, though, and in 1898 Spain ceded Puerto Rico to the United States. The migration of Puerto Ricans to the mainland began slowly in the latter part of the nineteenth century. They settled mostly in eastern cities and in areas where there was a demand for agricultural work. Although only about 1,500 were living on the United States mainland by 1910, a minor influx occurred after Puerto Ricans were made citizens of the United States in 1917 (Varona 1996, 129; Heyck 1994, 8–9). Few returned to the island after World War I. Migration of Puerto Ricans into the United States increased rapidly after World War II; most Puerto Rican immigrants chose to live in New York City. By 1970, the mainland Puerto Rican population had reached 1.4 million, having doubled in size in only one decade.[2]

Cuba was claimed for Spain by Columbus in 1492. Although it was captured by the British in 1762, it was soon returned to Spain. Situated in the West Indies, the island was inhabited largely by Euroamericans from Spain and a great many Blacks, mulattos, and Mayan and other Indians as a result of the Spanish slave trade. Spain gave up all claims to Cuba after the Spanish-American War of 1898. The United States established military rule, remaining in Cuba until 1909 when Cuba elected a democratic government. In 1953 Fidel Castro led an unsuccessful revolt against the ruling Batista regime. When civil war broke out in 1958, Batista fled in exile, and in 1959 Castro gained control of a dictatorship that continues to this day.

Like Puerto Rican migration, Cuban movement into the United States also began in the latter part of the nineteenth century. Cubans first settled in Key West and Tampa and subsequently in Miami where the population soared. However, the Cuban population in the United States did not reach immense proportions until after the Castro-led revolution of 1959. In 1960, Cubans in the United States numbered 64,000, and after the Cuban Missile Crisis of 1962, 181,000 more sought refuge here. The early 1960s brought 55,916 more, and a subsequent program to reunify families led to over 200,000 more refugees.[3]

In addition to these three larger populations of Latinas/Latinos in the United States, immigrants from Central and South America could be found in various places in the country, but those populations did not reach significant proportions until about the 1980s. As Earl Shorris points out in his *Latinos: A Biography of the People:*

> With few exceptions, the pattern of emigration from Latin America would be repeated throughout the century. At first, only a small number of poor people are driven to emigrate; the economic situation worsens, and there is a revolution; the left leads the revolution; the rich and well-educated elite flee the leftists; as the revolution goes on, the middle class and the poor follow the rich vanguard out of the devastated country. (Shorris 1992, 43)

Despite the broad range of differences between each of these ethnic groups, common links lie in a shared heritage of language, traditions, and religion. Shorris also adds their commonality in having experienced living as "minorities in a very race-conscious United States" (202). Through these links "there has been so much cross-fertilization" that we probably cannot even trace any one community's contributions to the mainstream; rather, we can appreciate the richness of the Latina/Latino culture as a whole and its "enhancement of American life" (203).

FROM THE DEPRESSION AND THE WORKS PROGRESS ADMINISTRATION THROUGH THE 1950s

Despite the end of professional theatrical activity during the Great Depression, theatrical activity of some kind was either maintained or established for the first time during this period in all cities and barrios where Mexican, Cuban, and Puerto Rican immigrants congregated. With an increase in literacy among these groups through the first quarter of the century came attempts at organizing theatre and dramatic clubs. These organizations were generally comprised of males, although in some instances women were also included, such as in the case of the Hispanic American Dramatic Club of Las Vegas, New Mexico (Rebolledo 1995, 20). In Los Angeles, barrio associations emerging after 1918 helped to maintain "the traditional culture and values of the homeland through the promotion of patriotic and religious festivals" and "[raised] both the ethnic and the class consciousness of the community," according to Ricardo Romo (1983, 149). He notes that the fiestas allowed new immigrants a chance to show group consciousness, pointing out that "the ethnic cohesiveness of the Mexican community also illustrated the slow rate of assimilation of this group" (161).

Community theatre emerged in most Spanish-speaking centers, and all kinds of plays and theatrical activity were produced, ranging from traditional Mexican and Spanish plays to *zarzuelas*, or musicals, and melodramas and variety. *Mutualistas*, or mutual aid groups, generally sponsored such events in order to raise funds for a wide range of community needs, which included helping the needy both in the United States and in México, striving to maintain cultures of origin, and guarding against injustices. These mutual benefit organizations were founded in the 1920s and 1930s. They became firmly entrenched throughout the Midwest, generally revolving around labor unions. Rodolfo Acuña tells us that "in the face of injustice, midwestern Mexicans remained highly nationalistic" (Acuña 1988, 175). He points out that in 1924, Mexicanas were less than a third of the Mexican population. Eleven years later they constituted over fifty percent, although it is always important to remember that Mexicans in the Midwest were undercounted by the census (177). The Mexican population of St. Paul, Minnesota, already settled by the 1920s, offered several venues for community benefits, including the Guild of Catholic Women formed by Mexican women in the fall of 1930 at the Mission of Our Lady of Guadalupe. In Chicago, there was a Mexican Social Center established in the early 1930s and the Mexican Mothers' Club there was formed in 1937. With these types of networks of communication, women were important contributors to the process of community building as participants in clubs, unions, and workers' associations, and were distanced more and more from México in a continuing process of urbanization (178, 243, 189).

Community participation in religious celebrations gave many young Chicanas/Chicanos/Latinas/Latinos unique opportunities to perform. Often entire families would play roles re-enacting important Church calendar events, such as the Christmas pageant, at which many angels and shepherds could appear along with the central figures of Mary, Joseph, the Wise Men, and so on. In many accounts, women played the part of the Virgin or angels, giving them their first encounter with performance and cultivating a future interest in the profession.

Estella Balli and Margarita Garza Cantú dressed in
Charro Day costume, Brownsville, Texas
(March 1946).
Private collection of Elizabeth C. Ramírez.

During the period of the 1920s through the 1950s, the Catholic Church continued its very long history of using theatre for didactic purposes. Historically, the Catholic Church has acted as an "agent of social control," as Acuña points out: "Most of its hierarchy as well as its priests have been Irish and/or German, rarely identifying with minorities such as Mexicans and their social struggles" (430). In the 1920s the Catholic Church in México had become distrustful as a result of the events of the Mexican Revolution. In the United States, the Mexican clergy was "anti–Mexican government and anti-radical," and many Mexicans held a strong anticlerical view as a result of anticlerical sentiments in México during and after the Revolution which led to the formation of male and female youth groups organized to propagate the faith. Ricardo Romo informs us that "throughout the 1910s and 1920s the progressive spirit within the Christian Church influenced the religious activities in the barrio," and "while the vast majority of Mexicans believed in Catholicism, church leaders from this denomination and Protestant sects as well felt challenged by the apparent weak bonds between the community and Roman Catholic parishes" (Romo 1983, 143). Church leaders did not always show empathy toward these immigrants, and both Catholic and Protestant churches faced serious problems with a shortage of Spanish-speaking personnel. Nevertheless, Church leaders did eventually aim religious activities at raising the standard of living for the Mexican family, and a wide range of activities, such as night schools, clinics, boys' and girls' clubs, and instruction in English, Spanish, music, and other areas soon occurred (146). The end result was an attempt to "Americanize the Mexican immigrants," with an "ultimate goal of stripping the immigrants of their old homeland attachments and making them over" (146). A variety of theatrical entertainment with this intent soon emerged.

In his important article about "Border Culture," Mario T. García mentions that for Mexican immigrants, "Catholicism provided a familiar cultural environment as well as institutional support for Mexicans' adjustment north of the border." He adds: "The Church not only took into consideration Mexican cultural traditions, but also became an agent of Americanization among its parishioners, especially those families, many of them political refugees, who could afford to send their children to Catholic schools" (M. García 1994, 75). "The mass of Mexican immigrants retained their popular religious beliefs and practices by transferring them across the border," he notes, and "regardless of economic or political backgrounds, first generation immigrants and political refugees, through their reestablishment of spiritual societies common in México as well as the reenactment of native Mexican religious celebrations, successfully maintained cultural continuity and helped create a sense of community in the barrios" (75). García provides us with an interesting account of amateur theatrical activities as a means by which the southside parochial schools, for example, under the direction of the American Sisters of Loretto, emphasized, as one part of their curriculum, the Americanization of their students, and attempted to change what they considered to be the Mexicans' bad cultural habits, utilizing what he calls "a bicultural approach in [their] treatment of Mexican immigrants" (76). The *Times* reported performances by a male choir and an instrumental performance by the Mandolin Club in 1904. García adds:

> Some of the girls who presented a drama in three acts entitled "The Little Waiters" received "round upon round of applause, and demonstrated the fact that several of the young ladies had real dramatic activity." Impressed, the *Times* gave credit to the students' teachers and praised the Catholic Church for its work among the Mexican children of the city. The performance had demonstrated, the paper concluded, "that there is an efficient and practical movement on foot to educate the Catholic youths and young girls of El Paso and teach them how to become good citizens and dutiable daughters and faithful wives." (76)

Years later, the Italian pastor of the parish lectured to the female members of the graduating class of Sacred Heart in 1919, and "encouraged them to adopt the best of other cultures but to never forget who they were: young Catholic Mexican girls, who were obliged to follow Christ and, as Mexicans, to conserve the beautiful customs and traditions of *la raza*" (76). Certainly, as more and more Chicanas/Chicanos attended Catholic schools, the standard European traditional theatre models served as the repertory on these stages from which performances would be drawn for the American stage. Several of the young girls in the photo opposite, for example, also performed in productions of *Cinderella* and *Little Red Riding Hood* as part of the parish parochial

Young girls as angels for nativity re-enactment. The
Virgin Mary is top right. San Juan Evangelista Catholic
Church, San Antonio, Texas, c. 1950s.
Private collection of Elizabeth C. Ramírez.

school's season. Informants discussed in later periods in this history have related their early theatrical experiences on amateur stages as a result of religious
and secular events. This traditional European fare as well as deeply rooted cultural events and festive occasions such as parades and civic affairs would eventually play a part in generating an interest in theatre and would serve as precursors that influenced many significant future practitioners.

Thus, theatrical activity could range from social to religious to cultural
and political in its intent and purpose, and despite the nation's dire economic
hardship during the 1930s, Chicana/Chicano communities would rally around
these kinds of supportive events. This type of community and amateur theatrical participation or combination of both amateur and professional productions
continued after the Depression in some form or another. Yet, perhaps some of
the most important theatrical entertainment revolved around one type of Spanish-language professional involvement.

Established in 1935 to combat unemployment, the Federal Theatre Project
(FTP) of the Works Progress Administration (WPA) undertook a variety of
projects of all types, primarily offering free theatrical fare. Access and availability enabled practitioners to build a community audience. Trained professionals provided quality in performance, although untrained amateurs were also
among the ranks of those who participated in this enterprise.

Between 1936 and 1937 the Spanish unit of the FTP, housed in the mag-
nificent Ybor City's Centro Asturiano, produced its own theatrical productions

close to other venues where mutual aid societies offered local Spanish-language fare. Even though they were noticeably absent from management positions, women appeared as actresses in highly demanding works. The public was able to witness women in dominant roles such as in the popular *zarzuela* and *La viejecita*, as well as in Jacinto Benavente's controversial *La malquerida* (*The Passion Flower*, 1913) from the modern repertory, which revolved around the story of a man's love for his stepdaughter and featured important roles for two women in the parts of mother and daughter. The Spanish unit of the FTP also participated in the multiple debut event of the adaptation by John C. Moffitt and Sinclair Lewis of *It Can't Happen Here* (Dworkin y Méndez 1996, 287).

The Spanish unit's version, *Eso no puede ocurrir aquí*, was among twenty-three simultaneous openings nationwide on October 27, 1936. It suffered from translation difficulties and also fell victim to the same kind of chaotically swift preparation and mounting of the production that the other units encountered. Yet despite these difficulties, the Spanish unit's version did an adequate job of portraying the main theme of the play—the emergence of a fascist dictator in the United States, which was interpreted by critics as a criticism of Roosevelt. Joining other ethnically based individual units that included Yiddish, Black, and other English-language groups, the Spanish unit's production contributed to the political and social debate that would ultimately undermine the WPA theatre project. Although chronicles of the period indicate that the WPA's goal of establishing a permanent professional theatre through the FTP was a failure, one must exclude the production of Spanish-speaking theatre from that analysis. The federal subsidy assisted an already established base of theatrical production and added to its sustenance and further grounding within the community.

In New York, Spanish-language theatres began to feature variety rather than the once-popular full-length plays and *zarzuelas*, or musicals, and by the 1940s, musical revues dominated theatrical activity. Also making its mark was the ever-increasing Puerto Rican audience, and tastes and demands were clearly changing for Spanish-language theatrical fare. Despite a climate of economic hardship and changing fare, some actors performing in variety remained active for a very long time, appearing in *carpas* or tent shows, and *tandas de variedad*, or variety shows. The latter forms provided the fare for an important Spanish-language vaudeville circuit in the United States that far outlasted Euroamerican English-language vaudeville and eventually became the resource for countless radio and television performances.

For example, after the demise of her first company due to the Great Depression, Chata Noloesca organized a second company, "Beatriz Noloesca 'La Chata' Compañía Mexicana," in San Antonio in 1938. She, her second husband, her daughter Belia, and four San Antonio natives hired to perform with the company formed the troupe. Their fare varied but generally consisted of Mexican, Mexican American, and traditional Euroamerican song and dance numbers and comedy sketches in which Noloesca starred. These sketches, performed by La Chata and a male partner, were the highlight of the productions. From the late 1930s to the 1950s Noloesca took her company on the road and performed to a range of Spanish-speaking audiences in the Southwest, Midwest, South, and Northeast, as well as in Cuba. Significant cities on the tour included San Antonio, Chicago, Tampa, and Havana. She performed with her company at the Teatro Hispano in New York City in the 1940s, and again appeared in an extended tour in New York in the early 1950s.[4]

By locating Spanish-speaking audiences beyond her native Southwest, Noloesca was able to sustain her company and her career. She was responsible for handling company finances, hiring and training performers, developing and directing the productions, and arranging contracts and tours. She was particularly successful in obtaining performance contracts and showed remarkable self-confidence in negotiating with theatre managers. Nevertheless, while Noloesca was among those select few who were able to sustain lengthy careers in their profession during this period when overall theatrical activity had come to a virtual halt due to film and television, severe economic conditions impacted greatly on theatrical activity throughout the United States. In a time of severe economic problems, theatres depending on unpaid volunteers for operations and subscriptions for financial support soon led to the growth of community theatre. By 1925, nearly 2,000 community or little theatre companies on the non-Spanish-speaking stage were operating in the United States (Brockett 1995, 496). By midcentury, the long history of Spanish-language theatrical entertainment was reduced largely to community efforts and infrequent amateur events.[5]

THE 1960s AND REVOLUTION: THE LEGACY OF LUIS VALDEZ AND CHICANA/CHICANO THEATRE FOR WOMEN IN THEATRE

During the 1960s, American society faced social and political upheaval. In this decade of protest, the struggle for civil rights demanded action and change, and passive resistance soon led to violence as the Vietnam War escalated. For Mexican Americans, militancy increased after the mid-1960s. In addition to the war in Southeast Asia, the invasion of Santo Domingo "raised Chicano political consciousness," and as Acuña notes, "the rise of the cult of Che Guevara, the anticolonial struggles, the anti–Vietnam War marches, and the continuing civil rights rallies legitimized street politics" (Acuña 1988, 356). Theatre played an active role in this period of turmoil, and theatrical activity in the Chicano Movement was a major contributor to America's cultural revolution.

The Chicano Movement is perhaps most characteristically identifiable as a social movement of political protest. The central issues of this movement are widely focused: social, economic, and educational inequality and injustice and self-determination for Chicanos in the United States. Some important book-

César Chávez, United Farm Workers of America boycott against
Gallo, near Sacramento, California, 1975.
Photo by Mario C. Ramírez.

length studies on the history of the Chicano Movement include Rodolfo F.
Acuña's *Occupied America: A History of Chicanos* (1981 and 1988), now in
its third edition; Juan Gómez-Quiñones's *Chicano Politics: Reality and Promise 1940–1990* (1990) and *Roots of Chicano Politics, 1600–1940* (1994); and
Vicki L. Ruíz's *From Out of the Shadows: Mexican Women in Twentieth-Century
America* (1998). The major struggles of this movement were regional in their
inception and were characterized by male leadership: the United Farm Workers
of America in California, the land grant issue in New Mexico, the Crusade for
Justice in Colorado, and the Chicano student movement and political activism
in Texas. In all of these and other struggles Chicanas were active participants,
but it was not until the 1970s that the Chicana voice distinctly emerged.

In "The Development of Chicana Feminist Discourse," Alma M. García
dates the development of the Chicana feminist movement in the United States
between 1970 and 1980 (A. García 1994, 175). Yet it was that earlier decade,
the 1960s, which served to formulate and develop a critical Chicana consciousness, and thus we can look at this earlier period in order to assess the influences
on Chicanas that led to the development of a feminist consciousness. Women
of all colors were highly politicized by the 1960s. Yet, as Acuña notes, "they
differed, ranging from the right to the left. And their agenda often clashed
with that of their leaders." Thus, this decade of the emergence of the Chicano
Movement can serve to help us understand the foundation for what David
G. Gutiérrez calls the "unprecedented politicization of thousands of Mexican
Americans across the country" that led to a new Chicana/Chicano identity and
discourse in which Chicanas participated (Pesquera and Segura 1993, 96, 101,
102, 105; Acuña 1988, 332; D. Gutiérrez 1995, 183, 184).

In the 1960s, the struggle to understand the Mexican's experience developed into a nationalistic perspective among political activists who were challenging the established Anglo-dominated mainstream society. Juan Gómez-Quiñones notes that articulating a historical understanding of the Mexican experience was of paramount necessity "in the struggle to shape a future for La Raza[6] in the United States" (Gómez-Quiñones 1990, 103). In challenging the fundamental ideology of the establishment, striving for national identity became pivotal. "Chicanismo" provided a voice and expression of hope and affirmation of identity in the most radical form, as Gómez-Quiñones defines the term:

> The emphasis of "Chicanismo" upon dignity, self-worth, pride, uniqueness, and a feeling of cultural rebirth made it attractive to many Mexicans in a way that cut across class, regional, and generational lines. In some way or other, most Mexicans had experienced, directly or indirectly, economic or social discrimination. These negative experiences increased the appeal of "Chicanismo"; it emphasized Mexican cultural consciousness and heritage as well as pride in speaking [the] Spanish language *and* economic opportunity. (104)

This emphasis on ethnic and political consciousness soon led to a distinct cultural nationalism in which the term "Chicano" represented the radically political and ethnically identifiable voice of this group. I will use the term Chicana/Chicano to include women. However, when I use the term Chicano, I will be referring to specific male and/or male-centered terms, such as the "Chicano Movement."

In the midst of this political revolution, a burgeoning cultural renaissance also surfaced. The arts became prominent, fused with protest, driven by politics, and charged with propaganda. This cultural and artistic flowering was evident in many forms, including music, art, and poetry; however, it was in theatrical expression that the entire spectrum of cultural expression coalesced.

While the historical antecedents of Latinas/Latinos in the United States provided the roots for theatrical expression, this heritage had largely remained dormant for several years before Luis Valdez reawakened it on the contemporary stage. The work of Valdez and the success of El Teatro Campesino (ETC) gave rise to a whole generation of Latina/Latino theatre groups and played a major role in influencing Chicanas/Latinas in theatre today.

Born in Delano, California in 1940, Luis Valdez has been credited with inspiring a national movement of Chicana/Chicano theatre groups, a movement that soon broadened to include the larger Latina/Latino community (Huerta 1994, 38). Although the works were created collectively, El Teatro Campesino was led by Valdez in its creations, and the troupe and its work soon inspired numerous other Chicanas/Chicanos/Latinas/Latinos to form their own *teatros,* or theatre groups. In light of recent scholarship which challenges the claim of Valdez's supremacy by countering with a unique and exclusionary women's re-visionist historical account, this study approaches and evaluates pertinent evidence in support of his influence from a theoretical and critical perspective that is augmented by the viewpoint and first-hand accounts of theatre historians and theatre practitioners.[7]

Founded by Luis Valdez in 1965, El Teatro Campesino first sought to show the plight of the farm workers in California and subsequently broadened its scope to include social, political, and cultural issues revolving around the Chicana/Chicano experience in the United States. Generally labeled agitprop or "guerrilla" theatre, the Teatro began with productions of short scenes aimed at educating and politicizing its audience about the particular problems of the farm workers, hoping to motivate audiences to take social action. For more than thirty years, the Teatro's history was one of creativity, work, and change. From its early *actos* that first demonstrated the plight of the striking farm workers to its eventual prominence as a leader in alternative theatre, El Teatro Campesino grew and evolved as it eventually began to reach a mass audience.

Certain models informed Valdezian production at its inception. As a theatre historian and practitioner it is my task to combine historical inquiry into theatre as a social and cultural institution, whereby the theatre can be distinguished as a reflection of distinct ideological assumptions framed by time and place, with an emphasis on critical individuals contributing to that activity and on careful scrutiny of the process by which theatrical practice and performance evolved. It is also my intent to describe and analyze the product itself, that is, the performative text as well as the event in production for an intended audience. A study of Valdez's work can further determine his influence on Chicanas within his own troupe directly and, even more far-reaching, his influence on Chicanas/Latinas in performance.

LUIS VALDEZ: THE SHAPING OF A GENIUS

Many studies have documented the political activism that motivated Valdez to fight for social justice in a manner which made a unique contribution to theatre history and served the Chicana/Chicano struggle for economic, cultural, and political survival.[8] Yet no study of Valdez's solid grounding in theatre exists. Valdez's experience in theatre stems from his work at San Jose State University, where he majored in English with an emphasis on playwriting. He was fully launched into the theatre when his first full-length play, *The Shrunken Head of Pancho Villa,* was produced by the Theater Department at San Jose State under his direction (Huerta 1989, 146). He joined the San Francisco Mime Troupe the following year after a trip to Castro's Cuba, and then in 1965 he joined César Chávez in his crusade to organize a union for farm workers and started El Teatro Campesino. Valdez brought to Chicana/Chi-

cano theatre a grounding in acting and playwriting and a familiarity with theatre history and practice that helped establish him as a recognized figure in this
theatre movement. What follows is an examination of the varied processes that
Valdez drew from as he developed a workable method of using theatre as a
radical weapon for change.

In his commentary "The Actos" that appeared as introductory material to
the 1970 publication of the early works of El Teatro Campesino, Valdez wrote
that the *acto* "developed its own structure through five years of experimentation." The form was

> developed into a short dramatic form now used primarily by Los Teatros
> de Aztlan, but utilized to some extent by other non Chicano guerilla the-
> ater companies throughout the U.S. including the San Francisco Mime
> Troupe and the Bread and Puppet Theatre. (Valdez 1971, 6)

He added that "considerable creative crossfeeding" had occurred on other levels, namely, "between the Mime Troupe, the Bread and Puppet and the Campesino." It is this cross-feeding that I wish to examine in relation to influences
on Valdez before determining how he influenced others.

Ron G. Davis's chronicles of the first ten years of the San Francisco Mime
Troupe reveal a great deal about how influential both Davis and the Mime
Troupe actually were on Valdez. The experience Valdez gained from this early
venture quickly had a visibly powerful impact on his own troupe formation. In
Ron Davis Valdez was working with no ordinary practitioner of theatre.

I was first introduced to the work of Ron Davis through Jorge Huerta in
1974 when Huerta shared an unpublished narrative by Davis entitled "Methods in Mime." This document, dated 1962, was used as an integral resource in
various acting, directing, and playwriting workshops I attended at the Fourth
Annual Chicano Theater Festival in San Jose, California in June 1973. The
festival terminated with subsequent informal discussions in nearby San Juan
Bautista, where the resident El Teatro Campesino hosted numerous directors,
actors, and practitioners of Chicana/Chicano theatre eager to continue dia-
loguing about varying topics that had engaged participants of the festival. Davis's techniques and approach and the work of the Mime Troupe during the
time he was heading the group came up often during the exchange.

Davis had studied with Paul Curtis's American Mime Theatre in New York
for two years and performed with them. Paul Curtis taught a combination of
Method acting (drawing from the Actors Studio approach and from Stanislav-
sky) and mime as he had learned it from Etienne Decroux. Davis tells us that
Curtis rejected Decroux's non-Method approach to movement and emphasized internalized calisthenics and modern dance instead. Davis, preferring to
study with the master, went on to study with Etienne Decroux in Paris for six
months on a Fulbright scholarship. Perhaps the most notable performative el-

ements Davis brought to his own troupe had to do with performing "gestures without a motivated frame of reference," that is, the approach we generally connect with Method or Stanislavskian-driven actor study.

The mime, essentially, "has to act on himself, and uses everything that is present on stage in front of an audience," according to Davis (1975, 14). At this juncture, we do not want to set aside or dismiss Davis's use of male-centered language, as we find others have done with Valdez's staging terminology.[9] Instead, we want to very carefully mark Davis's use of male-centered language because although the discourse derives from a pre-feminist period of analytical historical writing it also holds a valuable clue to the type of role Davis assumed within his own company. This language is significant in terms of how he influenced others who also assert a similar role in theatrical practice. Davis continues:

> The tools are the elements: audience, light, air, sound, clothes, body, wall (or curtains), floor. These become props. The Pantomimist . . . had to indicate emotions, props and scenery. He had to learn facial grimaces which Method acting had discarded as nineteenth century melodrama. The Mime's use of the immediate environment produced a realistic (not naturalistic) depiction of life. (Davis 1975, 14–15)

Davis returned to the United States as both a performer and a teacher. He joined the Actors Workshop in the Bay Area when it was under the direction of Herbert Blau and Jules Irving, serving as an assistant director. The San Francisco Actors Workshop became known for its experimental productions in which Blau and Irving pioneered stage work using Brecht and Beckett. Co-founded in 1952, this iconoclastic troupe was managed by the two San Francisco State College professors until 1965, when they left to manage a new theatre at Lincoln Center. In his *The Impossible Theater: A Manifesto* (1963), Blau vowed "to talk up a revolution" with "theatre as a social art" (Blau 1964, 3, 6, 9). The San Francisco Actors Workshop was called "the most daring American regional theatre of its era, pursuing vigorous artistic goals in bold versions of innovative European plays."[10] This was another experimental stage for Davis. However, he soon undertook his own troupe where his fundamental ideas and experience coalesced into the San Francisco Mime Troupe.

Davis's fundamental belief that "only half the work is done before it is presented to an audience" would become a determining principle for Valdez (Davis 1975, 15). Valdez recognized that the essence of theatre lay in the interaction of performers and audience within one place and one time as a crucial element of the theatrical experience. But other elements that served as experimental for Davis also informed the work of Valdez. The most critical factor had to do with how Valdez was influenced by and reworked theatrical conventions and practices in forming his own company.

When Valdez went to work with the Mime Troupe, Davis's company was in its sixth year of performing contemporary adaptations of Italian *commedia*. Along with the broad farce of the Italian form, the political consciousness and progressiveness that were hallmarks of the period were already hallmarks of the group. The bawdy, outdoor performances that would effectively serve to entertain and educate Valdez's own farm worker audiences featured body language, use of masks, and exaggerated gestures and dramatic action suitable for the noisy outdoor surroundings. Above all, the improvisational nature of this type of popular form of entertainment allowed Valdez's troupe to develop a repertory of plays where none had existed before.[11]

In *commedia dell'arte*, as we have come to understand the form in theatre history, there are two fundamental characteristics: improvisation and stock characters. We know that actors worked from a plot outline as the core from which they improvised dialogue and action. Generally, each performer played the same character with given business and distinct attributes and dress. Comic business, or *lazzi*, was often standardized, but unexpected and unplanned dialogue and action seemed to ensure a measure of spontaneity. The character types were generally divided into masters and servants, and when given certain normative types, such as the straight roles of young lovers, there was a means to establish the popular exaggerated types. The *zanni*, or servants, were the most varied of all the types, and at least one of these was ingenious and another witless. In stock *commedia*, these *zanni* were generally male, but one or two women might serve as maids.

We can only rely on theories to explain the origins of *commedia*. Possibly it stemmed from wandering mimes during the Middle Ages, improvisations on the comedies of Plautus and Terence (of which we have extant texts as examples; Valdez acknowledges having read Plautus's work),[12] or the Italian farce of the early sixteenth century. We do know that the troupes averaged ten to twelve members and that women were included. We also know that there was a designated leader or most respected member of the company who supervised productions. The responsibilities for this overseer involved explaining character relationships, delineating the *lazzi*, explaining the action, and obtaining the necessary properties. Rehearsals may or may not have taken place, but the leader was certainly in charge of clarifying what was expected of each actor. Because the companies were organized on a sharing plan, each actor had an investment in the success of the troupe, yet the nature of their operations involved extensive touring and playing on unplanned available stages so that adaptability was necessary to ensure their success.

Ron Davis tells us that his reason for utilizing the *commedia dell'arte* form stems from its working-class viewpoint (1975, 31). In his description of the traditional form, Davis very clearly specifies that the scenario was arranged by the lead actor or director who was loosely uniting the individual characters. Other elements that Davis identified in this form included assigning ownership of a part to one performer "for life" whereby the performer "learned closing and opening lines, poetry and physical tricks, *lazzi* and *burla* (particular business, solo or duo)" (31). Davis further noted that the company could be small, generally numbering seven or eight, followed a specific scenario, and performed on a platform with a back curtain for easy entrance and exit. Other important characteristics included exaggerated character types that included set costumes; each actor wore colorful and clearly defined costumes and masks were crucial, although Davis noted that the costumes of women and the male lover were exceptions to the practice of wearing masks.

The following elements of performance served Davis and the Mime Troupe and later surfaced in Valdez's work: using stereotypical characters as a means of describing social conditions rather than simply general types; improvising from old scenarios and available plays and writing new scenes; performing for an audience with the thought clearly in mind that "in comedy the audience is master" (Davis 1975, 32; Huerta 1982, 14). Davis's statement that "this *commedia* was 'Brechtian' in that the stage play was a game" (Davis 1975, 32) accurately describes the work of the San Francisco Mime Troupe—performers were totally committed to the event both on and off the stage platform, rehearsing and polishing the work to the point that improvisation became an inherent manifestation of the idea behind the work, and refining the *lazzi* to the point where they were an integral part of the whole rather than individual stage tricks.

Improvisation was at the root of the Mime Troupe's work. Among other resources, Davis was drawing from Viola Spolin's social work which resulted in the various theatre games and transformational role playing which eventually found their way to actor training and performance (Brockett and Findlay 1991, 388). Through the "happening" Davis utilized improvisation and performance. The "happening" form, not necessarily theatrical, was a form popularized by visual artists in the 1960s which was eventually the term used for any event in which improvisation or chance played an important role, including demonstrations and sit-ins (400). Davis's approach toward creating improvisation, however, very clearly indicates a leadership role as "instructor or director" who selected a situation. With actors subsequently taking on characters and deciding "the who, what, when, where and why of the situation[,] they then begin to talk to each other or 'improvise'" (Davis 1975, 20).

Davis's method was aimed toward simplicity and focus on the actor. He wrote, "To achieve the full benefit of improvisational skit-making, certain conditions are important. Obstacles are minimized; conflicts are few; people work together, allowing for easy flow of dialogue and action" (20–21). But Davis adds a critical note regarding his part in the process: "In the professional theatre the director calls the shots and selects portions of the improv to keep or rework. After the first improvisation the same pattern, or rehearsal, takes place as in any ordinary play production" (20–21). Thus, if one understands this type of organization and practice, it is comprehensible that Davis is the driving force, the organizer, and the person in charge of the troupe, or as Robert Scheer states in his introduction to Davis's book about the Mime Troupe: "Ronny Davis appears more as a force than simply a person who blew through where I happened to be standing" (9).

The San Francisco Mime Troupe, which began in 1959 as the R. G. Davis Mime Troupe, was described by Scheer as "the most consistently energetic and responsible element in the counterculture of the Bay Area" (9). But even though the work of the troupe was on the cutting edge of the counterculture, the management of the company was very traditional. Davis oversaw the hiring of staff and company and doled out those responsibilities. He brought his expertise in Method in which he had received more than generalized training, and he organized rehearsals and wrote text. What stands out in accounts of this troupe's history is the traditional Western European method Davis used of taking charge of his own company, despite its improvisatory ensemble nature.

Davis organized the troupe and lent his extensive expertise as the foundation for its style, approach to production, and practice. In an early program for the company, Jules Irving and Herbert Blau introduced Davis's new addition to their venue, referencing the method by which Jacques Copeau went about introducing "the art of Mime" as one of his many innovations into the modern theatre. In their program notes, Irving and Blau write that "the art of Mime might even be considered the soil of the art of acting. It is made of muscle, and gesture, and rhythm and motion, and may give birth by the devious route of internal action to the unexpected Word" (19).[13] However, Blau and Irving also noted that mime had not yet significantly found its way into modern American drama. Clearly, Davis was responsible for ushering in a new form and style for the American stage. Crediting what they called the R. G. Davis Mime Troupe, Blau and Irving explained the process: "The people in the troupe have trained together, and the work you will be seeing—though prepared for an audience [—]is an original account of what they have done together" (19).

Valdez also served as the overseer of his own troupe a year after he joined the Mime Troupe while he continued his very close collaboration with Davis and subsequent company members; his leadership style was very similar to that of Davis. Like Davis, Valdez is responsible for a troupe known to work collaboratively as an ensemble, yet he functions as director in the traditional Western European sense.

What other elements of the production process did Valdez take with him upon his departure from the Mime Troupe and his subsequent reappearance with a full company? Luis Valdez appeared with the Mime Troupe on September 12, 1965, as one of the cast members of *Candelaio,* an adaptation by Peter Berg of a play by Giordano Bruno that was directed by Ron Davis.[14] There were twelve performances at Washington Square Park in San Francisco, where it premiered. On August 7, 1965, Davis stepped into Valdez's role, the stock character Brighella, for the planned "special" arrest in Lafayette Park, where Davis would be "busted for performing in the parks without a permit" (201).

By November 1965, Luis Valdez had founded El Teatro Campesino with members of the National Farm Workers Association (NFWA), the earliest union organizing effort which merged with the Agricultural Workers Organizing Committee (AWOC) in 1966 to form the United Farm Workers Organizing Committee (UFWOC). Davis adds that El Teatro Campesino was formed "to dramatize the issues of the Delano grape strike and urge farm workers to join the union" (201). Although the period of time spent with the Mime Troupe may seem brief, given Davis's approach, Valdez would not have been given the Brighella role unless he had acquired considerable training and capability to play the part. What training and preparation, then, did Valdez acquire that helped shape and inform ETC?

We know that the Mime Troupe spent a great deal of time workshopping the use of *commedia* masks in performance. Carlo Mazzone, a mime from the Lecoq School who had played Brighella under Giorgio Strehler at the Piccolo, worked with the troupe in rehearsal. Mazzone owned twelve leather *commedia* masks made by Amleto Sartori (for whom the molding process was a family secret) that were carefully detailed props of distinct character traits, such as Brighella's constant "wise guy grin," which had room for an actor's shifty eyes. The importance of mask work cannot be underestimated in both the Mime Troupe and Valdez's staging process. Andrei Serban has been instrumental in more recent work with masks and integrating *commedia* elements into production. It is clear from my own participation in similar workshops with Serban and in work with Valdez and his company that actors cannot simply wear a mask without wearing the history and every aspect of the character role of that mask; thus, the object may be papier-mâché or some similar physical object, but the placing of the mask also includes assuming stereotypical gestures, attitudes, and very distinct business appropriate to the individual character. Davis's own integration of the mask led to one constant for the Mime Troupe actors, and it was a three-fold job: "Play yourself, play the character, play an Italian who was a *commedia* performer" (40).

Valdez immediately drew upon the theatrical device of using masks for his own application of *commedia* with ETC. He had conceived of mask work as an integral part of the performance, and used masks in creating and developing new and unique characters for his own company. Jorge Huerta, the first theatre historian to provide us with an in-depth history and criticism about Chicana/Chicano theatre, provides an important glimpse into Valdez's ability to integrate what he had learned from Davis's mask technique in the process of developing characters. Huerta tells us: "When Valdez took that pig-like mask to Delano, he was certain of its effect on the audience as well as the actors" (Huerta 1982, 19). Valdez had learned the process of bringing a character to life by adding a comic mask to the role and animating the false face with accompanying body movement. But Valdez also recognized the effective function of the mask as a means of separating the character from the real-life figures they wished to represent. Often, the performance required portrayals of some of the most negative figures in the lives of the farm workers. Huerta explains that: "Although the farmworkers were at first reluctant to portray the despised *esquirol* [Strike-Breaker], shielded only by a paper hung around their necks, the comic mask offered another alternative, for it *hid* the real person behind the disguise" (19). Huerta adds that fortunately "the instant anyone put it on, the howls of laughter showered the actor with a sort of approval," and the actor could then feel comfortable in knowing that the audience was only reacting to the character being represented rather than the person portraying the role. The character masks, often half-masks with exaggerated facial features that left the mouth area open for more flexibility in movement and vocal expression, quickly became an integral part of performance style.

Besides actor training and mask work, Valdez also instituted the use of experimental techniques in staging. Essentially, any open outside area on the ground or on a flatbed truck became a performance space which eventually evolved into a piece of canvas slung across a rope from one end of a pole to another to provide a backdrop for entrances and exits with any makeshift raised platform for the central playing space. Drawings in Davis's chronicles illustrate the basic models for staging that Valdez also utilized in his *carpas,* or tent show productions, that were inexpensive and easy to travel with as the company toured farther and farther afield. Valdez also drew upon the immediacy of the audience for the total effect he sought. At the first *commedia* presented by Davis's troupe, an intimacy and exchange with the audience became part of the performance. Davis wrote: "Our opening format was designed to help the performers warm up in front of an audience and let the audience in on the 'secrets' of backstage." He continued:

> We would set up the stage, get into costume and makeup (or masks), play music, loose and easy, gather into a circle and do warm-up physical exercises while singing songs. At first, the songs were from an Archive record of the Central Middle Ages, often simple rounds, Christmas tunes, and eventually, tunes from Wobblies and political songs from Italy, Mexico and even some we wrote. When inside we sang behind the drop or "off stage" in the dressing room. In the park, we sang and played to one side of the stage. . . . We learned to work with audiences before the show. (Davis 1975, 37)

While Ron Davis and the San Francisco Mime Troupe had a clear influence on Valdez's early work, other influences also helped shape his particular kind of theatre. Oscar G. Brockett distinguishes four radical theatre companies of the 1960s, the San Francisco Mime Troupe, the Bread and Puppet Theatre, the

Free Southern Theatre, and El Teatro Campesino. With the exception of the Free Southern Theatre, these groups have an interesting interrelated history that has direct bearing on how Valdez shaped his work. Besides the San Francisco Mime Troupe, Peter Schumann's Bread and Puppet Theatre, founded in 1961, provided an interesting dimension that informed Valdez's process. The Radical Theatre Festival of 1968 was sponsored by San Francisco State College. Davis had seen Peter Schumann's troupe in 1964 when they performed a Christmas pageant play in New York City. This performance

> contained some of the most interesting shapes, hand puppets, masks, live bodies with fake props, trips of scenery and action that I had seen. It was epic in its simplicity. Props were used as suggestions for total pictures. Images were conjured up in our minds through the use of a mask, a gesture or an element of the real thing. I watched and absorbed. (104)

For the three groups, the event allowed for workshops, open panel discussions while presenting their works in the evening, and extensive demonstrations of the work they were doing. Bread and Puppet demonstrated how to make puppets, make bread (which was an inherent part of its ritual element of performance), and produce banners. El Teatro Campesino presented its first full-length play, Valdez's *The Shrunken Head of Pancho Villa,* and the Mime Troupe workshopped *commedia* and puppet shows and theorized on the cultural revolution as part of performance. Participating in these events not only broadened Valdez's experience, but also provided actor training for the Teatro.

In addition to these joint ventures, Valdez would have future collaborations with other generations of Mime Troupe collectives, and Peter Brook would come to San Juan to work with Valdez. Valdez's work is clearly connected to Brechtian theory and to Artaud, who influenced him in both overt and less obvious ways, but it was those early influences which seem to be most responsible for formulating the techniques he would bring to performance. Yet, in addition to what he witnessed and participated in, Valdez was also engaged in creating his own use of theatre as a weapon of political activism. In a 1988 interview with David Savran, Valdez's response to what he considered the major influences from his theatre training was very broad:

> It's all important. It's a question of layering. I love to layer things, I think they achieve a certain richness—I'm speaking now about "the work." Those years of studying theatre history were extremely important. I connected with a number of ancient playwrights in a very direct way. Plautus was a revelation, he spoke directly to me. I took four years of Latin so I was able to read him in Latin. There are clever turns of phrases that I grew to appreciate and, in my own way, was able almost to reproduce in Spanish. The central figure of the wily servant in classical Roman drama—Greek also—became a standard feature of my work with El Teatro Campesino. The striker was basically a wily servant. I'd also been exposed to *commedia*

dell'arte through the Brighellas, Arlecchinos and Pantalones. I saw a direct link between these *commedia* types and the types I had to work with in order to put together a Farm Workers' theatre. I chose to do an outdoor, robust theatre of types. I figured it hit the reality. (Savran 1988, 17)

His links to Brecht came as early as 1960 when Martin Esslin's newly published book, *Brecht: The Man and His Work,* fell into his hands. Valdez tells Savran: "Brecht to me had been only a name. But this book opened up Brecht and I started reading all his plays and his theories, which I subscribed to immediately" (18). Thus, while one phase of his education in theatre was literary, dealing with the basic elements of drama—structure, language, music, and movement—the other aspect was "raw, elemental education," performing under the most primitive conditions in the farm labor camps and on flatbed trucks, with the constant threat of violence. Valdez drew from both a literary and a practical education.

Yolanda Broyles-González argues that the total effect and result of El Teatro Campesino's work should be attributed to its collaborative way of operating as a collective. She also feels that the Chicana/Chicano *teatro* tradition stems from the earlier oral and popular heritage. In contrast, I focus on the formative years of both the company and Valdez as theatre practitioner in order to establish both that Luis Valdez functioned as an artistic director, that is, someone who integrated the collaborative process of theatre into the whole, and that this work laid the necessary groundwork that enabled Chicana/Latina women to develop their performative skills. The role of Chicana/Latina women in theatre has built on this experience to achieve a new status at the center of performance.[15]

Jorge Huerta has already provided us with an in-depth study of the Chicana/Chicano theatre movement during its first fifteen years in his 1982 publication *Chicano Theater: Themes and Forms.* In this seminal work, covering the period from 1965 to 1980, Huerta analyzes plays about various topics related to the Chicana/Chicano community in order to define Chicana/Chicano theatre, its major dramatists, and its theatre groups. As a theatre historian, Huerta provides chronicles about events and practice through play analyses rather than attempting to offer a detailed account of any one particular group and/or their operations and practice. While a close examination of Huerta's study clearly shows attention to the contributions Chicanas have made throughout the long history of Chicana/Chicano *teatro,* in Huerta's analyses as well as in numerous other first-hand accounts about Luis Valdez and the integrative and ensemble process practiced by El Teatro Campesino, Valdez is situated in the period of the Chicana/Chicano Renaissance as a creative genius and true visionary.[16] This male-centered, Euroamerican/mainstream acknowledgement derives from a theatrical practice that collaboratively integrates the man and the ensemble, much as we have seen in Davis's work and operations, thereby creating art that is inseparable, finding its most essential path in a whole. As a poet, playwright, performer, and director, Valdez created effective theatre and skillfully brought his vision to the stage. What, then, is it about this practitioner that sets him apart, enabling him to re-create lost traditions, inform about the past, create new models and myths, and ultimately, inspire, encourage, and challenge Chicanas through theatre and performance?

VALDEZ THE PRACTITIONER: CREATING A STAGE

Valdez was working with people who were not trained in theatre. He had to go back to basics in actor training, educating the actors about stage presence, vocal projection, basic stage directions, and the basic essentials for performance that he already knew. Those of us who are practitioners generally use these basic acting skills and techniques as a means of grounding a company or ensemble with a common language and understanding, and as we have already seen, Valdez had trained and worked with highly experienced individuals and had developed his own expertise.

We know that the actors were farm workers in the earliest composition of the troupe. The stage was in the grape fields. The farm workers improvised the drama. In an early account of the troupe, we get a rare glimpse of the actors:

> Felipe Cantu was the star. He had been an obscure grape picker who had worked, he said, at everything, from "policeman to a clown." A volatile man, the father of seven children, he "resembles a Mexican version of Ben Turpin," Valdez says. "He speaks no English, but his wild, extravagant Cantinflas-like comic style needs no words." (Steiner 1970, 328)

Another actor, the 20-year-old Agustín Lira, described as "an intense and sensitive man" who became the group's guitarist and poet, was also a grape picker. Errol Franklin of Cheyenne, Wyoming, was referred to as "the Indian cowboy." Partly Black, he was "lean and thin," and had been a "horsebreaker, fisherman, apple picker, short-order cook, and longshoreman" before arriving in the valley as a strikebreaker. Soon after joining the *huelga* (strike), he joined the Teatro as well, becoming the mask maker for the troupe and doubling as the stage cop.

The work of El Teatro Campesino in these early years generated new cultural resources. Many actors joined the Teatro briefly and went on to become leaders in the Chicana/Chicano theatre movement. The work of the company generated a new theatrical literature as well. Valdez's dramaturgy can be divided into three types: (1) early works that were collectively conceptualized but that he scripted and produced, (2) longer plays he either fully conceived or developed beyond the work of the ensemble, and (3) experimental works that integrated forms by incorporating the *acto, mito,* and *corrido.* Here we want to deal with the first type, the early works.

The troupe's earliest dramas are described by Valdez as *actos.* An *acto* is a short scene, arrived at through improvisation, usually comic in form, which strives to "inspire the audience to social action. Illuminate specific points about social problems. Satirize the opposition. Show or hint at a solution. Express what people are feeling" (Valdez 1971, 6). It is important to understand the nature of these early works if one is to understand the evolution of Chicana/ Chicano theatre, for these *actos* inspired other Chicanas/Chicanos to form their own *teatros* or theatre groups, to also collectively create performance pieces about their own struggles.

The major characteristics of these early works are embodied in one of the first *actos* presented by El Teatro Campesino, *Las Dos Caras del Patroncito* (*The Two Faces of the Boss*). *Las Dos Caras* is concerned with educating the audience about the farm workers' strike in California and the need for the union advocated by César Chávez as a solution to the injustices against the farm worker. The piece pits two very dominant figures against each other, one the poor and humble farm worker and the other his exploiting archenemy, the *patrón*, or grower. Nothing in the dialogue other than sexist and racist attitudes toward the Euroamerican/White wife of the grower tells us anything about women, and we learn nothing specifically about Chicanas either. We can only imagine the presence of women as farm workers if we assume that the "universal" male pronouns used in the play include females as well.

Born in the early stages of the work of the Teatro with the union, *Las Dos Caras* conveys the urgency of that time. This *acto* shows how Valdez's knowledge of theatrical conventions and practice made for effective performance. Valdez had learned from Ron Davis's direction how to bring a character to life with the use of the comic mask and how to connect body movement to bring that face to life. But the mask also shielded the untrained actor who was coming directly from the fields in a manner which allowed a separation between real life and disguise. Valdez also knew the technique of improvising with the mask, and this double-sided venture led to the creation of stock characters. By hanging signs on the characters to indicate the types and using minimal props and exaggerated movements to enhance the figures, the very serious nature of the drama was presented as entertaining comedy amidst a very harsh social reality. The transformation of the Patroncito into the lowly Campesino is complete with the donning of the mask; the solution of the *acto* is to join the union.

We encounter no female roles in Valdez's work until 1966 with the second play, *La Quinta Temporada* (*The Fifth Season*). *La Quinta Temporada* is also centered around a farm worker's experience, this time one who is looking for a job. Yet, the characterization quickly essentializes this figure as symbolic of all migrant workers as he struggles through each passing season to survive.

The play is an allegory. Summer and Winter have brought no hope of survival in the *campesino*'s quest to earn a living. It is not until Spring enters, dressed as a woman in a spring dress and strewn with flowers as she sings a happy tune, that any sense of optimism is conveyed (Valdez 1971, 28). In sharp contrast to Winter, who has kicked and beaten the farm worker, leaving him helpless, Spring offers protection and physical warmth. Although first appearing passive and meek, she soon turns aggressively on Winter. Spring symbolizes rebirth and renewal as an integral part of the four seasons of a farm worker's life. Despite Winter's sexual reference to her as a "Mamasota" (Big Mama), this sexist language only serves to reinforce this figure as dominant, capable of wiping Winter away and helping the poor farm worker determine his own destiny: "There, there, you poor, poor farm worker, here, now, get up. You mustn't let this happen to you again. You've got to fight for your rights!" (29).

Up until this point, the farm worker has not been aware that he has rights, but Spring's ousting of Winter climaxes with the farm worker himself calling upon notable male figures in Mexican history who have also struggled for their rights, namely Pancho Villa, Francisco I. Madero, and Emiliano Zapata. By the end of the piece, Spring returns in the guise of a nun representing the churches; her part is doubled just as other parts were doubled. In this case, she returns representing a powerful institution that also brings food and money. When the farm worker tries to run away, cowering against the grower, he is held down by the Nun who is just as capable as the Unions and La Raza to confront the grower and help the farm worker usher in the Fifth Season, represented here by a character named Social Justice, as they get the grower to sign a contract that ensures better conditions for the farm worker.

During the summer of 1967, the troupe went on its first national tour, performing on campuses, at union halls, and in various civic venues in order to call attention to the *huelga* (strike). While these appearances brought much-needed money to the farm workers' union and support for the boycott and strike, the troupe was also gaining national recognition. Their East Coast appearances included performances in New York's Village Theater, at the Newport Folk Festival, and at the Senate Sub-Committee on Migratory Labor in Washington, D.C. Upon their return, they decided to leave the day-to-day demands of Chávez's union in order to devote more time to full-time professional work in theatre.

With this move, Valdez sought to accomplish his goal of reconnecting to culture through the arts. He established a cultural center in Del Rey, California, where the group was no longer singularly tied to the farm workers' struggle; they could broaden the scope of their explorations of the Chicana/Chicano experience. Valdez felt strongly that the company needed more training. At the Centro Campesino Cultural, situated in the small rural community of Del Rey, the troupe attended workshops to hone their skills and get formal training in theatre and performance. The move to Del Rey also gave the troupe more time for rehearsals and performance.

In moving to Del Rey, the troupe was able to begin its search for a lost culture. Stan Steiner asked Valdez why he had taken his theatre to "so god-forsaken a rural ghetto" and Valdez responded: "We are not aspiring to Broadway. We are aspiring to build a theatre among our people. That's the whole bit about the Teatro. We are not a theatre *for* farm workers; farm workers are our theatre." Valdez continued: "Besides, we are trying to build something bigger than a theatre. In English you could call it La Raza Folk Cultural Center. But it will be more than that. Someday it will be a center for Chicanos all through the Southwest" (Steiner 1970, 336).

One of the most significant pieces to emerge from the troupe's work in Del Rey was *Los vendidos* (*The Sell-Outs*), first performed in 1967 at a Brown Beret[17] meeting in Elysian Park in East Los Angeles. *Los vendidos* is an *acto* that demonstrates the multifaceted dimensions of being sold out and of selling out. In this piece we see how the group was able to broaden its scope to include issues about identity, assimilation, and acculturation above and beyond the very direct struggle of the UFW. *Los vendidos* was widely produced on the stage and reached millions of households in a Los Angeles KNBC broadcast in 1993. It is probably the most frequently produced *acto* by Chicana/Chicano theatre companies.

Only one female figure appears in this piece. Miss Jimenez is a state employee who has sold out her people to advance the political agenda of her employer. As the play begins, she enters a "Used Mexican Lot and Mexican Curio Shop," where she has come as "a secretary from Governor Reagen's [*sic*] office" to look for "a Mexican type for the administration" (Valdez 1971, 36). This text is central to the formation and history of *teatros* (other troupes); it provides a performative event in a cultural milieu that can no longer sustain a silenced female. Miss Jimenez, in fact, is one of the most dimensional characters we have seen up to this point in the *actos,* and although she suffers from all of the negative stereotyping generally cast upon her type, we know more about her than we do about the other characters.

A feminist reading of Miss Jimenez notes her prominence in a male-dominated arena. Miss Jimenez stands out—she is articulate, capable of taking charge of an important task, and able to bargain for what she wants. She is certainly no weak, timid, and humble figure like the earlier farm workers we have seen. Instead, she seems to be at the crux of the drama, and possibly suffers more than any of the others in a situation in which no solutions seem to be readily available. Perhaps the most frightening aspect of the piece is that it seems to offer no viable replacement for the very negative stereotypes represented on stage. Miss Jimenez illustrates the worst type of traitor in the barrio, the sell-out; yet she herself has been duped through dubious and dishonest bartering that sets her up as the ultimate victim. Here we realize the powerful reversal of the Spanish title, for *Los Vendidos* can also refer to those who have been sold or sold out. Translating the title literally pointedly calls attention to how far too many Chicanas/Chicanos have been "bought or sold by somebody or something," as Jorge Huerta writes. Miss Jimenez enters the shop as the buyer, but she is in fact also bought and sold by the state government and by the very models around the shop who presumably constitute the society in which she exists. Audiences coming from first-hand experience in this society of sell-outs must stop and ask themselves whether they have also been bought or sold (Huerta 1982, 66–67). In effect, the presumed victims of society have victimized one of their own. In this kind of environment, there is little hope that she or anyone else like her can turn things around in her society, a tragedy indeed in this seemingly comic act.

VALDEZ THE HISTORIAN AND EDUCATOR IN EL MOVIMIENTO

The Centro Cultural allowed the group to offer and partake of art classes and guitar lessons and Teatro. Valdez listed the cultural offerings of the Centro: "We have 'history happenings,' every two or three weeks, dealing with the history of La Raza. We have *actos* about La Conquista, the Alamo, Gold Rush, the Cisco Kid and Pancho Villa." Steiner provides us with a valuable glimpse of this Center and Valdez's vision of it. He quotes a Centro Campesino Cultural brochure:

> Campesinos are far from "culturally deprived." They possess and live with-
> in a "culture"—one which is, however, largely unfamiliar to the mass of
> English-speaking North Americans. It is a culture native to a great part of
> the land mass of the United States and has been for the last 400 years. It is
> an untapped resource of human experience. . . . The Mexican American
> farm worker in the Southwest has long been denied the tools of [his] cul-
> tural expression. . . . El Centro Campesino Cultural is an attempt to hand
> over these tools—the tools of the Arts—directly to the Spanish-speaking
> people of the Southwest. (Steiner 1970, 336–337)

For Valdez it was time to make a change: "We know we have our own culture. . . . It's just that there has been nobody to express it—until now. We will change that. We are on the verge of it. The whole country will be amazed!" (337)[18]

In *La conquista de Mexico* (*The Conquest of Mexico*), a puppet show dated 1968, the group presented the kind of cultural history they had intended to provide from their new base of El Centro Campesino Cultural, and this work debuted there. This farce deals with broader social and historical issues; it re-creates the conquest through a comparative process which sets pre-conquest society against colonialism and against contemporary Chicana/Chicano strug-gles against mainstream domination. Although the "Piedra del Sol" (The Cal-endar of the Sun) which serves as the narrator of the Mexican history carries the feminine-sounding "Piedra" in its name, the word for rock is not gendered in Spanish—although it ends with an "a" and may sound feminine. The character itself seems to have no gender, although, when called upon to organize, it is portrayed as a masculine figure and suggests the male figure with the final response, "Simon," a term generally associated with male street language slang although not exclusively.

Interestingly, gender-specific terms are omitted both for "Sol" and "Raza." Yet, Cuauhtemoc very clearly specifies how masculine gender has functioned in the downfall of México when he concludes that *los mexicanos* of antiquity were not united with "nuestro [*sic*] carnales de la raza y porque creiamos que esos hombres blancos eran dioses poderosos" [our brothers of la raza and because we believed that those white men were powerful gods]. The only clearly female figure in the story, then, is "La Malinche," here presented by the Narrator as a "sell-out" within a historical context:

> This woman was to become infamous in the history of Mexico. Not only did she turn her back on her own people, she joined the white men and became assimilated, serving as their guide and interpreter and generally assisting in the conquest. She was the first Mexican-American. (Valdez 1971, 58)

Cordelia Candelaria, in her article entitled "La Malinche, Feminist Prototype," refers to this description as Valdez's interpretation, telling us that his saying that "'she turn[ed] her back on her own people, she joined the white men and became assimilated,' becomes little more than weak slander. What else could this outcast from the Aztecs, 'her own people,' have done?" (Candelaria 1980, 6). But the characterization from Valdez is in the form of the Narrator's words and not Valdez speaking that view himself. Nevertheless, in an endnote, Candelaria tells us that in speaking with Valdez in 1976 he had "acknowledged that his characterization of Doña Marina [as La Malinche was "christened by Cortés's *padres*" (1)] was "historically invaded" (6). Candelaria finds that the account of La Malinche "might be read as an account of the prototypical Chicana feminist," adding:

> La Malinche embodies those personal characteristics—such as intelligence, initiative, adaptability, and leadership—which are most often associated with Mexican-American women unfettered by traditional restraints against activist public achievement. By adapting to the historical circumstances thrust upon her, she defied traditional social expectations of a woman's role.

The figure herself, as presented here, is never inconsequential. She is set against the most powerful men in Mexican and Spanish history, including Moctezuma II, Cuauhtémoc, and Hernán Cortés, and she is more than able to carry her weight. She is strong, articulate, and knows her own mind. She is also ingenious, knows her geography, and capably leads her oppressors, skillfully commanding attention. She is able to survive by drawing from her knowledge of her indigenous surroundings and background. However, at this juncture if we consider how La Malinche was portrayed in the early stages of Chicana/Chicano theatre in the Chicano Movement, we can understand how she functions as a central figure in the recovered cultural history of Chicanas/Chicanos that Valdez scripts from the improvised work.

Tey Diana Rebolledo tells us that "Chicana writers do not view La Malinche as the passive victim of rape and conquest but instead believe her to be a woman who had and made choices" (Rebolledo 1995, 64). Rebolledo also points out that many Chicana writers today personally identify with La Malinche, as evidenced in their work. Yet Rebolledo designates the personification of La Malinche in the early Chicano Renaissance as the traitorous woman. She is like the women who ruptured the much-guarded collective unity sought in the Movement whenever women voiced their own call for action on women's issues. In this *acto,* however, the role has been staged to show a powerful figure with the ability to wield resistance and opposition. When presented before an audience who is being asked to renegotiate history, identity, and self-determination, this Malinche disrupts the paradigm she has always appeared in, the hegemonic structure of patriarchal practice. Instead she is appearing as a model for a new cultural climate and cultural history.

La Malinche is often synonymous with La Llorona, and we have already witnessed the portrayal of that historical figure in *La Llorona*. Both figures would become important cultural symbols for Chicana dramatists and writers. In *La Conquista de Mexico* she may have initially appeared as a simple object of sexual desire, but upon closer examination we see that she exhibits an incredible ability to negotiate languages and other cultures, displaying a keen political acumen to ensure survival. A feminist reading of the text illustrates how the downfall of an entire culture is attributable to this figure, and with that kind of weight she represents an empowering voice of authority.

In contrast to the Aristotelian silenced woman who lacks an authoritative voice, we are here provided with a legacy of a real woman of power, one resisting suppression, who visually and emblematically portrays "Woman" onstage. She not only carries and sustains her own bloodline, but also creates a new lineage, the *mestiza,* or combination of Spanish and Indian. La Malinche essentially foregrounds difference and resistance by raising questions of identity and race representation—she has acquired a new color; the mixed blood of the *mestiza/mestizo* stems from her. Positionality is staged between historical figure and contemporary Chicana, and the *acto* shows how historical moments shift, depending on their context: Here La Malinche is in the center rather than on the periphery. While it can be argued that in this *acto* Malinche remains a symbol of hegemonic/patriarchal/historical representations of the first "Mexican-American," or "sell-out," other dimensions of this character are certainly worthy of consideration (Cypess 1991, 138–152).

In 1969, the group moved again, this time to Fresno and to another Centro Cultural. Valdez was hired to teach courses in Chicano theatre at Fresno State College, and the composition of the troupe changed from farm workers to students. Here the new ensemble created *No saco nada de la escuela* (*I Get Nothing Out of School*). Notably longer than the other published *actos,* this work was divided into three scenes, taking us from elementary to secondary to college classrooms. At a time when education was one of the most heated issues in the Chicana/Chicano Movement, it is not surprising to find that this work was a success.

Masks and very basic properties create the setting for this *acto,* which uses exaggeration and satire to address the very serious issue of the nature of the educational system in the United States for those outside the mainstream. The only Chicana in the group, Esperanza, prefers to be called "Hopi" from the English translation of her name in an attempt to detach herself from her Mexican background. By the end of the piece, she discovers herself and her ethnic identity, and she exits in the guise of a *pachuca,* the archetypal figure of a streetwise, dominant woman recognizable by this time in the Chicano Movement as a symbolic agent capable of commanding power and enacting change.

All of these *actos* were important in accomplishing Valdez's goal of educating Chicanas/Chicanos about their culture and background. By the close of the 1960s, the Chicano Movement had witnessed a collective expression of militancy and protest which manifested itself in significant ways through theatre. The language, culture, and traditions of Chicanas/Chicanos were continually reinforced by their proximity to México. The decade of the 1970s would bring a further awakening, often referred to as the Chicano Renaissance, whereby Chicanas/Chicanos were no longer "deprived of their birthright, but, instead participated in an American literary heritage that was also theirs" (Ortego 1973, 334). Philip D. Ortego's summation contextualizes this period: "The Chicano Renaissance came into being not in relation to the traditional past but rather in the wake of growing awareness by Mexican Americans of their Indian, not Hispanic, identity. The Chicano Renaissance is but the manifestation of a people's coming of age. It has been long overdue" (331–350).

The early stage of the Movement during the 1960s was significant in theatre history because of the work of El Teatro Campesino and Luis Valdez. We can see through the available playtexts how that reconnection with history and myths reached as far back as an indigenous ancestry. Valdez combined commitment to social and political activism with his search for a Chicana/Chicano cultural identity, and he brought to the annals of theatre history a wide range of experience, experimentation, and innovation that encouraged and inspired others. He was also responsible for training his own troupe who in turn trained others in the field.

It was a long road for the troupe and Valdez from the earliest stages of experimenting with performance to building a cultural mecca where all of the arts could be integrated. In 1969, El Teatro Campesino filmed Rodolfo "Corky" González's "most famous poem of the Chicano Movement in America."[19] This epic poem had impacted greatly on the Chicana/Chicano community, but the film version extended that influence even further. Initially, the troupe had presented a reading of the poem along with music and slides as part of their repertoire, but the film allowed for broader distribution and a significant means of expanding their outreach. We will witness new directions and other dimensions of Valdez's contribution to American culture and society as we step into the 1970s, during which Valdez taught in higher education and changed his troupe into one composed of students. As an educator and historian, Valdez made a lasting mark that would influence future practitioners.

Raymund A. Paredes tells us in his overview of "Mexican-American Literature" that "nothing exemplified the integration of literature into a program of Mexican-American cultural and political activism more than the Teatro Campesino" when Luis Valdez "seized an opportunity to combine his theatrical ambitions with the goals of César Chávez's farm workers' union" (Paredes 1993, 42). Paredes adds: "More than any other literary activity of the time, the Teatro Campesino demonstrated to Mexican Americans the power of art to provoke consideration of critical cultural and political issues." In Paredes's view, Mexican American literary activity expanded rapidly upon being "stimulated by the Teatro Campesino."

As an activist in the Movement, Valdez seems to have always viewed his role as both historian and educator and found in performance a means to access the Chicana/Chicano past which had always been so "invisible" to Euroamerican/ Anglos. Not only did Chicanas/Chicanos have to "preserve their language," but they also had to "create and publish their new literature without the *simpático* and commercial help of the educational institutions" (Steiner 1970, 224). Valdez noted: "We have to rediscover ourselves," recognizing that "there are years and years of discoveries we have to make of our people" (218). He added:

> People ask me: What is Mexican history in the United States? There is no textbook of the history of La Raza. Yet the history of the Mexican in this country is four hundred years old. We know we pre-date the landing of the Pilgrims and the American Revolution. But beyond that? What really happened? No one can tell you. Our history has been lost. Lost! (218)

The 1960s were a time of discovery, and a desire for cultural nationalism emerged from militancy and protest and awareness. More Chicana/Chicano social and political involvement was evident than had previously been witnessed, and by the end of the decade issues surrounding education dominated the Movement.

Valdez's role as historian was clear from his explorations with performance in telling of the past as well as in creating new myths, and the tours and his published forms of the group's work began to reach across the United States and abroad. In 1969 El Teatro Campesino was one of the featured performance groups in a theatre festival in Nancy, France. The Centro offered another venue to study culture and traditions, and Valdez's operations brought greater attention to the search for an indigenous past that would reconnect Chicanas/Chicanos with their origins. Although the schools had failed them before, now Chicanas/Chicanos could challenge Euroamerican mainstream society and reconstruct their history, their culture, and their identity in order to determine their own destiny. Valdez's voice profoundly guided and inspired the Chicana/Chicano ideological re-evaluation, self-determination, and new cultural nationalism that was at the heart of the Movement. For women, writing themselves for the stage was still at the threshold, and Luis Valdez and El Teatro Campesino would soon prove to be important influences and precursors toward that end. We can now turn to the next two decades which bear witness to the emergence of Latinas on the American stage through the continuing influence of Valdez and other distinct theatre practitioners.

4
THE EMERGENCE OF
A LATINA STAGE
The 1970s and the 1980s

According to the census, the total population of Mexican origin in the United States in 1970 numbered 6,293,000. In the 1980s the estimated figure rose to between eight and ten million persons in addition to a half million to two million undocumented Mexican workers. Juan Gómez-Quiñones writes that at one point in the 1980s there were six million Latinas/Latinos eligible to register to vote, yet only two million actually registered, leaving 65 percent unregistered (Gómez-Quiñones 1990, 173). Despite the difficulty in assessing distinct Latina/Latino groups as part of the whole, what we do know is that the Chicana/Chicano group continued to be a fast-growing population in the United States; figures from the 1970s through the 1980s indicate record growth. According to the most accurate estimate, about 49 percent of the growth of the total population in the 1980s was attributable to growth in the Latina/Latino population (Bower 1998, B2).[1] In 1980, the majority of these persons of Spanish surname origin (Latinas/Latinos or Hispanic), "about 7 million in number," as Gómez-Quiñones tells us, lived in the five southwestern states (Arizona, California, New Mexico, Colorado, and Texas) and, he adds, "most of these persons, 86 percent, were of Mexican origin." In addition, over a million and a half persons of Mexican descent resided in the midwestern cities of Chicago and Detroit and their surrounding areas (Gómez-Quiñones 1990, 190).

Within this extraordinarily large population of Spanish surname origin, in which Mexicans are unquestionably the largest subgroup, the number of women was significant. Gómez-Quiñones found that for March 1979, "partly because women in general usually marry at younger ages than do men, there were proportionally more single Spanish surname-origin men than women." Approximately 35 percent of men of Spanish surname origin at twenty-four years of age and over were single, compared with only 27 percent of Spanish-origin women. Yet he notes that the average Latina in the 1980s was entering her peak child-bearing years, from nineteen to twenty-nine, and forecasted "an unprecedented population growth" for Latinas/Latinos during the next ten to twenty years. In addition, divorced and single women heads of households continued to increase (191). As significant as the count of the subgroup in this population has been, Chicanas for the most part have been left out in chronicling the history of the Movement. As historian Vicki Ruíz tells us, even U.S. women's history has overlooked Chicana feminism (V. Ruíz 1998, 100). The Chicana/Chicano Movement provides us with a wealth of archival resources, oral interviews, and notable stories which are beginning to offer scholars opportunities to include women within this period. An important aspect of this history is the chronicling of the emergence of a Latina stage.

As the Chicana/Chicano Movement developed during the 1970s, Chicanas began to assess their role within the Movement. Chicanas viewed their oppression in a context that went far beyond male domination. Women's voices began to emerge on issues of class, race, and gender. More and more, Chicanas questioned traditional gender roles because these conventional positions so severely restricted women's participation in the Movement and their acceptance as full partners in Movement work. Significantly, El Teatro Campesino continued as a major force in the Chicana/Chicano theatre movement through the early 1970s, and both Luis Valdez and the company continued to impact greatly on the flowering of the written expression of las mujeres.

Valdez provided a voice for cultural nationalism in the Movement, calling for a search for an unknown indigenous past to inform the present. In his continuing attempt to educate La Raza on its historical past, Valdez co-edited with Stan Steiner one of the most widely distributed anthologies on the Chicana/Chicano experience, *Aztlan: An Anthology of Mexican American Literature,* in 1972. Although only one section was devoted to La Mujer (The Woman), under *La Causa* (The Cause), out of six portions devoted to the broad topic of the Chicana/Chicano struggle, this limited amount was important because little attention to the woman in this struggle had appeared anywhere up to that time. In this rather brief coverage, with eleven entries on women, some segments were translated from Spanish into English with no specified translator. Stan Steiner translated three songs about women, and two entries were poems written by Chicanos about women, namely José Montoya and Augustín Lira, both works which would become some of the most highly recognized expressive works chronicling the Chicana/Chicano voice of the time. Hence, despite their significance, it must be recognized that women's voices were filtered through male conceptualizations in each of these instances.

José Montoya's poem "La Jefita" ("The Little Mother") recalled his mother as "a symbol of life-giving sacrifice" (Valdez and Steiner 1972, 266). Montoya was one of the pioneers of the *teatro* movement and was co-founder of the Centro de Artistas Chicanos in Sacramento, California in 1970. Largely dominated by male artists, the Centro de Artistas, which also became known as The Royal Chicano Air Force, operated as a collective and included theatrical activity in its wide variety of artistic expression. Lira, the farm worker–poet who was also a member of El Teatro Campesino, wrote "Cruz," a poem in which he presented his mother as "an image of holiness and earthiness" in a world where women cry but men do not (268).

Perhaps the most significant entry about Chicanas in Valdez and Steiner's anthology was one entitled "The New Chicana." Here, the editors refer to the "Raza Renaissance" (271). More often referred to as the "Chicano Renaissance," which Philip D. Ortego describes as "the greatest outpouring of Mexican-American writing since 1900," it appeared "in prose, all of it essential in laying the foundation for what was to erupt as the Chicano Renaissance in the last years of the 1960s" (Ortego 1973, 344). The choice by Valdez and Steiner of the term "Raza" indicates the inclusive nature of the Movement at this stage; it involved both men and women, and the commentary they provide indicates their attention to this embrace. They place Chicanas in a pivotal position when they note that "in the 'Raza Renaissance,' there are few 'leading men' who do not have a woman devotedly and actively by their side" (Valdez and Steiner 1972, 272). Still, this point of view was not shared by all, for as the editors add, "as a leader of the Chicano movement has explained, 'Our women are equal with the men. If they stay one step back.'" The editors were quick to censure such exclusion: "The new Chicanas in the universities and barrios no longer accept this separate, but unequal, heritage of the Aztec and the Spaniard; nor do they express the 'silent strength' of the pioneer woman of La Raza; nor do they acquiesce to the 'goddess/mistress' imagery of the male ego—his *machismo*" (272). These early historians and collectors of documents about this watershed period for women's writing about themselves include two works that serve as representative voices for the time: one is Enriqueta Longauez y Vasquez's narrative about "The Woman of La Raza," and the other is Mary Lou Espinosa's poem, "La Madre de Aztlan."

Through Enriqueta Longauez y Vasquez, a writer for the New Mexico Chicana/Chicano newspaper *El Grito del Norte,* we discover the female activist's voice. She writes about the historical woman, the woman as provider and the liberator of men who calls the Chicana to action in this 1969 piece. Longauez y Vasquez is "sure that *La Chicana* will leave her mark upon the Mexican-American movement in the Southwest" (Longauez y Vasquez 1972, 273). She states: "When we talk of equality in the Mexican-American movement we better be talking about TOTAL equality, beginning right where it all starts, AT HOME" (278). Of Mary Lou Espinosa's poem, "La Madre de Aztlan," which also first appeared in 1969, Valdez and Steiner write, "in her hardlined poem," Espinosa "evokes the elemental 'life from within' that women bear to strengthen their status in contemporary life" (Valdez and Steiner 1972, 272). In seven stanzas, Espinosa's definition of equality moves from "the function of man as father/woman as mother" to a new construction in which both operate as "independent" humans "capable of change" (279). Ultimately, "a free woman can creatively / contribute with radical solutions / because she knows life from within" (280).

Chicanitas performing in Chicana/Chicano barrio park,
Sacramento, California, 1975.
Photo by Mario C. Ramírez.

Within two decades after the beginning of the Movimiento, as Juan Gómez-Quiñones asserts, "these years of sustained conflict and struggle had yielded some positive results," for they had led to "a cultural and artistic flowering," a predominant feature of the late 1960s, the 1970s, and the early 1980s (Gómez-Quiñones 1990, 190–191), and the new articulation by women must be counted among them. In her 1998 publication *From Out of the Shadows,* historian Vicki Ruíz devoted an entire chapter to "La Nueva Chicana" (Ruíz 1998, 99–126). Ruíz notes that "whether through *commadrazgo* [*sic*] [godmothering], *mutualistas* [beneficial social service societies], labor unions, or political organizing, some women recognized what they had in common as women" (102). During the period of Chicana/Chicano student activism, "picking up the pen for Chicanas became a 'political act.'" Many *teatros* were born on college campuses primarily centered in California, although the work of El Teatro Campesino was helping to broaden the scope of Chicana/Chicano performance farther afield, and women were beginning to play a vital role in this aspect of the Movement, that is, a renaissance of performance.

TENAZ AND WOMEN IN TEATRO (W.I.T.)

In 1970, El Teatro Campesino hosted the first national festival of Chicano theatres, and sixteen groups from throughout the United States attended. El Teatro Nacional de Aztlán, known as TENAZ, was founded in 1971 as a coalition of *teatros* for the purpose of coordinating national and regional events, publications, and interaction between groups. Summer workshops were also organized under the auspices of TENAZ, and the first of these was sponsored

Members of El Teatro Campesino in rehearsal (left to right: José
Delgado, Andrés Valenzuela Gutiérrez, Diane Rodríguez, and Socorro
Valdez). Socorro Valdez is Luis Valdez's sister. The actors are creating
the illusion of a moving train, using movement, music, and sound.
La Gran Carpa de los Rasquachis, 1975–76.
Photo by Al Balz, San Juan Bautista. Courtesy of Diane Rodríguez.

by ETC. The ETC influence was evident from the outset. Luis Valdez and his
brother, Danny, and other troupe members led workshops for representatives
from the other groups that were participating. The TENAZ festivals and workshops played a major role in ensuring better networking between groups, and
allowed for the flowering of new trends in Chicana performance within Chi-
cana/Chicano theatrical practice.

The earliest account we have of a women's *teatro,* Teatro Raíces, was
formed in San Diego, California in 1971. Felicitas Nuñez and Delia Revelo
founded the group with the intention of focusing on women. Although lasting
until 1982, working largely on a part-time basis, virtually nothing is known
about this group.[2] Perhaps the most important historical moment for a study
of women in theatre is the formation of El Teatro de las Chicanas, a women's
group which performed at the 1973 festival in San Jose. Their work seriously
examined the divisiveness caused by the sexist stereotyping that was hampering
the Chicano movement. The significance of the performance was made evident
in the series of discussions that were part of this festival. Serious debate and
censure surfaced in a session designated for criticism of the performances at the
festival. Participants walked away taking sides: Some felt that the issue of Chicana feminism was divisive to the Movement and others felt strongly that wom-
en's voices needed to be heard. As Alma M. García points out in her article
entitled "The Development of Chicana Feminist Discourse, 1970–1980," Chicanas were beginning to examine the issues that were impacting on them as

women of color (A. García 1994, 175–183). In developing this feminist consciousness, Chicanas were assessing their participation in the Movement.

The *pláticas* (talks) at the 1973 festival made it clear that women would be active participants at subsequent festivals and that they would continue to be a part of the Chicana/Chicano theatre movement. This was the first time the issue had surfaced of whether certain topics would be addressed at the festivals, or whether certain groups would even be permitted to participate. The discussions were heated; radical women who wished to participate felt censured and found very little support for their voices and their type of activism. The lines were clearly drawn; participants either adhered to the traditional forms, styles, and approaches to performance which they had garnered from studying with or about the leading troupe of the period, El Teatro Campesino, or they took new paths. By opposing the type of *teatro* typical of the Movement up to this time, namely, that which was most distinctly characterized by male domination in themes and forms, women began to pursue new directions, with attention to a changing ideology and political agenda. Chicana feminists were striving toward social equality and an end to sexism and racist oppression. Regardless of which side festival participants took, though, all agreed that the lack of a clear story line in *teatro* performances, poor preparation, lack of performance skills, and departures from loyalty to Chicano ideology left much to be desired. Almost everyone supported the commitment to strengthen the craft and the performance itself.

The result of the conflict at the 1973 TENAZ festival was that a growing number of women began to make their own unique contributions to Chicana/Chicano theatre. By 1978 a women's caucus, Women in Teatro (W.I.T.), was formed within TENAZ. The objectives delineated by W.I.T. were to create professional space for women playwrights and directors, to emphasize strong female roles in order to educate Chicana/Chicano audiences, to address individual women's needs such as child care, and to garner support from Chicanas and Chicanos in the development of women in *teatro*. W.I.T. has functioned to provide a network for communication and broad-based support in a wide range of theatre organizations. TENAZ has often included workshops on consciousness-raising and getting started in Chicana/Chicano theatre.

The formation of Chicana alternative theatre groups increased the number of Chicanas working in *teatro*. For example, in her article "The Female Subject in Chicano Theatre," Yvonne Yarbro-Bejarano discusses the work of Dorinda Moreno and Las Cucarachas in their performance of a work entitled *Chicana,* first performed for a small festival in San Francisco's Mission District and subsequently in Mexico City for the Fifth Festival organized by TENAZ. In the *teatropoesía* form, a combination of poetry, prose, music, and other forms which owed much to the choral poetry style,[3] *Chicana* brought numerous Chicana figures to the stage under the auspices of a narrative history. Yarbro-Bejarano also chronicles another women's group, Valentina Productions, based in San

Jose, California. This group performed *Voz de la mujer* (*Voice of the Woman*), also in the same *teatropoesía* form, and added other Chicana figures to the stage as well. In 1984, Carolina Flores co-founded Teatro Huipil, named after a woman's garment in the Mayan tradition and eventually changing its name to Teatro Vision (Yarbro-Bejarano 1990, 139).

VALDEZ'S INFLUENCE CONTINUES

TENAZ continued to grow in membership, largely comprised of student groups and groups affiliated with community organizations, but Valdez remained the recognized major force in the Chicana/Chicano theatre movement. Evidence of his influence was seen in the ideology of the groups and in their performance. Groups drew from the style of performance, the language, the distinct symbols and images, and especially the forms that El Teatro Campesino presented. Most of the groups had no formal training, except for Adrian Vargas and Manuel Martínez, graduate students at the University of California, Irvine, who served as co-directors of Teatro de la Gente, and Jorge Huerta, the founder of El Teatro de la Esperanza when he was completing his doctoral studies in theatre at the University of California at Santa Barbara. But it was Luis Valdez and his collective organizational approach that dominated the work of other *teatros* in the early 1970s, and thus we must examine the continuing influence and role that Valdez and ETC played in the reshaping of Chicano *teatro* and understand why Latinas are compelled to create their own voice on the American stage.

Out of the sixty-four known groups of Chicana/Chicano *teatros* that I studied in 1974 (excluding eighteen groups that never responded to my queries), most had benefited from some influence stemming from Luis Valdez and/or ETC; if not from its playtexts, then from word of mouth or from witnessing their performances. In fact, because the *acto* form as well as the Teatro Campesino style became so dominant for other forming groups, *Tenaz,* the publication of the organization, published an article in 1972 addressing the shortage of new materials, stating:

> Material for performance has been a problem which all teatros have suffered. During the past festivals one fact became obvious and that is that each group seemed to be performing the same material. Recognizing this shortage, an *Acto* workbook was compiled and made available for developing groups. A problem which is foreseeable is the danger of different teatros directing the *actos* in the same style as Teatro Campesino. This has its good and bad points. Good in that the *actos* are being performed and bad in that experimentation in different styles may not take place. ("Chicano Theater," 1972, p. 8)

There was a call for new methods, noting that: "It should be made clear that this is not a criticism against student teatro groups," of which most *teatros* were comprised. "On the contrary, the work they do is important and should be recognized and worked with." The article added that "Teatro Campesino has suffered also from the same problems. Problems which each new group will undoubtedly experience" (8). Despite the call for change and new directions, many groups continued to be influenced by Valdez and the Teatro Campesino style and approach. With the publication of *Pensamiento Serpentino* by Luis Valdez, which emphasized the cosmic vision of ETC, and with "Notes on Chicano Theatre" by Valdez and a list of "Teatro Campesino (Warm-Ups)" for performance preparation, the dominance of ETC ideology and approach was solidified (7–23).

As Valdez delved more and more into the project of connecting an indigenous past to the present, he began to integrate the cultural heritage of Chicanas/Chicanos with the *mito* form. Valdez noted that "our rejection of white western European (*Gavacho*) proscenium theater [made] the birth of new Chicano forms necessary—thus, *los actos y los mitos* (the *actos* and the myths): one through the eyes of man; the other, through the eyes of God" (Valdez 1971, 5). Valdez had begun seeking ways to relate indigenous myths to the present in response to a growing desire among Chicanas/Chicanos to investigate the roots of Chicana/Chicano culture. A return to the *mito,* he felt, would help Chicanas/Chicanos rediscover their long-forgotten cultural heritage as well as help regain that spiritual strength which even the Catholic Church had been robbing Chicanas/Chicanos of for hundreds of years (Huerta 1974, 113). *Bernabé: A Drama of Modern Chicano Mythology,* written in 1969, was the first drama in this vein.

Valdez wrote of content that

> The teatros must never get away from La Raza. Without the *palomía* [the people] sitting there, laughing, crying, and sharing whatever is onstage, the teatros will dry up and die. If the Raza will not come to the theater, then the theater must go to the Raza. This, in the long run, will determine the shape, style, content, spirit and form of el teatro Chicano. (Valdez 1971, 4)

Valdez began to work with the *mito,* or myth, as a new way to educate audiences about the Chicano experience. The *mito* was Valdez's "new, more mystical dramatic form" which could complement and balance the *acto* in an effort to distinguish Chicano theatre from Western European performance. With this form, he returned to writing longer plays instead of developing material within the collective. He directed his first *mito, Bernabé: A Drama of Modern Chicano Mythology,* in 1970, five years after the founding of ETC.

Just as Artaud had intended, Valdez was able to create new myths. *Bernabé,* a "modern Chicano mythology,"[4] offered the story of a *loquito del pueblo,* or village idiot, who experienced rebirth through La Tierra (Mother Earth). Mother Earth appears first in the guise of a *soldadera,* or woman who fought in the Mexican Revolution, and subsequently as fresh *maíz* growing from within the *milpa* (ear of corn growing on land where corn is cultivated), which represented rebirth. La Tierra appears as an activist, powerful enough to make Bernabé want to fight for her, die for her, and even kill for her. Her ability to fend for herself is never questioned, and she is positioned to empower a man in order to fight for justice and enact change. She symbolizes a spiritual union, and this *soldadera*[5] or La Adelita, as the woman soldier of the revolution was known, is a warrior who can be owned by no one. Through her the new Chicana/Chicano can acquire indigenous ideology and spiritual freedom.

Bernabé introduces us to three figures who contrast sharply with each other: the mother, the prostitute, and the new woman of power. Each character begins with traditional roles, but in the context of socio-political events she moves from victim to liberator and activist. These women are pivotal in Bernabé's life. Valdez uses the universal theme of male supremacy over land, power, and wealth to illustrate that man's wish to attain land frequently creates the antithesis of that desire in man's exploitation of the land. He draws parallels between the exploitation of the land and the exploitation of human beings by society. By the end of the drama, man has been redeemed by woman, who has been able to renew and revive him within a higher, spiritual realm that is part of a cosmos in which Chicana/Chicano ideology reigns supreme.

Valdez is concerned with the Chicano's quest for his deepest roots in La Tierra (the Earth). Bernabé, the central character, is the village idiot, who through his innocence seeks to marry La Tierra, who for him is a woman. Valdez draws from the Aztec belief that a male child, upon reaching puberty, must first copulate with the earth, thereby attaining manhood.[6] He draws parallels as well between the exploitation and prostitution of the land and female prostitution. The play also illustrates the exploitation of the Chicana/Chicano in many ways: landowners control Torres, a hotel and bar owner who owns the land that the farm workers work on for little pay and under poor working conditions; Eddie, a young Chicano, is used by Torres as his go-between in his dope-smuggling business; and Connie, the prostitute, is controlled by her pimp, Torres.

Bernabé is seen in two spheres: the realistic setting in which Bernabé lives and the sphere in which he encounters the world of the Aztec gods, of which he eventually becomes a part. Valdez makes use of specific scene divisions in this play. Seven scenes are held together by the central character's continual desire to be with his girlfriend, La Tierra, and more important, to achieve that goal so that he may attain complete happiness and truth. Only through the Earth can Bernabé be a complete man.

It is in Scene 6 that the change in reality occurs as the *llano,* the plain of soft dirt behind Bernabé's house where he meets with his girlfriend, becomes his refuge from the real world. This world consists of a spiritual reality in which Bernabé encounters La Luna, the brother of La Tierra, who introduces Bernabé to his "girlfriend." In order to marry La Tierra, Bernabé must give himself

La Tierra (The Earth) as *maíz,* or ear of corn growing from the ground, with death mask at her belly in Scene 6 in the *llano,* or open plain, in *Bernabé* by Luis Valdez, California State University, Sacramento, directed by Elizabeth C. Ramírez (May 1975).
Photo by Mario C. Ramírez.

up to her father El Sol, the Sun, to nourish the Sun so that he can rise each morning.[7] Bernabé will continue the long lineage of powerful men who constitute the Chicana/Chicano heritage, the forefathers who knew and cherished the land.[8] He is symbolically sacrificed in a ceremony in which his heart is wrenched out as a source of life for the Sun in a manner similar to the bloody sacrifices of the Aztecs.[9] Bernabé becomes a new man, no longer an idiot but a man instilled with a greater knowledge of the universe. He has found his deepest roots in La Tierra and after being united with her for all eternity, she turns into Death. Bernabé embraces his deadly bride with the enlightened knowledge that "life is death and death is life," a concept deeply rooted in the Chicana/Chicano indigenous mythology.[10]

The major differences between the female characters in this play and those in the earlier *actos* lie in their greater depth. We get an insight into Bernabé's conception of his surroundings, and he becomes a complete person as other major figures reveal his circumstances. Valdez purposely costumes the allegorical figure of the earth and the moon to represent distinct familiar characters in Chicana/Chicano history. La Luna was developed from the earlier zoot-suiter who first appeared in *Los Vendidos,* and La Tierra undergoes several changes as she continues to manifest notable figures in Chicana history. Through the figures presented in the sixth scene, Valdez supplies the audience with visual images by which he can educate them about mythology and instill in them a sense of pride in symbols of the Chicana/Chicano heritage.

Other plays by Valdez also utilized the forms now typical in his dramaturgy. *Dark Root of a Scream,*[11] first produced in 1971, combines an indigenous past with the contemporary setting of the Vietnam War, creating a modern myth in the process. This work seems to have evolved from the earlier collective ETC *actos, Vietnam Campesino* and *Soldado Razo,* both profoundly anti-war. Highly emotional in content, the history Valdez writes links the most recognizable cultural hero of the Chicana/Chicano, Quetzalcóatl, with the fallen Chicano hero who returns from the war in a coffin. Although the focus of analysis of this work has primarily been the tragedy that befalls the Chicano hero, an examination of the women's roles in this work reveals important performative elements that contribute to the emerging female voice on the contemporary stage.

The setting very deliberately contrasts the spiritual with reality, with the apex of the cultural site of a pyramid situated in "an abstract mythical-religious peak at the top," with realistic "artifacts of barrio life at the broad base" where we can see a street corner and an interior home scene (Valdez 1973, 79–98). The street is the signifier for both displacement and cultural loss. We see three *vatos locos,* Lizard, Conejo, and Gato, "huddled against the wall." The brick wall is covered with "Chicano writings in pachuco script." However, we are soon drawn from an outer reality into a spiritual indigenous awakening via a *velorio,* a wake, in a living room. Three figures, a *madre* (mother), Dalia (a young woman), and a priest enter the room, where we see a metallic black coffin draped with an American flag. Here is true representation of the American scene, and the cultural codes are those of Chicanas/Chicanos in crisis.

The title of this play comes from a line in Federico García Lorca's *Blood Wedding,* an excellent example of a world in which women, especially mothers, suffer. But the shift in focus in this work from the surrealism of García Lorca brings to the fore issues that highlight women as subjects. In both worlds women are shown in a male-dominated universe and we see them struggle to survive. But the roles in the contemporary Chicana/Chicano setting are not the traditional roles. Instead, we begin to hear women's voices and, more important, to view them as active participants in the complexity of the dramatic action.

Dalia, the dead soldier Indio's *ruca* (girlfriend), comprehends and speaks Spanish, reminding us that not all Chicanas have lost their language. She is the character who links Chicanos to what they should be proud of, "their culture, their heritage" (86). Dalia uses this link when she initiates the discussion in Scene 10 about the mythology surrounding Quetzalcóatl and the Indians of México. The next scene, driven by Dalia, further develops the efforts Indio was making to enact change for Chicanas/Chicanos.

In explaining to the Euroamerican local priest what the victim's contributions to his barrio were, she reveals how she too was taught about her Indian heritage. She recites a litany of the power the modern-day savior brought to his barrio: "He wanted the Raza to be close to God." "He wanted our people to have enough to eat." "He wanted Chicanos to express and educate themselves." "He wanted us to live free and equal." She turns on the priest, accusing him of having hampered Indio in his efforts. As the play progresses, Dalia seems to reach greater insight than the rest.

The figure of the mother at first seems to merely replicate the stereotypical fainting and suffering madonna—she lost her husband when her son was just eight years old. But it soon becomes clear that her character has greater depth.

Although it was his father who taught Indio about the Aztecs, we can surmise that when the mother was left alone to raise her three sons she continued the lessons. Not only does she naturally and easily pronounce their given Indian names (in clear contrast to the white priest who keeps exclaiming about his limited abilities to speak Spanish and uncomfortably struggles to understand the unfamiliar terms), but she also serves as the link in the drama to that indigenous blood lineage, the Aztec heritage.

Indio returns with the Congressional Medal of Honor, "the highest award his country could give him," as the priest points out. But the mother has lost three sons to war, one killed in France, one in Korea, and now Indio in Vietnam. She calls Indio *corazón de tu madre,* the heart of his mother, and her continual moaning and wailing and grief build to the climactic moment when she rushes to the coffin and reveals her strength as the only one willing and able to open the lid. She discovers Indio's heart in the coffin, giving out light "in the descending darkness," along with a "brilliant headdress of green feathers and a cloak of Aztec design," indicating the powerful visual emblem of that Chicana/Chicano icon, Quetzalcóatl, the long-awaited savior for the Aztecs— now linked to the blood of the new Chicana/Chicano in Aztlán, the Southwest (98). It is difficult to view the female subject as subordinate in this story; it is women who drive the dramatic action and control the outcome of the drama. The Madre is pivotal; the setting situates her as a dominant survivor who has the ability to penetrate everyday reality toward another greater spiritual understanding. Positioned at the heart of the home and within her barrio surroundings, she transcends even the religious and mythological toward a deeper indigenous realm.

In examining these representative plays of the early 1970s written by Luis Valdez and developed by El Teatro Campesino, clearly the shift from male centrality to a growing attention to the changing role of Chicanas in the Movement began to surface. However, the major shift in attention to women in performance did not occur until Valdez's longer plays made it clear that women's voices not only had to be heard but also made pivotal within the Chicana/Chicano experience and the broader societal spectrum. The extraordinary exposure brought about by the production of *Zoot Suit* made it evident that change was on the way.

Zoot Suit represents Valdez's greatest popular dramatic success to date.[12] This Chicana/Chicano drama with music was first produced in 1978 by both El Teatro Campesino and the Center Theatre Group of Los Angeles, commissioned by Gordon Davidson and the Mark Taper Forum. Considered the first Hispanic American play to reach Broadway, it opened at the Winter Garden Theatre on March 25, 1979, in a revised version. The play, an adaptation of real events that occurred in Los Angeles during World War II, was directed by Valdez and featured Edward James Olmos and Daniel Valdez. It combines symbolism, the Living Newspaper technique of the 1930s, and agitprop theatre, along with "elements of the *acto, corrido, carpa,* and *mito*" in a spectacular documentary play with music (Huerta 1982, 177).[13]

Zoot Suit brought a half million people to see it in Los Angeles. In Valdez's words, it was "because I had given a disenfranchised people their religion back." But essentially the playwright's own story is the story that has to be told. Valdez has said that "it deals with self-salvation" and that "you can follow the playwright through the story—I was also those two dudes," referring to the central character, Henry Reyna, and his "Jungian self-image, the super-ego," of the Pachuco (Savran 1988, 20).

The zoot suit serves as a symbol of protest and dignity in the face of racial intolerance, injustice, and inequality. The play centers on gang leader Henry Reyna, who is arrested and convicted in a trial for murder that occurred during a purported gang fight. The trial in court and through the press was so one-sided that the conviction was later overturned. The women's roles in the play are few and limited. The demands on Henry Reyna to have a woman at his side who will be loyal to him and offer a family background and culture similar to his own are sharply contrasted with his desire for Alice Bloomfield, the Jewish American woman who provides him with a fresh and lively exchange of intellect and equality that he has never before experienced. He is torn between Della, who on the surface may seem to be portrayed as the traditionally meek and silent woman of the Chicana/Chicano community who stands by her man, and the independent and opinionated Alice. Yet his loyalty and connections to his family and his Chicana girlfriend prevent him from reaching out for someone outside his class and culture.

Although limited, the roles of Della and the mother are crucial in the drama. The Chicana/Chicano family was at the heart of the Movement, strategically functioning as a means of power and protest. This Brechtian open-ended play allows us to consider that one possible ending to this tragedy is that Della and Henry marry and that their children not only attend university but also call themselves "Chicanos." The political consciousness that Della and Henry have acquired would certainly produce educated offspring who would also be politically aware. Henry's mother serves as a cohesive force by sustaining the family unit; the food she provides and the home she maintains ensure survival. The story ends with the mother reminding us that Henry Reyna is "our son," with the full realization that he would not exist without both parents who have nurtured and guided him. Yet feminist critics have found it difficult to acknowledge the mother, who rolls tortillas and tearfully holds the family together without a voice in the political resistance that was at the heart of the Movement. But when critics such as Yolanda Broyles-González tell us that "the deplorable representation of Mexican and Chicana women is a chronic weakness and signature of Luis Valdez's mainstream productions" (Broyles-González 1994, 160), I immediately recall Valdez's call to all participants in playwriting workshops to write their own stories. He stated that Chicana/

Writer/director Luis Valdez as El Maestro and singer Linda
Rondstadt in *Corridos! Tales of Passion and Revolution.* A production
of KQED/San Francisco in association with El Teatro Campesino.
Photo by Allen Nomura.

Chicano theatre was "theatre as beautiful, rasquachi [rough and unpolished],
human, cosmic, broad, deep, tragic, comic, as the life of La Raza itself" (Valdez
1971, 1), and *Zoot Suit,* perhaps more than any other play, led Valdez and ETC
toward a new path: identifying plays written by women to include women's
voices as an integral part of their work.

Clearly, Chicanas were on the verge of making an indelible mark on performance. In her critical analysis of the "Female Subject" in *teatro,* Yvonne
Yarbro-Bejarano notes that the "representation of female subjectivity and sexuality" in Chicana/Chicano theatre is linked to the historical development of
the Movement:

> The phase that coincided with the heyday of cultural nationalism produced
> ordering narratives that tended to exclude the Chicana from the subject
> position and define her sexuality in terms of *La Malinche* or *La Virgen*
> within the heterosexual hierarchy of the family. (Yarbro-Bejarano 1990,
> 148)[14]

In the 1970s, she adds, "a materialist analysis countered the mystified racial
and cultural identity of cultural nationalism with class identity, producing representations of revolutionary subjects, both male and female" (148). By the
1980s, more and more representations of women in the Chicana/Chicano and
the broader Latina/Latino theatre movement had surfaced. (The work of Josefina López and Evelina Fernández, produced by ETC, will be discussed in

the following chapter.) Valdez and ETC also had a significant influence in the area of production; male and female actors from ETC would soon appear in some of the major theatrical venues in the United States. Valdez and ETC were clearly paving the way for numerous Chicana voices and faces in performance and before long they would impact on Latinas throughout the United States as well.

TEATROS IN THE ACADEMY AND ACTOR TRAINING PROGRAMS[15]

Another significant influence on Chicana/Chicano theatre came from academe. Jorge Huerta, who was completing his doctoral work at the University of California, Santa Barbara, formed El Teatro de la Esperanza (The Theatre of Hope) in 1971, along with other students. The early history of this company is generally glossed over in order to get at its more recent collective history, one which has been highly successful and significant in terms of work by women. But in the early days of the company Huerta, like Valdez, served as the overseer and director of the company, taught in a theatre department, and worked with students that entered the field. Huerta's wife, Ginger Huerta, who served as the musical director and business manager of the company, was also a core member of the troupe, often conducting workshops and organizing rehearsals. This troupe was important for its published collection of works written collectively and by individuals in the group. Above all, however, Huerta has emerged as an important leader second only to Valdez in the areas of actor training and performance specifically related to the Chicana/Chicano experience. A recognized scholar in the field, Huerta has lectured extensively and has directed numerous workshops in style and performance in his area of expertise.

In addition to guiding the group and serving frequently as a director, Huerta has been responsible for training many Chicanas/Chicanos/Latinas/Latinos in theatre in higher education. Diane Rodríguez was one of the core members of Esperanza. She worked first with Huerta as a theatre major, and after her work with Esperanza joined ETC and eventually went on to work farther afield (Rodríguez will be discussed further in Chapter 6). Huerta eventually moved to the University of California, San Diego, where for a time he led a Chicana/Chicano theatre program.

I founded and directed a Chicano theatre program at California State University, Sacramento. An ongoing program since 1974 that was subsequently directed by Romulus Zamora and then by Manuel Pickett, this program also served as a training ground for undergraduate students to specialize in theatre studies and for some to continue in graduate programs. Performances generally included numerous community members integrated with students and there were many opportunities for generating new works and holding performance workshops.

The university setting was responsible for the formation of many *teatros* as the Chicana/Chicano student movement broadened. Most group members had little training but were driven by activism and militancy and a shared political message; groups formed and fell apart as urgent circumstances pulled them from the community to classes to performance. In the groups with longer histories, however, it seems that when members had further and/or formal training in performance their involvement in *teatros* was longer-lived. By the beginning of the 1980s all of the members of ETC were graduates of a drama department or had had previous experience with other *teatros* or, in some cases, had experience in both academic and applied arenas.

The Chicana/Chicano theatre movement was sustained through academic training, and the history of Chicanas/Latinas in performance was influenced by those practitioners who eventually settled in the academic arena. However, another figure emerged who provided the kind of professional practice relatively alien to and alienated from the American stage. She honed her craft by writing for the stage and struggling for a means to effectively ensure that her work would be heard.

THE 1980s: MARIA IRENE FORNES

During the 1980s, probably the single most influential Latina on other Latinas in theatre and performance was Maria Irene Fornes. Born in Cuba in 1930, Fornes emigrated to the United States in 1945. This distinguished Cuban American playwright has been the recipient of numerous awards, including the John Hay Whitney Foundation Fellowship (1961), the Centro Mexicano de Escritores (Writers) fellowship (1962), two Yale University fellowships (1967, 1968), two Rockefeller Foundation grants (1971, 1984), a Guggenheim fellowship (1972), two National Endowment for the Arts grants (1974, 1984), numerous Obie Awards for Playwriting and Directing, an Obie for Outstanding Achievement in the Theatre in 1982, and the New York State Governor's Arts Award in 1990.

In the mid-1950s, Fornes was on a tour of Europe to study painting. She saw Roger Blin's production of Samuel Beckett's *Waiting for Godot* in Paris. Blin has been described as Antonin Artaud's "most devoted disciple," and through Blin's work many of Artaud's ideas were brought into the French theatre. Blin had also worked with Charles Dullin and Jean-Louis Barrault, bringing absurdism to international attention in a period under the threat of the Cold War and atomic holocaust (Brockett and Findlay 1991, 313, 319). Clearly, Blin was a leader in the avant-garde movement, and the production Fornes witnessed was no ordinary production. Fornes has often spoken about the impact of this production on her subsequent work in theatre, particularly emphasizing the visual imagery the production used. Upon returning to the United States in 1957 she worked as a textile designer before turning to playwriting. Her first work, *Tango Palace,* was produced in 1963 at the Actors Workshop in San Francisco, the same venue where Ron Davis had worked. In the same year she joined the Actors Studio playwriting unit and became a member of the Open Theatre's playwriting unit. She received her first Obie Award, for Distinguished Playwriting, in 1965 for *Promenade* and *The Successful Life of 3.*

Soon after Fornes began writing plays she began to direct as well. Her first Obie Award for directing, which also included recognition for playwriting, came in 1977 for *Fefu and Her Friends.* Recognized for her contributions to Off-Broadway theatre in her concerns and style, she is also acclaimed for her innovative staging techniques. Numerous articles, dissertations, and two recent books have been written about this acclaimed playwright's work. Assunta Kent's *Maria Irene Fornes and Her Critics* is a rather disappointing attempt to bring a dramaturg's perspective to the work of Fornes; it is greatly hampered by the excessive explication of the methodology she wishes to apply to a vast amount of data about this major American playwright.[16]

Dianne Lynn Moroff's *Fornes: Theater in the Present Tense* does provide a worthwhile and in-depth study of the work of this leading contemporary American dramatist both as a theatrical practitioner and playwright.[17] Fornes's explorations of political, feminist, and absurdist theatre emerge as striking elements in production, but Moroff transcends strictly literary analysis to arrive at crucial issues dealing with the exploration of subjectivity, social relations, language, and representation. Central to this study is the power of spectacle as Fornes foregrounds the visual image over the word, and Moroff effectively examines how the interplay between various theatrical elements is an integral aspect of this playwright's work, particularly as applied to the spectator and the theatrical event. A broad glimpse of Fornes's thirty years in theatre precedes a detailed look at such works as *Fefu and Her Friends* (1977), *Mud* (1983), *Sarita* (1984), and *The Conduct of Life* (1985).

The most extensive criticism available on Fornes, of course, is found in the countless reviews of her work both in New York on Off-Broadway stages and on many of the most recognized regional stages across the country. Yet, critical work to date on Fornes fails to provide comprehensive and in-depth analyses of the Cuban/Latina ethnic and cultural explorations this playwright offers. The influence of this individual on other writers and practitioners is impressive; it is important to examine her contribution in bringing new Latina voices to the American stage.

Although her work is extensive, we will examine a representative work by Fornes in order to shed light on the type of political theatre that exemplifies an evolving Latina feminism. Through investigating structures of race, gender, class, patriarchy, and other issues experienced by Latinas, we can arrive at the consequences of these issues for Latinas, women of color, and all women in American society. In *The Conduct of Life* (1985), as Alma M. García suggests, we witness "a rephrasing of the critical question concerning the nature of the oppression experienced by Chicanas and other women of color," with Chicana/Latina feminists, like Black feminists, "asking what are the consequences of the intersection of race, class, and gender in the daily lives of women in American society, emphasizing the simultaneity of these critical variables for women of color" (A. García 1994, 183).

First produced in New York City at Theater for the New City on February 21, 1985, *The Conduct of Life* was directed by Fornes. *The Conduct of Life* presents us with a world in which it seems that Orlando is the central figure. At the outset of the play he is an army lieutenant but he soon advances to lieutenant commander. The opening scene reveals his physical abilities, and his monologue, the only text in the first scene, complements that strength with his command of words and political position: "Thirty three and I'm still a lieutenant. In two years I'll receive a promotion or I'll leave the military. I promise I will not spend time feeling sorry for myself." At the end of his monologue, Orlando states his mode of operation: "Man must have an ideal, mine is to achieve maximum power. That is my destiny.—No other interest will deter me from this." This vow includes even his sexual drive: "My sexual drive is detrimental to my ideals. I must no longer be overwhelmed by sexual passion or I will be degraded beyond hope of recovery" (Fornes 1986, 68). His strategy is set.

The world of the play shifts from one which seems to be a universal world to one which tells us about this culturally specific experience: it is set in the present in a Latin American country with no specified name (1985 is the date of the premiere). Although it would seem that any Third World nation could be inferred here, the targeted group becomes immediately specific when Spanish character names and terms are used, when we witness a clearly delineated class structure and severe economic hardship, and when we hear of the horrors of torture, domination, and oppression described in this world. The countries quickly narrow down to those known and recognizable countries from which our American immigrants have poured in: Cuba, Argentina, Chile, and Central America. But the militarization described in the Latin American world called for here, in what Diana Taylor describes as "criminal governments in Argentina, Brazil, Uruguay, Paraguay, Chile, Guatemala, and El Salvador (to name only the most brutal)" that "deliberately used destabilizing tactics to terrorize and atomize their populations," offers more distinct possibilities (Taylor 1991, 20). In fact, Taylor recommends thinking of Latin America as "twenty-five different countries—each with its own particular combination of races and populations, languages and dialects, traditions and cultural images—that share a similar history of conquest, colonization, economic and political instability, and continuing sociopolitical and economic dependency" (8). But the far reaches of an unknown Latin American country that Fornes calls for are much more immediate: minorities or marginal peoples within the U.S. itself, and of course, Latinas/Latinos exist within a Third World community right in their own backyard. As Robert Blauner points out, "members of the third world within the United States are individually and collectively outnumbered by whites, and Anglo-American cultural imperatives dominate the society—although this has been a true cultural minority" (Blauner 1994, 160). He adds, "In the United States, the more total cultural domination, the alienation of most third world people from a land base, and the numerical minority factor have weakened the group integrity of the colonized and their possibilities for cultural and political self-determination" (160).

Whether or not Fornes has Cuba in her mind when she calls for an unidentified Latin American locale, unquestionably the incredible U.S. involvement in militarization in Latin America allows us to zero in on that country, but we must keep in mind that the Third World community within the United States is more than a suitable arena in which to situate the world that Fornes's characters inhabit. What better way would this powerful force in American theatre have than to provide a venue for Latinas to challenge their subject position by reclaiming their identity? Orlando states: "I must eliminate all obstacles.—I will make the acquaintance of people in high power." The hierarchy of class is at the apex, and how he will get to that position is what the play revolves around. The oppression that derives from class is inseparable from the oppression that derives from race and ethnicity; economic factors abound throughout this universe. But the play is not what we think we see.

The dramatic action seems to want to seduce us toward male-centered domination and oppression. Orlando says: "If I cannot achieve this on my own merit, I will marry a woman in high circles. Leticia must not be an obstacle." Leticia, his wife, is ten years his elder. Fornes refers to relationships between older women and younger men as distinctly Latin American; such relationships are generally based on the ability of wealthy women to buy men. In fact, for any other reader/spectator this age difference may hold no bearing, but for the Chicana/Latina viewer, gender issues are often economically driven, that is, money can buy Leticia anything in this patriarchal society but it is certainly not controlling her. There is also Olimpia, the servant who wields incredible power over Leticia, whom she manages to intimidate into action. Olimpia is physically able to overpower Orlando but careful not to overstep her boundaries, and she chooses to take Nena under her wing by comforting her but is unable to stop the abuse of the young girl. Within this household of three women and one man who more often than not has his friend Alejo, a lieutenant commander, with him as well, issues of race, class, and gender are immediately foregrounded in this play.

The way Fornes positioned women in this work lends itself to both a materialist feminist and a radical feminist analysis: we at once enter a world in which (1) class is central to Latinas and is inseparable from color and the community and (2) we also view the conflict in sexual roles in society. Clearly, if we buy into this supposed patriarchal system in which Orlando represents an elevated power position, the lines are drawn and his is the privileged position of dominance and control. We have, in fact, entered an entire universe in which all-consuming oppressive forces are at work.

The entire scope of this drama is exploitation, and everyone is affected. Anger and aggression emerge at all levels, and sexual politics matters just as much as race and class politics. Orlando's power bases are represented by his work for the state, his physical and verbal dominance over Leticia (who desires freedom and is desperately striving to educate herself), and his very visible sexual abuse of the 12-year-old girl he has taken captive.

Fornes draws from her background in the visual arts to carefully construct the visual environment and composition of this play. The scenery is deceptively simple; the division of the floor into four horizontal planes creates a setting so immense and far-reaching that it cannot be contained within one vista. Archways and hallways broaden the space. The areas include a living room downstage, situated close to the audience; a dining room is center stage; the cellar is upstage, with steps leading up; and above the cellar there is another level where the warehouse is situated. Floors and steps serve as further extensions beyond the immediate visible layering, underscoring the imagistic montage we also get from the dramatic action.

Through a series of short, episodic scenes, the fable explores changing representations of power in relationships between individuals of different class and gender. The drama of Self versus Other surfaces as we see visual layering of shifting socio-political and historical relationships of authority. We witness what Diana Taylor has identified as a key element of Latin American dramatists: "They approach specific issues that are key to an understanding of Latin America and its cultural images—among them, colonialism, institutionalized violence, revolution, identity and self-definition, and socio-economic centrality versus marginality—in a variety of strikingly powerful ways" (Taylor 1991, 9). But the alarming crisis in this play is not in Latin America. It stems from Fornes's experiences in America.

Fornes is not importing a Latin American world for spectators to observe at a distance. Instead she is offering the perspective of someone coming from a culture that has been colonized and exiled. She has been oppressed and driven from a homeland by the dominant regime, but in the United States she finds herself to be oppressed and living in a Third World condition. The world is distorted and in the midst of political crisis, but the oppressor and the oppressed are reversed. By the end of the drama, the simple analysis that it is Orlando who is the oppressor is no longer possible. His blatant repression is replaced by the more subversive repression of Leticia, who murders him and then asks Nena, the young girl he had sexually abused, to take the blame.

But what does this play say about culture? When I asked Fornes what was distinctly Latina/Latino in this universe, she immediately referred to the names of the characters, the foods they ate, the activities they undertook. These elements bring us to the issues of eroticism and the political nature of torture, the disruption of family units, border conflicts, the loss of language, and ignorance and educational deprivation at all levels. Why is it that all of the named characters are distinctly Latinas/Latinos, but the Spanish language is lost/missing within their text/consciousness? When we are told they are eating flan, avocados, boiled plantains, and mangos, "before all the fresh stuff is bought up," Fornes is situating the core of the drama in that Latina/Latino world.

The power of the colonizer hits us hard in this play. The loss of language, the disrupted family, the marginalized women, the struggle for identity, and the exclusion of the colonized are issues that fragment the Latina/Latino world. Fornes questions what it is even permissible to know, given the long history of hostility between the United States and Latin America. We are compelled to go beyond Cuba in order to understand how this Latina can be so tremendously impacted by imperialism, oppression, and revolution. The education Fornes offers is distanced through the Latin American setting, but it gives us the same issues we have already encountered in the earlier Chicana/Chicano political theatre, namely, countering repression through revolution and shifting from the colonized position to self-determination. But where do we end up? The repeated acts of subversion, repression, and continual exploitation result in chaos and death.

In a personal interview, Fornes has said to me that in no other country, in no other arena, will you find the kind of male/female relationship you find here. Orlando has tapped a resource who can help him attain the social position he strives for; he has married an older Latina who can afford to help him gain "high power."[18] In another interview, when asked whether she believed in a female aesthetic in drama, she replied: "How could there possibly not be? Not only is there a women's aesthetic, each woman has her own aesthetic and so does each man." She added: "It's like saying 'Is there a Hispanic aesthetic?' Of course there is" (Fornes in Worthen 1995, 927).

Fornes has stated that her "life in Cuba has not been an important influence" on her work. "But the life in Cuba had a strong effect on me," she adds.

> In many ways I still think like a Cuban, or maybe just a Latin, or maybe like a European. In 1945 Cuba was much closer to Europe than to the United States—in the sense of values, the order of things, what you were and were not allowed to do. I have a strong accent, and I think it's because there's a part of me I don't want to eradicate. (Fornes in Osborn 1987, 47)

Yet, while everyone has their "own universe," Fornes adds, "How could we, as women, have nothing in common? That's not possible. We are different from a man, who is not a woman, who has never had a menstrual period in his life." What Fornes provides with her dramaturgy is the centering of woman.

In *Mud,* the characters portrayed are distinctly non-Latinas/Latinos, and Fornes points out the universality in this distinctly feminist arena:

> I feel that what is important about this play is that Mae is the central character. It says something about women's place in the world, not because she is good or a heroine, not because she is oppressed by men or because the men "won't let her get away with it," but simply because she is the *center* of that play. (Fornes in Worthen 1995, 929)

For Fornes the play is "a more important step toward redeeming women's position in the world," which is more important to her than whether or not there is a prevailing feminist theme in the drama. She adds:

> I believe that to show a woman at the center of a situation, at the center of the universe, is a much more important feminist statement than to put Mae in a situation that shows her in an unfavorable position from which she escapes, or to say that she is noble and the men around her are not. (Fornes in Worthen 1995, 929)

Fornes points out that presenting a mind that is "in a woman's body makes an important feminist point." This view is one we must consider in an analysis of this playwright's work.

In 1981 the Ford Foundation made possible a four-year grant of $150,000 to help launch a playwriting lab for Hispanic playwrights. Max Ferra, the artistic director of INTAR (International Arts Relations), a not-for-profit organization incorporated in 1972, invited Maria Irene Fornes to conduct what became known as INTAR's annual Hispanic Playwrights-in-Residence Laboratory. Operating from 42nd Street's Theatre Row, INTAR's major contribution to Latina/Latino theatre has been in developing and staging new works.

The Lab, as it came to be called, was designed by Fornes as a workshop for "ethnic, underprivileged or minority writers" (Worthen 1995, 923). This work has led her into discovering "a Hispanic sensibility." Part of the lab work has also led her and her students to direct their own work. Mindful of Valdez, she stresses that playwrights need to educate themselves about directing and acting techniques as well. At the Padua Hills Theater Workshop (where she usually goes in the summer), directing became an integral part of the process, for if one did not direct one's own work then a search for a director had to be mounted. Her abilities in actor training stem from acting classes at the Actors Studio.[19]

Many Chicana/Latina playwrights have been influenced by Fornes's work, either through direct training or from indirect influence by virtue of her recognized position in American theatre, feminism, and Off-Broadway experimental avant-garde performance. The following chapter covers representative playwrights and the emergence of political voices in performance. One of these, Milcha Sanchez-Scott, was among those playwrights who attended one of the

INTAR workshops. Sanchez-Scott credits Fornes as a major influence on her work: "That year was the best thing that ever happened to me" (Osborn 1987, 246). The experience enabled writers to meet other Latina writers. We will turn now to consider how Chicanas/Latinas have contributed to the growing body of work, drawn from experiences in their own communities, that contemporary women of color in theatre have written as they have emerged as political activists on the issues of race, ethnicity, and feminism.

5 THE EMERGING CHICANA PLAYWRIGHT
The Political Act of Writing Women

Chicana/Chicano/Latina/Latino theatrical history clearly reflects the reality that performative activity has served as a means of empowerment. From the male voices that dominated during the Mexican Revolution to the work of Luis Valdez and Maria Irene Fornes, the forerunners of contemporary Chicana/ Latina theatre used their art and the history of their people to empower their audiences. But until recently, when Chicano women began to write their own playtexts, it was not possible to assess the distinct contribution of women to this medium of public expression. Fortunately, contemporary Chicana/Latina playwrights have emerged, and their work is garnering critical and popular acclaim, thus enabling us to begin to more fully examine their voices as powerful cultural, socio-economic, and political forces.

Ramón Saldívar points out that "contemporary Chicana writers challenge not only the ideologies of oppression of the Anglo-American culture that their Chicano brothers confront, but they also challenge the ideologies of patriarchal oppression evinced by Chicano writers and present within Chicano culture itself" (Saldívar 1990, 173). The dialectics within these texts help us to understand the construction of socially symbolic acts of resistance to oppressive class, race, and gender structures within contemporary culture. From this perspective we can see that the writing itself is a political act, just as the performance of the work is an act of empowerment.

Hegelian or pre-Marxist ideological constructs of identity posit that identity is formed in a stable, fixed, and identifiable fashion. Adorno's *Negative Dialectics* (1966), in contrast, negates any hope of a synthesis of subject and object. The self and other cannot unite, and this unfixed, decentered identity alters the pattern by which a society must position the subject (Saldívar 1990, 174). In this sense, identity in Chicana playtexts is being analyzed and worked through, demonstrating the dialectical tension that Adorno theorizes. That is, it is disunified and nonlinear, revealing no synthesis or reconciliation. Instead, the apparent subjective identity evident in these works tends to be complexly dialectical, without bridging or synthesis.

In turning to Chicana playtexts, then, we see playwrights rejecting traditional, linear structures, searching for new and different approaches to writing for performance. Identity is established along the lines of a continuously unstable borderline of difference between Mexican and American social ideologies. Chicana identity expresses itself as the historical working out of the contradictions implicit in both Mexican and American ethnic, cultural, and political economies. Chicana subjectivity within these texts thus is represented as both Mexican and American and also neither one nor the other, completely. It falls more along the lines of the "intercultural" view of performance that Richard Schechner offers as an ideal term; namely, the confrontation and ruptures between cultures and difference, at the marginality institutionalized in geopolitical terms by the border between the sovereign states of México and the United States.

Chicana playtexts resist the male-dominant ideologies of Valdez and other Chicano playwrights. Several significant examples show how Chicana playwrights are following the path already set forth by Chicana narrative writers, particularly in their insistence that "identity politics" that do not account for the social construction of gender and sexual orientation merely reproduce the hierarchies of oppression embedded in bourgeois Anglo-American society.[1] The task of Chicana playwrights seems to rely on building an instructive alternative to the exclusively phallocentric subject of the work of Valdez. While these playwrights are influenced by him and generally acknowledge that resource, they also strive to discover their own means of dramatic expression.

Estela Portillo Trambley has laid important groundwork for the development of plays by Chicanas/Latinas, and the works of Milcha Sanchez-Scott, Josefina López, and Cherríe Moraga have made significant strides toward writing and staging a dialectics of difference. For these women, a subjectivity in process seeks to resist a positive, fixed identity. Specified gender roles explode in performance in profound ways. These artists have written deliberate acts of symbolic resistance, desiring to reclaim ethnicity both inside and outside themselves. Even further, they are performing culture and their ethnicity. These dramatists speak to stark oppression of women in their own male-centered Chicano world. They live between worlds, cultures, and histories, situated at what Sonia Saldívar-Hull has termed their "feminism on the border" (see Saldívar-Hull 1991). Yet one does not for a moment forget that as they confront their own culture and explore their ethnic connections, they also target the dominant Euroamerican/Anglo culture surrounding them.

ESTELA PORTILLO TRAMBLEY: AN EARLY CHICANA VOICE

Estela Portillo Trambley represents the first Chicana playwright to gain recognition within the Chicano cultural movement.[2] Born in El Paso, Texas, Portillo Trambley (b. 1936) has also written poetry, short stories, and novels. *The*

Day of the Swallows (1971),[3] her earliest work, appeared in *El Espejo—The Mirror: Selected Chicano Literature*, an anthology compiled under the auspices of Quinto Sol Publications. In the introduction to the anthology a list of 123 names of writers, poets, and artists was included with the following statement: "Some may say that there are no Chicano writers. Others will say there are no Chicano works. These are lies. The following writers readily dispel these allegations" (Romano-V and Rios 1972, xiv). Out of 123 names, eleven were women and the gender of four others is uncertain, since they could be male or female names. Out of twenty-nine entries this was the only full-length playtext entry. In 1973 Portillo Trambley was awarded the third annual Quinto Sol literary prize for her first two works.

The story of *The Day of the Swallows* revolves around the lesbian relationship of the central figure, a Mexican Indian, with a young woman she has rescued from a whorehouse. Sue Ellen Case perhaps best describes this work when she calls it homophobic. In Case's critical article about both Portillo Trambley and Cherríe Moraga, she notes Moraga's reaction to this play: "I've always loved *Swallows* although it is a 'classic' lesbian work in the worst sense of the 1950s view. . . . In this play . . . Portillo as author is the obedient daughter. Those who follow the law of the father will be rewarded. . . . Those who transgress are punished (the lesbian suicide)" (Case 1994, 92). Case has devoted much attention to this work in her examination of the destructive forces of heterosexual ideology the playwright imposes on the lesbian leading character. It is unfortunate that for the playwright herself, the entire work was primarily an exercise in attempting to write in the dramatic form for the first time.

Case discusses this work in her article entitled "Seduced and Abandoned: Chicanas and Lesbians in Representation," where she examines the destructive forces of heterosexual ideology the playwright imposes on the lesbian leading character. In many conversations I had with Portillo Trambley during a Chicana/Chicano conference at California State University (1975), the playwright spoke about having written this play in her search to create a marketable commodity. Case notes that "lesbian critics may find the play homophobic" and refers to another similar comment by Portillo Trambley about her motivation for writing this play:

> When my first book was rejected, someone told me to do fiction. I had just seen the movie *The Fox* . . . and someone said, why don't you write something like that and make millions? I'm always thinking of a buck. So in a month and a half I wrote *The Day of the Swallows* and I put everything in. The plot is about lesbians; I knew nothing about them, but I was going to sell it. (Case 1994, 93)

Despite being driven by the desire to make her work marketable, Portillo Trambley not only brought a new voice to the growing Chicana/Chicano literature in print but she also brought a new female voice to the stage.

Portillo Trambley did not seek to create new myths and/or new forms; she instead chose from paths already taken, namely, the repertoire of long-established male dramatists from the Spanish theatre. In an interview in 1974,[4] Portillo Trambley explained that one could go back to Federico García Lorca to develop the skills needed to hone the craft. Thus, it is not surprising that "Josefa," taken from the crazed and outcast grandmother figure in García Lorca's *The House of Bernarda Alba* should appear here as well (prior to the advent of plays by women that included substantial parts for women, this play was often produced in English on the American stage because of the large number of women's parts). The playwright merely extends the story by pursuing the intriguing unknown facts about this illusive figure with which García Lorca tempts us as he chronicles Spanish life at the turn of the century. Despite the play's significance as the first work by a Chicana woman to be published in dramatic form, as Jorge Huerta notes, the taboo theme of homosexuality in the barrio probably explains why the play failed to go beyond college campuses in California and Texas at least through the early 1980s (Huerta 1982, 218).

Portillo Trambley had some obvious difficulties as she delved into the uncharted waters of female playwriting, but she persevered in honing her craft. She also had to stretch her scope since she was writing about Chicana/Chicano topics for the first time. In 1974, I invited Jorge Huerta to speak and provide workshops in Chicana/Chicano theatre at California State University, Sacramento, as part of activities related to the Chicano Theatre Program. Estela Portillo Trambley had coincidentally also been invited to the campus. Primarily because of the great attention that Portillo Trambley was receiving in early anthologies, conferences, and events related to the Chicana/Chicano experience, Jorge Huerta began to raise the question with me about whether a play by a Chicana/Chicano was enough to pronounce a work of art Chicana/Chicano. In a panel discussion and workshop on Chicano *teatro* and in numerous subsequent *pláticas* and workshops in Chicano theatre, factors such as themes and ideas, acting and actors, and other elements of style began to mark distinctions between Chicana/Chicano and non-Chicana/Chicano works. Huerta has continued to adhere to the view that content "determines whether or not a play is, indeed, Chicano," explaining that "neither the ancestry of its author, nor the fact that it is written in a particular language, determines whether or not a play is Chicano. If the theme explores the nature of being Chicano, I would call it Chicano and more particularly, ethno-specific theatre" (Huerta 1994, 39). While challenged by some, this view very directly led Estela Portillo Trambley to continue working to bring Chicana/Chicano topics to the stage.

Puente Negro deals with the problems faced by undocumented workers trying to reach a border town who are caught in a shack that serves as a way station for *coyotes*. *Blacklight* explores the alienation of a Chicana/Chicano family as its members confront hardships and personal crises. In *Sor Juana* the difficulties in comprehending the essence of existence are revealed through a series of episodes that shed new light on La Décima Musa as she suffers inner turmoil and faces the oppression of society and the Church. Unlike the other plays, *Autumn Gold* does not have a distinctly Chicana/Chicano or Mexican milieu, and one wonders why it was included in this anthology. The play deals with non-Hispanic middle-class characters who are faced with the comic dilemma of what to do with a corpse.

Of these plays, two deserve some scrutiny. *Blacklight* underwent various problematic stagings and revisions for a number of years before at least one production reached some success. Roberto Pomo's Elenco Popular in El Paso staged a noteworthy production to some acclaim in that region. The play's major problem is that the language used never seems quite appropriate to the character types drawn. Unfortunately, the characters quickly settle into the more upper-middle-class, well-educated language typical of Portillo Trambley's writing. The infrequent use of Spanish terms or slang is not enough to establish recognizable characters such as street corner *vatos* or older Mexican Americans. Similarly, the language of *Puente Negro* does not reflect the language a group of undocumented workers might use.

While language poses major concerns about believability of characters in terms of class, age, and overall appropriateness, *Blacklight* has other issues that make the entire work problematic. Because the play only tiptoes on the fringes of myths, indigenous ideology, and the creation of new cultural heroes, one act after the next fails miserably to bring the three-act drama to complete fruition. Set in a border town with a population largely comprised of "Mexicans who crossed the river into the United States," almost the entire world of the play is filled with men. A gang of teenagers, "Los Vatos," are comprised of four men, one young woman, and the central character, Mundo.

Although 18-year-old Mundo tells us he is doing his best to help his father, the issues at stake are vague and fail to rise to any level. We are asked to view the ever-present railroad tracks as a constant threat to Mundo's life and surroundings, yet these iron obstacles are almost negligible. These tracks took his uncle's life when a train killed him, and the memory of this tragedy threatens to bring on a frightening paralysis, not only threatening Mundo but also affecting his whole family's existence. Unfortunately, this malady never clearly surfaces or figures significantly in the total story.

Because Mundo, his mother, and his sister all fear his father's impending death by the same train, Mundo fails to see that other forces are also controlling his destiny. His primary flaw is his inability to let go of Shirley, his *gringa* or Euroamerican/White lover, already married and clearly leading Mundo to perdition. Although he attempts to break away from her, it is too late. Her husband discovers their affair and shoots Mundo. Yet throughout the play there is an irrational or at least unknowable force at work, as evidenced in Itzamna, the Mayan god of Night and Day, and Mundo's father's unyielding desire to know and serve that god. Itzamna calls for sacrifice, taking the son for the father. Although the plot is structurally weak, the idea is interesting. Portillo Trambley exercises the kind of mythmaking that Valdez had called for through the *mito*, and her attempts to reclaim a myth did not go unnoticed. Jorge Huerta worked with her on script development, and I read the manuscript and provided some notes about strengthening the development of the story.

Time and place are unclear in *Blacklight* since the play works on separate levels of reality. The dance and ritual in which four male gods appear occur only within the father's reality, apart from the reality which the other characters inhabit. However, the indigenous world is never connected to the rest of the story. Many questions remain unanswered in a somewhat scattered plot, and the play does little to bring attention to significant roles of women in this society.

Relegated to stereotypes and predictable roles, the three women in *Blacklight* are one-dimensional and poorly constructed. The mother, Amelia, speaks far above her presumed lower-class station, and she does little to tell us about her role in the family other than that she has slept with the uncle, ignored her husband, and failed to support her children enough to get them even to want to stay within that household. She ridicules the myths and indigenous past that the father espouses, and appears selfish, self-centered; she seems to seek only physical fulfillment in life. The daughter, María, is equally disappointing in terms of shedding any light on the story that is meant to be told. She is pregnant and nearly ready to give birth, and laments the fact that her lover has abandoned her. We know little else about her other than that her father has renamed her with an Indian name and that he loves her deeply. Suggestive connections to her role in the father's otherworldly visions fail to bring her to any significant function within the total story.

Lastly, the role of Mundo's lover Shirley is perhaps the most disappointing. She is selfish and lustful and victimizes Mundo for her own interests rather than because of any deeply rooted sentiment for him. Both Mundo and the father are blinded by love and desire to the point where they meet their tragic ends—Mundo dies from a gunshot wound, and the father offers little hope that by staying alive he will bring any value or hope to anyone in his household. The multiple male gods and the *vatos* offer even less hope that any of these men can bring anyone to a higher realm of spiritual or physical existence. Thus, Mundo and his uncle have, in effect, lived out their lives for no apparent purpose. We are left with the view that women are victims, victimizers, and prostitutes, and they too offer no hope of a better life for themselves or for others. The baby who is born at the end of the play will obviously also suffer a similar fate of death and destruction within this universe.

Of all of the plays in this collection, by far the most developed character portrayal appears in *Sor Juana*. Leaving to one side some of the unbelievable and stereotyped characters (most particularly the poor slaves), the central figure belongs to a milieu with which Portillo Trambley is definitely familiar and comfortable. Sor Juana is portrayed as an educated, middle-aged woman who intermingles her philosophical insights with everyday reality. The historical setting allows for a story line to develop between the main character and the particular individuals who affected her life. Unfortunately, the dramatist has selected a very narrow segment of Sor Juana's life with which to begin and end the play, that is, from when she is forty-two years old to the time near the end of her life two years later. More unfortunate, however, is the absence of historical context in the re-creation of the life of this notable figure in Chicana/ Chicano history.

With the exception of the brief segment of flashbacks with which the play begins and ends, the play is constructed around scenes in which Sor Juana appears in various stages of her life as she searches for meaning and fulfillment, confronting many obstacles along the way. *Sor Juana* consists of three acts, each divided into two scenes. The last act is rather brief and somewhat unsatisfactory because it comes to a sudden end without specificity about actual details of her final days. The flashback technique is utilized often, primarily through the use of light and a few stage properties to show a spatio-temporal change. While presenting us with more depth in the character of Sor Juana than heretofore seen in other texts, this work is also plagued by weaknesses in character development, and we never fully glimpse the complexity we have come to expect of this historical figure.

The language is often stilted, lacks believability, and raises issues about whether the character would be more appropriate if she spoke in Spanish rather than with the abbreviated, more informal, English terms she uses. None of the supporting characters are ever fleshed out; they remain weak and lack depth. There are twenty-four named characters. Overall, the playwright tries to encompass too much with the multiple scenes and many characters, but the most problematic aspect has to do with the direction the playwright takes with this figure. What Estela Portillo Trambley had attempted in *Blacklight* with dance, ritual, and music in combination with realistic scenes now appears as a theatrical ploy to create one reality. But the spectacle is presented as literature to be read rather than as literature to be performed. We are asked to enter Sor Juana's mind as a chamber in which we experience her thoughts and vivid memories, enhanced by aural and visual stage elements.

While the theatrics are problematic and weak, the play itself fails to provide new insights into the life of a woman who is today considered a feminist heroine by many Chicanas/Chicanos/Latinas/Latinos. Unfortunately, the work never really goes beyond the narrative form, failing to create believable and fully fleshed characters. The most problematic material presents a figure who espouses change and intellectual freedom through writing and using performance to reveal a powerful, fresh, and unique female voice in a time when women were uneducated and expected to stay that way. Here Sor Juana is presented as drawing this voice not from her own essential being; its source rather is her passion first for a young man whom she can never have due to her lower station and then for a priest whom she desires and pursues. The story insinuates that Sor Juana could not be driven without the passions stirred in her by the men she has encountered. In the end, the story fizzles out of steam upon the death of Father Antonio, for whom her love remained unrequited. The playwright merely leaves Sor Juana in the convent and adds a note in italics announcing his death, and her own death "two months to the day after the death of her beloved confessor" (Portillo Trambley 1983, 195). Clearly, the playwright has relegated this woman to traditional subjugation to men, and the result remains disappointing in terms of historical context. Nevertheless, despite any weaknesses, it is easy to understand why prizes for Portillo Trambley's works in print were given, for she stood out in a time when there were few Chicano playwrights and no known Chicana dramatists, and in a time when women's voices were actively being sought. Portillo Trambley is important for her worthwhile attempt to explore the dramatic form as a means to broaden the scope of the total Chicana/Chicano/Latina/Latino experience, and her efforts must be recognized.

MILCHA SANCHEZ-SCOTT: A CHALLENGE IN ETHNIC CLASSIFICATION

Many labels could be used to describe the ethnicity of Milcha Sanchez-Scott, born on the island of Bali in 1954. Her ancestry on her mother's side is Indonesian, Chinese, and Dutch. Her father was Colombian and was raised there and in México. Her parents met in Indonesia. Sanchez-Scott explains that while she prefers to remain unclassified by ethnicity, she has most often been classified as Chicana rather than Latina. Perhaps having lived primarily in the Southwest has led to this categorization, but for the most part she has been recognized as a Chicana playwright by many rather than by the Latina identity she probably more truly represents. In M. Lizabeth Osborn's collection *On New Ground: Contemporary Hispanic-American Plays,* Sanchez-Scott tells us that when she was invited to join Maria Irene Fornes's 1984–1985 workshop at INTAR she met some "extraordinary Hispanic writers." She continues: "And I felt more accepted. I'd always been grouped as a Chicana writer, and part of me is. But a larger part is not. My roots are in South America" (Osborn 1987, 246). This playwright has been difficult to classify for those who view her work as distinctly representative of the Chicana/Chicano experience despite the fact that her heritage clearly indicates otherwise.

The major influence on her work has been Maria Irene Fornes. Sanchez-Scott has workshopped and been affiliated with the Mark Taper Forum more than any other regional theatre in the United States, although her work has been performed nationally and internationally. Her first play, *Latina,* was premiered by L.A. Theatre Works in 1980, garnering seven Drama-Logue awards.

Dog Lady and *The Cuban Swimmer,* two one-act plays written in 1982, were produced in 1984 by INTAR and selected for Theatre Communications Group's Plays in Process series. *Dog Lady* was also published in *Best Plays of 1986.* Sanchez-Scott has been the recipient of the Vesta Award, given each year to a West Coast woman artist, and she has also won the Le Compte du Noüy Foundation Award, given to "a young writer with a unique voice."[5] She won the First Level Award for American playwrights from the Rockefeller Foundation for 1987.

The works that stand out in Sanchez-Scott's repertory are *Dog Lady* (1988), *The Cuban Swimmer* (1988), and *Roosters* (1987). Her most recent work, *The Old Matador* (1995), has been workshopped and performed in numerous venues, remaining a work in progress. She is now preparing a new play, *La Carmen,* based on Bizet's *Carmen.* Above all, *Roosters* remains her most recognized work, one which has been produced as a feature film by American Playhouse with limited release due to mixed reviews. In terms of a stage work, however, the piece has been favorably reviewed and is notable in the brief history of new works by Chicanas for the stage. *Roosters* appeared in *American Theatre Magazine* as the featured new playscript in September 1987, with photographs of the INTAR production.

Sanchez-Scott's work stands out for its attention to the young female coming of age in a world that revolves around men. A recognizable theme in the universe she creates in her work has to do with the changing roles of men and women. She emphasizes women's discovery of their own voices, girls' discovery of their womanhood, and the dominance over men that women acquire through circumstances of sheer survival in the context of the family and the larger community that surrounds them.

Dog Lady tells the story of a young girl's quest for success in a running race. Factors that lead to her success include a neighbor woman, her mother, and ultimately, the spirit of her deceased father. Sanchez-Scott tells us that in both *Dog Lady* and *The Cuban Swimmer,* "I really bore the community in mind, the Hispanic community, especially the girls in the Hispanic community. I wanted to say to them 'You can do anything. You have the power to do anything'" (Waite 1993, 44).

Dog Lady illustrates Sanchez-Scott's earliest manifestations of the characters who would become trademarks in her work, namely the mother, the father, and their children, who are struggling for success and recognition above and beyond the normative patterns and expectations of American children. The young adolescents are striving for distinction and screaming for independence as they do so. The play is unquestionably race specific through the use of language, character descriptions of typical figures in the barrios of Los Angeles, and the attention to themes and ideas revolving around Catholicism, indigenous history, and deeply rooted cultural beliefs and ideas. It also provides a more universal appeal in its broader attention to all women who strive for success when faced with the impossible. The same is true of *The Cuban Swimmer*, a play that is frequently produced alongside *Dog Lady* because both are short works that can be combined for an entire evening's fare; the plays have similar themes and ideas that run parallel in many ways.

The Cuban Swimmer, also set in California, tells the story of the Suárez family. This time, however, the family is Cuban, and the political connotations of the world of this play are remarkably telling in relation to Cuban-American relations. Driven to succeed by a demanding father, a young woman is coached and pushed to win a swimming race. However, what stands out in this play is the way that female characters counter the father's physical drive through their use of history, tradition, and identity that contribute in major ways to the young Margarita's success. While the father seems to push her endurance physically, a challenge she must accept in order to win the race, the seemingly underlying figures of the grandmother and mother take on significant roles that contrast to his undue pressure on the daughter.

The struggle Margarita experiences in the water takes on magical proportions very much in the vein of the magical realism typified by many Latin American writers. This special world reveals a reflection and refraction from everyday realism to a world filled with power amidst the sheer physical struggle for survival. The grandmother, Abuela, tells the story of Margarita's ancestry as she struggles to stay afloat:

> Sangre de mi sangre, you will be another to save us. En Bolondron, where your great-grandmother Luz Suárez was born, they say one day it rained blood. All the people they run into their houses. They cry, they pray, pero your great-grandmother Luz she had cojones like a man. She run outside. She look straight at the sky. She shake her fist. And she say to the evil one, "Mira . . . (Beating her chest) coño, Diablo, aquí estoy si me quieres." And she open her mouth and she drunk the blood. (Sanchez-Scott 1982, 39)

Through language, traditions, bloodline and heritage, and the transference of women's power from one generation to another, we witness the coming of age of the young girl both physically and spiritually, but above all, culturally and historically and politically. The grandmother sets up the dialectic of difference and opposition in terms of identity. The young girl has her heritage and her culture, yet she can make her own contribution to the long family history. The past in which Cuban Americans had no place in the United States transitions to a politically charged present in which they cannot be ignored.

While the two earlier works are important steps in the development of her dramaturgy, it is *Roosters* that stands out for its remarkable attention to the heretofore unheard voice of the Chicana in crisis amidst political circumstances. When we examine the empowerment of women in moments of crisis, the body politic and the struggle between gender and ethnicity emerge as dominant. In *Roosters*, women are caught in the struggle of familial change, impending loss of culture, and difference. We can place this work among those that contribute in a profound and substantive manner to the nature of the performative act and the dramatic voice of the Chicana.

Roosters may appear to some critics as the typical ordering of the Valdezian drama that yet again shows "the virgin, the mother, and the whore" (Huerta 1994, 43) ruled by an ex-con father in battle with his son for the position of power in the family. Chicana feminist critics might attack this play for its reinforcement of those traditional female roles that yet again negate the power of women, relegating them to inferior positions as dominant males determine the direction of their lives. While it may seem that its narrative supports the tendency to represent women's subordination, always in the context of tarnished sexuality, closer examination of the role of women in this play can disclaim these negative views about the power of women.

The representation of Chicana subjectivity and sexuality is related in this play to the historical development of the Chicana as she emerges with a distinct voice in the broader Chicano Movement. Instead of excluding the essential narratives of this emerging figure in the barrio, we witness directly before us the dialectic between "the Virgin" position and "La Malinche" and the young girl as a powerful agent of change and resistance to traditional roles. By presenting all three in opposition, we can see the growth from the subject position of the Virgin/Madonna/Mother to the Malinche/sell-out/prostitute to a new position.

Angela, the young girl, enacts a miracle that stops bloodshed. The power of the miracle, however, does not come from God, does not come from the angels and saints whom Angela prays to, but it comes from within herself as a culmination of her exploration of racial and sexual identity. Angela emerges as a desiring subject from the dialectical unfixed status of a changing cultural construction of gender and sexuality. As she states, "My old man, my Holy Father, my all powerful Father, sees no problems. If there are problems, I am the angel of this yard. I am the comet. I am the whirlwind. I am the shooting stars. Feel my vibrance" (Osborn 1987, 271). Sanchez-Scott has created woman in a new construction, empowering herself above and beyond all expectations.

The playing space becomes ritual, and the young daughter is set up for sacrifice. As Angela is mocked and ridiculed for her aspirations to become an angel, she is both a desacralized sacrifice, a victim of abandonment and unfulfilled patriarchal attachment, and the agent for catharsis between father and son, mother and father, sister/aunt and nephew, and daughter/mother/sister/brother and father. Sacrificial violence is utilized here just as effectively as it is used in the dramatic convention in the *Oresteia* or other Greek crisis dramas; crisis, event, and ritual enact the transference of power from father to daughter, empowering her to resolve the struggle, the turmoil, and save the day for the family and for the community around her.

The parameters are small when seen in the context of the hills surrounding

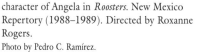

Costume design by Tina Cantú Navarro for the character of Angela in *Roosters*. New Mexico Repertory (1988–1989). Directed by Roxanne Rogers.
Photo by Pedro C. Ramírez.

Costume design by Tina Cantú Navarro for the character of Juana in Los Angeles Theatre Center's production of *Roosters*, directed by José Luis Valenzuela.
Photo by Pedro C. Ramírez.

Costume design by Tina Cantú Navarro for the character of Chata in New Mexico Repertory's production of *Roosters*.
Photo by Pedro C. Ramírez.

the small community, but are enlarged when the scope broadens to the critical stakes of the violent tragic act about to unfold as the young girl empowers herself to take charge. Her brother and father struggle in a knife fight where they may kill each other. When Angela proclaims, "I have lost my faith. . . . I am cast down! Exiled!" (Sanchez-Scott 1988, 45), she calls on the Holy Father, Abuelo (her grandfather), and Hector to "breathe" on her. But Angela restores order with her ability to be "launched" as her brothers says: "Oh sweet hummingbird woman, shooting star, my comet, you are launched" (46). She attributes this miraculous ability to "Abuelo, Queen of Heaven, All the saints, All the Angels. It is true, I am back. I am restored" (46). Her saints are St. Teresa and St. Lucy, and the Queen of Heaven is always in her litany, and she has already told us that if the Holy Father takes her, claims her, and launches her, she will be his "shooting-star woman," his "comet woman," and his "morning-star woman," all drawn from the powerful pantheon of the Chicana/Chicano indigenous past. Just as other contemporary playwrights have done, Sanchez-Scott raises the common man/woman/person "to a new level of participation in societal self-examination," and through the performative act, challenges the spectator "to move beyond identification and witness to analysis and action" (Dahl 1987, 132).

Sanchez-Scott's dramaturgical exploration sets in motion a use of theatre as ritual that allows the spectator to investigate the essential experiences of life. But we may go further when we consider the impact of the violent deed on the family as part of the larger community. We are positioned to assess the efficacy of violence as a political strategy that leads to political action when the victim can cleanse her social order and society by halting death and redeem society by saving the executioner. She is able to do so by halting Gallo's execution of his son; she stops the pollution of the community by positioning herself over her father and brother who formerly served as the powerful emblems in the family.

Sanchez-Scott's contributions to the American stage are considerable. She stands out among the few Latina playwrights who have gained critical success in writing about the Latina/Latino experience. She draws from her culture which comes from many traditions, and she integrates a deep adherence to her Catholic faith. She is also among the first of many Latinas highly influenced by Maria Irene Fornes, and she brings to the stage fascinating explorations of magical realism, language, themes, and ideas as she creates new and multifaceted characters that represent her Chicana/Chicano/Latina/Latino world.

JOSEFINA LÓPEZ: VALDEZIAN PROGENY

Josefina López's (b. ?) work centers on the problem of immigration and survival in the United States. The Mexicans in her work who pursue the American dream find exploitation instead of streets paved with gold. López's first play, *Simply María,* was first produced in San Diego and later aired on PBS television. This surreal examination of the life of a Mexican woman in the United States occurs largely in a dream state after the young María fails to convince her family that she should go to college. Conflicting voices inside of María set her against the cultural myths that lead to her role as Mexican mother and wife. Her rebellion leads to an assertion of self and the play ends with her determining her own destiny. Leaving behind fighting parents whose marriage breaks down as they accuse each other of mistrust and deception, María decides to find herself on her own. She promises not to forget the values of her roots, but wants to find "the best from this land of opportunities" and goes in search of an education and a "struggle to do something with" her life. Through three girls who represent varying manifestations of her being, she tells us that she will not forget her parents, that México is in her blood, and that America is in her heart (Feyder 1992, 140–141).

Simply María was produced by El Teatro Campesino and toured extensively along with a short work by Evelina Fernández, *How Else Am I Supposed to Know I'm Still Alive* (to be discussed later). Bringing attention to the position of women as active agents in the Chicano Movement, *Simply María* is beholden to the early Valdezian *acto* form as well as to *La carpa* of El Teatro Campesino. This work served to meet the growing demand for women's voices in the work coming out of ETC, and the staging and performances paid tribute to the skills and abilities of the acting company to produce an effective work to support this vital emerging female view of life in the United States.

In another work, *Real Women Have Curves,* López's message more fully grapples with sensitive issues at the very crux of the border of female identity. Set in a sewing factory in Los Angeles, *Real Women Have Curves* shows six women encountering anger, frustration, and enjoyment as they face the growing problems of women forced to work in dangerous and unsatisfactory conditions when they cross the border from México into the United States. Hand in hand with the very real threat of deportation, these women also discuss food, abusive relations, male/female interaction, and their own sense of being.

The plot revolves around five women: Estela, the owner of a sewing factory where her mother, Carmen, and her sister, Ana, work for her along with two other women, Pancha and Rosali. Although ages are generally not disclosed, Carmen, the mother, believes she is pregnant until she learns she is really beginning menopause; thus she is older than the others. We know Estela is twenty-five because her birthday is celebrated, and the other women seem to be about that age as well. Ana is trying to make enough money to enter New York University where she plans to study writing, thus she is older than high school age but younger than Estela. While Pancha laments being unable to bear children, Rosali tells us she is a virgin but does have a boyfriend.

In the context of constant fear of being found and deported by the *migra,* or immigration authorities, the story centers on helping Estela with an unusually large order of dresses that must be completed in order to help her meet the charges resulting from a lawsuit against her for failing to meet her payments on the sewing machines. Despite a large settlement she received from an unnamed accident, she still has to purchase a new steam iron in order to meet the demands of her business. The crisis revolves around the fact that Estela is an undocumented worker. Out of all of the women who initially feared being deported because they were threatened so often due to their status as "illegal aliens," Estela is the only one who still does not have her temporary residence card or any other legal documentation that would enable her to remain in the country (López 1992, 3).

The point of view is that of Ana, who represents the playwright in this largely autobiographical work. When López received a scholarship to attend New York University, she had to defer college while waiting to receive a temporary residence card. She took a job at her older sister's sewing factory. She recalls her experience as an overweight young woman whose teachers advised her never to "play Lady MacBeth or Juliet." In her words: "I wasn't that marketable so I thought, if there is nobody writing for me, I'll have to write myself."[6] In this work, Ana pens her thoughts about everyday life throughout the piece; her writing serves as a unifying factor. About midway through the story, Ana reflects on the dire circumstances around her—the low wages, the little hope for improvement, and the constant fear of Estela's deportation and closing of the sweatshop. Audibly reciting her discovery she states: "So why do I stay? . . . It's true. I stay. Because no matter how much my mother could try and force me to come, I could decide not to come back. But I do. . . . Why? . . . Maybe I'm trying to make a connection with these women. Maybe they and this place have something to offer me." However, she asks: "But what?" (38).

It is the response to this question that drives the story. Ana tells us at the end that while she had planned to get educated and go back and teach the women about life and women's liberation, and "all the things a so-called educated woman knows about," instead "they taught me about resistance. About a battle no one is fighting for them except themselves. Perhaps the greatest thing I've learned is that we women are powerful, especially when working together" (78). Mindful of the shedding of the serpent skin that Luis Valdez had spoken about in a notable poem he wrote about Chicano theatre, "Pensamiento Serpentino" (c. 1973), the women physically shed their outer garments on the stage to reveal their bodies, at least down to their underwear. Their startling surprise comes when they discover that underneath it all, they are just the same, but even more, they begin to feel a sense of pride in themselves and soon become cognizant of their accomplishments as well. When banding together, they are a powerful force. The women come together to help each other succeed, and they discover that their larger-than-average sizes and unusual shapes could in fact be applauded rather than criticized. The shadowy figure who haunts Estela's dreams, "El Tormentor," ends up being the one carted away by police for illegal possession of drugs while the women, on the other hand, complete their job and, by pooling their salaries, take possession of their lives and abilities by helping Estela open her own boutique, appropriately named Real Women Have Curves by the creative genius of the young Ana. They proudly pattern and model Estela's creations with their unique variety of body shapes and sizes (68).

The point of the play is that women can determine for themselves what they will do with their lives and actively take on the charge of resistance to the inequality and oppressive circumstances surrounding them. The political nature of this work lies in its exploration of how women's bodies, their skills, and their sense of community and bonding are always being challenged and abused. The discovery of self and the power of sisterhood reigns strongly in this work, and the simple technique of the Valdezian showing of character types is employed here to maximum effect. López centers on the female as subject on display not only with regard to beauty, but also in relation to how she can be a participant and agent of change rather than a merely submissive figure whose life reinforces the long history of oppression Chicanas have encountered as undocumented workers in the United States.

CHERRÍE MORAGA: CHICANA RADICAL FEMINISM AS EXPERIMENTAL NARRATIVE

Born in Los Angeles (b. ?), Cherríe Moraga is an acclaimed poet, essayist, and playwright probably best known for *This Bridge Called My Back: Writings by Radical Women of Color* (1981), an acclaimed anthology of feminist writings which she co-edited with Gloria Anzaldúa. In her work for the theatre, we witness the type of oppositional theatre that was very much at the heart of the political and cultural movement that was the benchmark of the 1960s. Jorge Huerta has written an interesting article about the similarities between Moraga and Luis Valdez in their approaches to topics about the Chicana/Chicano farm worker families in crisis, and how radically different the approach has become in exposing the problems and attempting solutions in the theatre of the 1990s as evidenced by Moraga's work.[7]

Moraga's dramaturgy can clearly be situated as an extension of that arm of the Chicano Movement of resistance, namely, mainstream cultural and economic domination. Through her explorations of gender roles and creating alternatives to the dominant Chicano theatrical representations in the Movement, Moraga significantly broadened the scope of Chicano theatre to include women. Breaking away from the cultural nationalism that idealizes the Chicana/Chicano indigenous culture and historical past, she provides a feminist perspective that challenges race, culture, and class oppression. She uses sexual politics to create new expressions in the broad spectrum of Chicana/Chicano dramatic tradition (see Yarbro-Bejarano 1990, 132–133).

Moraga not only ignites but also charges Chicanas with political and social commentary as she reappropriates female figures in the community and gives them notable roles within the larger world of gender politics. While Valdez had centered many of his stories that had to be told on males as subject, Moraga foregrounds females as subject. But in her author's notes to her published play, *Heroes and Saints*,[8] she both acknowledges and expresses her appreciation to Valdez for his play *The Shrunken Head of Pancho Villa*, whose lead character became for her a point of departure for her own central character.

Moraga's plays reveal her ability to reverse typical "power relations created by sexual difference" where an active male subject is represented opposite a passive female Other in such instances as when a woman is "bound in loving servitude through *La Virgen* or in fallen sexuality through *La Malinche*," as Yarbro-Bejarano found when comparing the narrative form of Valdez and ETC with Moraga's *Heroes and Saints* (137). Instead of reinforcing such conditions as poverty and economic exploitation, perpetuated through the female off-spring in Valdez's *Shrunken Head*, for example, Moraga turns the world upside down for the Chicana/Chicano, thereby forcing us to re-examine that universe. Moraga is clearly influenced by Valdez but surpasses him in relation to female representation, which removes her from the realm of the dominant Chicano narrative form and distinguishes her work from that of other playwrights.

In her first play, *Giving Up the Ghost* (1986), Moraga focuses on the female as desiring subject in varying stages of a girl's trek to young adulthood. The political action of the work revolves around the dialectics of difference, culminating with an affirmation of a new ordering of cultural identity. Moraga tells us about her work in theatre:

> I did not come to the theater quickly. My plays grew out of that place where my poetry and autobiographical essays left off, a place where having told my own story as honestly as I was able (*Loving in the War Years*, 1983), a space opened up inside me inviting entrance for the first time for fictional characters to speak their own stories. (Moraga in Perkins and Uno 1996, 231)

Moraga began writing *Giving Up the Ghost* in 1984, a work which she says "reflects my transition from poetry to theater. A kind of *teatropoesía*,[9] *Ghost* is a Chicana lesbian love story." In 1985 she worked with Maria Irene Fornes for one year in the Latino Playwrights Lab at INTAR Theatre in New York City, and in 1990 Fornes directed *Shadow of a Man*. Moraga views the latter play as her "family" play, in which she "tried to expose the secrets and silences affecting both men and women in the traditional Chicano household." She adds that as they moved "from the intimate relationship of lovers (*Ghost*), to the familial place from which lovers are created (*Shadows*), to the community that houses them both (*Heroes and Saints*)," her plays have "always occurred in dialogue with the Chicano/Latino community" (Perkins and Uno 1996, 231).

In her view, these dramatic works were providing what she refers to as "an intra-cultural critique and celebration." She was not writing "with the Anglo audience in mind because to do so would mean writing in translation." She adds: "As any writer of any culture should, I try to write as specifically as possible of the complexities in our lives. In that the universality of the Chicano experience is found and the work becomes 'cross cultural' in the deepest sense" (231).

Jorge Huerta notes that the significance of this playwright is in her insistence on writing her plays bilingually. Moraga is a poet; the dialogue is simple "yet stunning imagery permeates the language of her characters" (Huerta 1994, 44). The choices Moraga makes consciously pay heed to her activist politics, for here language serves to reveal very specific segments of the Chicana/Chicano population found in quite distinct communities. The portrayals reveal very carefully wrought differentiations in character drawn along lines of class, gender, age, and ethnic identification. As Huerta notes, "Moraga has made a very conscious choice to capture the nuances of working-class Chicano dialogue," even though those choices may cause limitations in terms of producing the work (44). Unfortunately, a very real disadvantage for regional stages or theatre companies who may wish to produce her work lies in the fact that they may not have developed bilingual audiences capable of readily grasping these nuances. But there is no question that the work has enjoyed success at least in venues where such usage can be comprehended. The production history of *Heroes and Saints* shows that certain stages do exist that are willing to support such work.

Initially commissioned through the Los Angeles Theatre Center's Latino Lab headed by José Luis Valenzuela, *Heroes and Saints* was performed as a staged reading under the direction of José Guadalupe Saucedo, formerly of El Teatro de la Esperanza. Another reading occurred under the auspices of the Latin American Theatre Artist Staged Reading Series under Moraga's direction. The world premiere on April 4, 1992 at El Teatro Misión of San Francisco was produced by Brava! For Women in the Arts under the artistic direction of Ellen Gavin and under the direction of Albert Takazauckas (Perkins and Uno 1996, 232). However, it remains to be seen whether non-Latino producers will take on the task of producing her work, for unlike Sanchez-Scott, who writes primarily in English, here the use of language does not lend itself to translation. For example, when the mother, Dolores, tells the daughter, "Mira todos los libros que tienes [Look at all of the books you have]. One a these days your brain's gointu explode por tantas palabras [because of so many words]" (Act I, 112, translation mine), code-switching from English to Spanish is so intricately woven that any attempt to translate either of these two languages will result in losing the effect it is meant to produce. The text is aimed at reaching a Chicana/Chicano audience accustomed to this language, and trying to change it would lose the intended resonances.

In *Heroes and Saints* children are dying of pesticides in the fields. In the town of McFarland in the San Joaquin Valley of California, a disproportionate number of children were diagnosed with cancer and born with birth defects. The documentary video of the United Farm Workers of America, *The Wrath of Grapes,* describes the situation during the ten-year period from 1978 to 1988. Moraga writes about viewing this video and being influenced by the image that remains in most viewers' minds:

> a child with no arms or legs, born of a farm worker mother. The mother had been picking in pesticide-sprayed fields while her baby was still in the womb. This child became Cerezita, a character who came to me when I wondered of the child's future as we turn into the next century. (Moraga 1994, 89)

The play is dedicated to the memory and legacy of César Chávez, immediately calling attention to the political nature of the work. In the character of Doña Amparo, the activist *comadre,* Moraga pays tribute to Dolores Huerta, the co-founder of the UFW, and one whom Moraga describes as: "a woman whose courage and relentless commitment to Chicano/a freedom has served as a source of inspiration to two generations of Chicanas" (89).

Written in two acts with thirteen scenes in the first act and eleven scenes in the second, the plot revolves around the problem a community of farm workers face with the agricultural pesticides that cause an unusually large number of children to fall victim to cancer, skin diseases, or severe birth defects. Although César Chávez's United Farm Workers union serves as an underlying force in the play, the focus of the story is a family faced with a severely deformed Chicanita, Cerezita, who emerges as the Virgin/Savior for an entire community. Reminiscent of the collective play *The Weavers,* or *Fuente ovejuna,* in which the protagonist is an entire community, here we witness an entire populace attempting to fend off impending doom from the menacing growers who spray pesticides at all hours of the night, the imposing media represented by a Chicana news reporter who fails to aid in disclosing the problems, and the Catholic Church, represented by a priest who is a misguided savior who follows rather than leads his flock.

Out of this chaotic world, where both father and brother abandon the women in the family—the mother, her two daughters, and a dying grandchild—the deformed Cerezita emerges as new woman/Virgen de Guadalupe who dies in her fight for justice and a better life for others. Despite her deformity, Cerezita is described in the stage directions as having "a head of human dimension, but one who possesses such dignity of bearing and classical Indian beauty she can, at times, assume nearly religious proportions" (Perkins and Uno 1996, 233). Throughout the play, the character suffers being ignored, bypassed, trampled on, and ridiculed, yet by the end she takes action in the most profound and dangerous way by means of leaving her home and family in the persona of virgin and martyred saint. The townspeople join her in acknowledging the dead and deformed children as they pray to La Virgen. Cerezita, addressing the entire universe now as the television cameras focus on her, speaks for the people and about them to the rest of the world, asking that they put their hand inside her wound where

> There is a people. A miracle people. In this pueblito where the valley people live, the river runs red with blood; but they are not afraid because they are used to the color red. It is the same color as the river that runs through their veins, the same color as the sun setting into the sierras, the same color of the pool of liquid they were born into. (261)

Cerezita is drawing from history and tradition—the indigenous past—as well as from the spirituality drawn from organized religion, yet the scope becomes broader as she encompasses the suffering of a devastated land where "bread is a tortilla without maize, where the frijol cannot be cultivated" (261). Her words point out the exclusion of the Chicana/Chicano within the dominant society and the devastation an entire people has faced through adversity. Into this picture she includes those from Guatemala, El Salvador, the Kuna, and Tarahumara, indicating all of those Latinas/Latinos whose "same blood runs through" each other's veins. She broadens the canvas to include everyone as "the miracle people because today, this day, that red memory will spill out from inside you and flood this valley con coraje. And you will be free. Free to name this land *Madre*. Madre Tierra. Madre Sagrada. Madre . . . Libertad. The radiant red mother . . . rising" (261). By taking action, Cerezita is released from her constraining makeshift *raite*, the platform which allowed her to get around. She is now free to position herself in the midst of the fields at the point where she can take charge in order to enact change. Machine-gun fire is heard and helicopters overhead resemble the sounds of the pesticides being sprayed over the fields, and the entire *pueblo*, or town, demands an end to the slaughter of the innocents. Burning the fields, they call out "¡Asesinos! ¡Asesinos! ¡Asesinos! [Assassins! Assassins! Assassins!]" to the planes (261).

No longer marginalized, the Chicana now takes control and serves as an agent of change. Yet, the political act results in tragedy. This Chicana appropriates space for its maximum effect. Ramón Saldívar, in discussing her narrative, refers to the "combative nature of Moraga's version of resistance" as one which acknowledges from the first the "difficulty and the costs of the Gramscian 'war of position'" (R. Saldívar 1990, 187). Women of color are pitted against multiple obstacles. Set against the patriarchy of everyday existence, they become prisoners of war in the class, racial, and sexual struggle not only with and against Chicano men but also with and against the dominant Anglo culture, and with and against Euroamerican/White feminism, as Saldívar points out. But in this world in which the patriarchy is absent and has abandoned and caused loss for the family, Moraga turns the tables.

Moraga engages in a politics of love and matriarchal caring and nurturing. Through the use of iconic representations of Mexican womanhood, the Chicana's emergence is juxtaposed with the central cultural symbols of Mexican spirituality and purity in the Virgin and the political activist real woman who counters that idealized emblem. Although the Catholic faith promises to end suffering and conquer oppression, such an occurrence can only be enacted if the new, reborn Chicana leads the way. Moraga's politics and writing set up the oppositions of identity: a chaotic blending of images of love, faith, and struggle set against the suffering represented by the young Cerezita, who receives true nurturing and support from Amparo, the childless activist who represents a true mother, in contrast to her own mother, who has kept her hidden from the world. Ultimately, the mother sets her free, recognizing the spiritual level her daughter has attained in her new position of power.

Cerezita both draws from and pulls away from her culture's claim on her, accepts and then rejects religion until she takes ownership of it, and distances herself from her family's attempts to define her and control her until she gains consciousness and is capable of reclaiming herself by embracing and celebrating difference. Thus, Cerezita ends up symbolically representing far more than farm worker, more than the Virgin/Saint emblem. Parallel to the autobiographical figure of Moraga in *Loving in the War Years,* we can apply Saldívar's assessment of the girl figure in Cerezita, that is, the emerging adolescent who also names herself by the discovery of place and identity politics in terms of body difference and Third World liberation movements (191).

Furthermore, Moraga's attempt to uphold the bond between mother and daughter sets up one of the strongest political acts found in Chicana playwriting. We witness the creation of a new version of the mother-daughter bond whereby the cultural political work of women serves as the agent that creates change (Jay 1996, 95–116). The final tableau is one of a violent means of destruction to effect change, and sexuality is the form of power to enact that change. The family as it has been constructed at the onset of the drama must be thought through again, for here the crippled child becomes the dominant force around which not only family but the entire community can rally behind and take action.

A significant voice for Chicana, feminist, and lesbian/gay studies, Moraga's plays have provided valuable contributions to new visions of cultural history in which women are instrumental. As Huerta points out, "both Valdez and Moraga's plays explore and expose problems of cultural identity, assimilation and economic survival," but Moraga's work "also exposes the issue of sexual identity." He adds: "For the traditional Chicano/Mexican audience, the theme of homosexuality can be very uncomfortable, and very few plays by or about gay or lesbian Chicanos and Chicanas have been produced to date," for "unlike the helpless head in Valdez's play," Moraga's "bodiless character [in *Heroes and Saints*] takes action, assisted by the people, as she sacrifices herself in an effort to bring more attention to their cause" (Huerta 1992, 51). In effect, Moraga has recaptured the essential theatrical intent we first discovered in Valdez's farm workers' theatre to use *teatro* to provoke social action. As Huerta points out, "Moraga has dramatized some of the more complex issues of our time" and can now "take advantage of professional Latino theatre artists and companies to interpret those concerns: individuals and companies that were non-existent in 1964" when Valdez first began using theatre for social change.

An assessment of representations by Chicana writers of Chicana women as subjects set against the context of the Chicano Movement reveals women as signifying and signified agents grappling with personal, body, and sexual politics; threats of deportation; the need for education; and race, class, and gender issues. They also work for social justice for themselves and others. Instead of being excluded from the subject position, the new narratives by women began to define Chicana sexuality, placing women in history and in the present as primary players within the developing Chicana/Chicano Movement and the broader Latina/Latino arena. Female playwrights broadened the parameters of ethnic and cultural identity as more and more productions featured significant representations of female subjectivity. Within this flowering of the Chicana dialogical imagination, more and more voices began to be heard into the 1990s, and a wider spectrum of the Latina experience began to be seen in performance.

6

CURRENT TRENDS AND PRACTICES[1]

CONTEMPORARY WOMEN PLAYWRIGHTS

In 1994 Jorge Huerta made a list of the five Chicana/Chicano plays most produced by mainstream theatres. Three were by women: Milcha Sanchez-Scott's *Roosters,* Edit Villareal's *My Visits with MGM (My Grandmother Marta),* and Josefina López's *Real Women Have Curves.* The other two were Valdez's *I Don't Have to Show You No Stinking Badges!* and Octavio Solis's *Man of the Flesh* (Huerta 1994, 42–43). Until the early 1980s Chicana/Chicano theatre was found only within the Chicana/Chicano communities where *teatros* had been born; Chicano/Chicana playwrights began their work in that milieu. However, with the critical acclaim and financial success of two productions, the New York Public Theatre's production of Miguel Piñero's *Short Eyes* (1974) and the Center Theatre Group's co-production of Valdez's *Zoot Suit* (1978) in Los Angeles, mainstream theatres took notice and began to produce more works by Latinas/Latinos (37–38).

Throughout the last three decades, as Vicki Ruíz has observed, we "have witnessed the emergence of distinct Chicana feminist identities: collectively and individually" (Ruíz 1998, 124). The 1970s brought an increased awareness of sexism in the Chicana/Chicano community (Acuña 1988, 394). Chicanas began to interact more and more with other feminists and women with a widening ideological base. Ruíz cites Teresa Córdova, who has stated that "Chicana feminists have struggled to find their voices—have struggled to be heard. Our struggle continues, but our silence is forever broken" (125). Ruíz says that for Chicanas, the act of picking up the pen is a "political act" (107). Since the early days of the Movement the parameters of their writing have continued to broaden, and, as Ruíz states: "Through their writings, Chicanas problematized and challenged prescribed gender roles at home (familial oligarchy); at school (the home economics track); and at meetings (the clean-up committee)" (108). The increasing presence of Latinas in the United States has widened these voices even more, introducing new directions in dramatic expression, performance, and production practices.

Sexuality is an issue that has arisen in the new spectrum of Chicana/Latina voices. Vicki Ruíz brings up the topic of claiming public space and its relationship to this issue. Lesbians in general, as Ruíz points out, "have struggled to create their own identities and to build their own communities in the midst of the most hostile environments. Carving a sense of sexual self amid such oppression was a courageous act of preservation, both personally and politically" (Ruíz 1998, 121; DuBois and Ruíz 1990, xv). One arena by which Chicanas/Latinas claimed public space for articulating their experiences has been through performance art; gender-specific topics soon surfaced in direct first-hand accounts in performances created by the actors.

LESBIAN PERFORMANCE ART: MARGA GOMEZ, MONICA PALACIOS, AND CARMELITA TROPICANA

Several Latinas have made their mark in performance art, including Marga Gomez, Monica Palacios, and Carmelita Tropicana. Perhaps the most widely known of these performance artists is Marga Gomez. Gomez was born in Harlem and is now based in San Francisco. She has worked professionally in both theatre and comedy venues (Perkins and Uno 1996, 191). She is a founding member of Culture Clash and has also performed with the San Francisco Mime Troupe and the Lilith Feminist Theatre. One of her best-known works, *Memory Tricks,* which premiered at the New York Shakespeare Festival at the Public Theatre in 1993, has toured extensively in the United States and at the Edinburgh Fringe Festival in Scotland, and has been optioned by American Playhouse as a feature film. Her more recent work, *Marga Gomez is Pretty Witty & Gay,* has also toured nationwide and at the Edinburgh Fringe Festival.

The daughter of a Cuban comedian-impresario and a Puerto Rican dancer and aspiring female actor, both of whom were well-known stars in their Latino community in Manhattan where she grew up, Gomez started in stand-up comedy and moved to solo performance art when she was invited to perform in a multicultural theatre festival at the University of California at San Diego in 1990. Written as an autobiographical monologue, *Memory Tricks* deals with her mother's Alzheimer's disease and with their relationship. *Marga Gomez is Pretty Witty & Gay (MGisPW&G)* is a powerfully staged performance monologue that, in her words, flaunts "my queer credentials, and at the same time says 'fuck you' to those members of the mainstream, and my own community," who had initially criticized her lack of gayness and excessively mainstream performance (192).

This piece is well-written and impeccably staged under the direction of Roberta Levitow.[2] It shows off Gomez's mastery of comedy while also reflecting material about her life. She tells us in her monologue: "I made sure to put that homophobic expression on my face. So my mother wouldn't think I was mesmerized by the lady homosexuals and riveted to every word that came from their lesbian lips" (196). The central factors in the politics of Gomez's staged self have to do with how her identity has been formed and is being re-formed. The published segments of her autobiographical trilogy in Perkins and Uno's *Contemporary Plays by Women of Color* take us through a comic exploration of lesbian identity that is deeply rooted in her Latina family and heritage.

Monica Palacios (b. ?) takes what she calls "the Latin Lezbo approach" in her effort to reach "a segment of audience that has been almost out of reach," as Al Martinez noted in the *Los Angeles Times.* "I didn't want to do just lesbian stuff," she says, adding "I am a Mexican-American vegetarian lesbian writer/performer and I wanted society to be aware we all exist, we all have human stories to tell" (Martinez 1991, B2).

Born in San Jose, California, Palacios began doing open-mike stand-up acts at age twenty-three in gay and lesbian clubs in San Francisco. She moved to Los Angeles in 1987, and like Gomez, is a founding member of Culture Clash. Palacios has become a voice in the Latina/Latino gay community, and is best known for her three one-woman shows: *Confessions,* described by Nancy Churnin in the *Los Angeles Times* as a "sexplosion of tantalizing tales"; *Greetings From a Queer Señorita,* encapsulating her life as a Chicana lesbian feminist; and *Latin Lezbo Comic.* In the latter, a thirty-minute excerpt from an autobiographical work, she sees the political in personal details as she encounters her Catholic family's reaction to her coming out. She gets laughs playing "the Don Juanita luring women into her 'girl trap' and portraying her life as a waitress trying to liberate her female patrons into giving her their order directly instead of through their men" (Churnin 1991, F1). Although her work focuses on the Latina lesbian experience, her humor is often described as universal in scope. Yet, with performing for the mainstream largely "out of the question until attitudes change," Palacios makes her own opportunities by self-producing and touring her show at alternative venues, art spaces, and theatres as well as pursuing writing projects. She recently received a playwright fellowship from the Mark Taper Forum's Latino Theatre Initiative to develop an individual project and to become more integrally involved with the Taper.

The New York–based Cuban American performer Alina Troyano, aka Carmelita Tropicana, began in theatre in the 1980s. Noted as a dancer and musical comedian, she says: "I went to acting classes, but I thought, 'Forget about it. Nobody's going to pick me.'" "I don't look like Grace Kelly—I'm a little shorter than Grace Kelly, that's the only difference," Troyano stated in an interview from New York, and added: "I want my accent. But when you realize you're not represented, you start writing your own stories" (Graham 1994, 58).

Candela shows a "flaky Latino lady" in a preposterous plot of Keystone Kops–style antics in which Tropicana's character, in a green polyester mantilla, a red feathered loincloth, and pink petticoat that turned her into walking cotton candy, is involved in a complicated murder plot. In *Milk of Amnesia* she gives a personal account about the identity problems of a transplanted child.

The work transcends social satire and humor to reach highly political proportions.

She is described by one reviewer as a performer with two very distinct personalities within one body:

> One is Carmelita Tropicana, a tangy bon bon, a spitfire, the spiritual daughter of Carmen Miranda (sans fruit but just as smashingly bedecked with flora and fauna), the perfect hostess for a Havana-themed bacchanal; the other is Alina Troyano, a thoughtful writer who wears glasses and, being a bit on the shy side, barely attracts attention on a crowded city street corner. (Obejas 1996, 34)

In *Milk of Amnesia* Tropicana brings the two personas closer together than ever before. The writer views this work as "definitely my most personal play," in contrast to *Candela* and another work, *Memories of the Revolution.* The other works are autobiographical, "but you wouldn't necessarily know that because they're so stylized. The others are more about Carmelita, the persona: very campy, humorous, ironic. In this one, there's a different tonality." It is based on her 1993 visit to Cuba, where she recalls not recognizing anything: "I had a lot more fear than if I had just been going to a Latin American country; this is the place where I was born. There were a lot of questions: Would I like the place? Could I relate to the people?" (34).

The trip began on a disconcerting note when Troyano arrived in Havana only to find that her visa, which she expected to be ready for her, was not there. She had to return to the States. When she was finally able to enter Cuba, she found herself overwhelmed by a sense of dislocation. She wandered the streets of Havana, looking for something familiar (34). Troyano recalls: "There was so much personal fear, which, of course, Carmelita would never have." In *Milk of Amnesia* Carmelita tells this story, which raises serious issues about identity and ethnicity, yet does so with a "rollicking good time," according to the reviewer. Her style seems to be surprisingly close to the style of the Cuban popular theatre, thus calling attention to the fact that her sense of estrangement coexists with a kinship with her people (34).

STAGING THE BORDER:
LAS COMADRES AND COCO FUSCO

Both perception and reception when crossing identity borders surface as pivotal moments in the work of many Latina performance artists. Yet, at least in two cases permanently split borders and a ruptured post-colonial history stand out. Las Comadres and Coco Fusco are excellent examples of highly politicized performers exploring the complexity of a binary and bifurcated existence between borders. Here, intertextual connections are finely entwined with the performative space. The dislocation of being is itself assaulted in the narrative, challenging the very roots of cultural past, present, and future.

Perhaps most closely aligned with interculturalism, these performers attempt, in Richard Schechner's words, to "probe the confrontations, ambivalences, disruptions, fears, disturbances and difficulties when and where cultures collide, overlap or pull away from each other." These "intercultural fractures, ideological contradictions, and crumbling national myths" explore "misunderstandings, broken messages and failed translations—what is not pure and what cannot successfully fuse" (Schechner 1991, 30).

Las Comadres, a multicultural women's group that is active in the U.S.-Mexico border region that includes Tijuana and San Diego, began in 1988. Several women artists, including Chicanas and Euroamerican/White women, came together to "counteract the isolation they felt, as a result, they thought, of jobs, family responsibilities, and the male domination of the arts community," as chronicled by Marguerite Waller in her account of the event as an active participant. What these women had in common was their "sense of invisibility, claustrophobia, isolation, or exploitation in relation to the webs of sociality and power" within which they usually operate (Waller 1994, 68–69).

Through a collective version of performance art, this group has explored issues of border conflict and the notion of representing the border. The performance piece *Border Boda* (*Border Wedding*) drew from past and present. María Teresa Marrero describes the visual and spatial effects of this performance/ritual:

> Here La Virgen de Guadalupe is deprived of a literal body. . . . Since the space is empty, it suggests that any woman can occupy it by positioning herself there. The border, then, can be seen as a construct, a state of being, which those who literally "place themselves" there can experience. . . . The Virgin, taken out of the institutional patriarchies of the Catholic Church and the Mexican government, and also taken out of the sanctity of the Mexican traditional home altar, becomes an appropriated icon. (Marrero 1992, 85–86)

The point of the drama is not to reach an Aristotelian resolution, but rather to confront the complexities of identity as constant issues for negotiation, filled with "painful histories and conflicted relationships" (Waller 1994, 82).

Laura Esparza, the director of the piece, approached the work as a means to "renegotiate relationships between past and present, sacred and secular, performers and audience, women and institutions" (77). Using two distinct performance spaces, two cultural arenas are presented. In one a Chicana granddaughter/niece is preparing for her upcoming wedding. Traditions of all types emerge, such as songs, foods, and *cuentos,* or stories. In another sphere, a "media" room, two Euroamerican/White performers question cultural representations of Chicanas/Chicanos set against recognizable images of conflict such as injustices toward farm workers, rape and murder by an Anglo, and other narratives that relate to "violence and loss" (79).

The back-and-forth banter results in the performers moving into and out of each other's spheres and eventually into the space occupied by the audience, thus engaging the audience in that world of "cross-cultural representation" as they enter to drink *calientitos* with the performers. Waller observes that the group viewed the work as "a ritual/performance," drawn from "collective (if heterogeneous) memories, to give ourselves and our audiences the strength and spirit to come to terms with our painful histories and conflicted relationships to each other" (82). The significance of this account lies in the fact that the chronicler discusses the failed performance, that is, its failure to bind interculturally what has historically and culturally been in opposition, struggling through too many centuries of "racist, misogynist colonial and postcolonial history" (67). In Schechner's definition of interculturalism, this disruptive juncture could instead be viewed as a success.

Coco Fusco, the second example of an artist who performs on the borders of identity, was born in the United States of Cuban parents (her mother was a Cuban immigrant), and views herself as a "border crosser." She was born and raised in New York. Fusco recalls, "My parents weren't directly involved in politics, but anybody who grew up in the shadow of Cuban immigration had politics thrust on them whether they wanted it or not" (McKenna 1993, F1). Fusco earned a B.A. in semiotics at Brown University and an M.A. in literature at Stanford University. She is most closely associated with performance artist Guillermo Gómez-Peña as his artistic collaborator. The two met in 1989 and performed together nationally and internationally through about 1998, although they are no longer together. Her link with an artist known for his exploration of the crisis at the U.S.-Mexican border resulted in numerous highly political and controversial performance works.

One critic says of their comedy *The Year of the White Bear,* performed in 1993, that the work argues the "need to rethink five centuries of New World history. It is not an anti-Columbus diatribe" (Pincus 1993, E1). The two artists tell us in their accompanying statement: "We are not trying to bury Columbus, or to deport all European-based culture back to the Old World. We are reviewing the many legacies of the conquest and colonization of the Americas in order to understand where to place ourselves in that history" (E1). Their work shows how the split culture of the border reveals a Latina/Latino community struggling with the politics of identity.

One of their most talked-about pieces is *Two Undiscovered Amerindians Visit New York,* described as "an exercise in faux anthropology based on racist images of natives" (McKenna 1993, F1). Because this work is available on videotape, under the title *The Couple in the Cage,* it has been widely seen. The piece was presented eight times in four different countries from Madrid to Sydney and was exhibited in a cage in various museums. One reviewer's account of the videotaped performance refers to this "provocative tape" as a documentary which satirized colonial stereotypes. The two appeared portraying two "undiscovered" natives from a fictitious island in the Gulf of Mexico as they toured internationally. In their performance at the Field Museum in Chicago, another performance artist, Paula Killen, donned a zookeeper's uniform while she "disinformed visitors about the anthropological specimens on display, explaining that Mayor Daley donated the color TV set inside the cage" (Stamets 1994, 233). According to the reviewer in the *Austin American-Statesman:* "By traveling around the world displayed in a cage like 'native' specimens, Fusco and her partner, Guillermo Gómez-Peña, poignantly addressed cross-cultural misunderstanding and the way human beings treat each other as exotic curiosities" (Goldman 1994, 13).

The reviewer for *The Herald* in Glasgow, where the two artists were appearing for the National Review of Live Art, tells us that both were "highly sought after on the international circuit" (Brennan 1994, 24). The reviewer noted that in *Mexarcane International,* which was subtitled *Ethnic Talent for Sale,* these artists dealt with identity, appearing as commodities being traded at the marketplace, namely, Mexarcane International, where the encaged two were up for sale. The reviewer added: "It's a piece about ethnic art as a commodity, about promoters, festivals, exploitation," and that the effect was "laceratingly clever. She [Fusco] sat, like some Carmen Miranda with a laptop, working out our individual profiles as consumers of ethnic goodies. He, tricked out in a marvelous agglomeration of ethnic uniform—bangles, beads, feathers and so forth—sat like some captive exhibit in a cage" (21). The desired effect of this work as "ethnic art as a commodity," complete with its dehumanizing exploitation, clearly made an impact on this reviewer.

Despite the recognition she has earned through her collaborations with other artists, Coco Fusco must be respected for numerous independent ventures. She is a critic and a solo performance artist. She has given numerous lectures about art and identity. She is also the author of *English Is Broken Here: Notes on Cultural Fusion in the Americas,* a collection of essays on cultural identity, gender issues, multiculturalism, and living a bifurcated life; it is about people born in the United States who live between borders, whether they are from México or anywhere else. This type of bifurcation is an inherent driving force in the work of Puerto Rican dramatists.

NUYORICAN THEATRE: MIGDALIA CRUZ

The Nuyorican theatre has had numerous women playwrights, including Carmen Rivera, Yolanda Rodríguez, and Eva López, whose works were anthologized in John V. Antush's *Nuestro New York,* a collection of Puerto Rican plays (1994). Perhaps the most produced is Migdalia Cruz (b. ?), whose work has been seen in London, Montreal, New York, and on numerous U.S. stages, including Playwrights Horizons, New York Shakespeare Festival's Festival Latino, and the Cleveland Public Theatre. This prolific artist has written over twenty plays, musicals, and operas: her most recognized plays are *Miriam's Flowers, The Have-Little, Telling Tales, Lucy Loves Me,* and *Frida: The Story of Frida Kahlo.* Stemming from that generation of Latinas who studied with Maria Irene Fornes in her INTAR playwriting workshops, her work, which initially focused largely on women's lives in the Bronx and the difficulty of surviving poverty, has gone farther and farther afield.

An INTAR Theatre Playwright Resident from 1984 to 1988 and recipient of a McKnight Fellowship, Cruz was selected to participate in the revived Taper Lab at the Mark Taper Forum. The lab helped to develop sixteen plays and performance pieces at Taper, Too, the 99-seat space under the John Anson Ford Theater. Included in this group of playwrights were several who would go on to gain recognition: Bill Cain, Philip Kan Gotanda, Jude Narita, John Fleck, John Stepplin, Shem Bitterman, Michael Henry Brown, Tim Miller, Ariel Dorfman, Doris Baizley, Doug Wright, Steven Morris, Robert Schenkkan, Tony Abatemarco, and Pavel Kohout. Migdalia Cruz, too, quickly made her mark.

Miriam's Flowers[3] was produced at Playwrights Horizons' second-floor Studio Theater in 1990. In the play, Cruz tells about a 16-year-old Puerto Rican girl in the South Bronx in 1975. We witness the breakdown of her family following the accidental death of her 7-year-old brother, Puli, who was hit by a train and terribly maimed as he ran to catch a ball. This depiction of an already fragile and crippled family brings out the suffering that both Miriam and her 36-year-old mother, Delfina, undergo as a result of this senseless loss. There appears to be no hope for this family as the father's excessive love for the mother turns into destructive abuse, and Miriam's own relationship with her father completely deteriorates as she witnesses his excessive lust and eventual abandonment of the family. Miriam's relationship with Enrique, who loves her, also deteriorates. At the end, the mother's death in the bathtub in which Miriam would bathe her almost ritualistically in an attempt to help them both confront their demons and soothe their pain leaves Miriam praying at the altar in what seems a continual path of sacrifice to atone for the death of the young Puli (Bommer 1991, CN6).

Puli's death leads the young Miriam to connect her pain "to the physical suffering of the crucified Christ," as Feyder observes, thus seeking her own means of "self-inflicted torture to feel she's alive" (Feyder 1992, 7). After its premiere in London at the Old Red Lion, *The Independent* reviewer noted: "Miriam's 'flowers' are the patterns a young Puerto Rican girl carves into her arms with razor blades and offers up to a statue of the mutilated Christ" (Bayley 1991, Arts 19). Cruz's drama follows an ominous and disjointed episodic structure to offer a fascinating exploration of Catholicism and interconnections to that deeply rooted faith and to modern-day society. This dark and foreboding portrayal tells us something about the women in the world as Cruz conceives her universe. In her introduction to *Shattering the Myth: Plays by Hispanic Women,* in which this play was published, Linda Feyder, the editor, offers some important commentary about the play's connections to the lives of Latinas through its suggestion of "the sacrificial element in the sexual act for Hispanic women, the close relationship between suffering and sex. The women in this play become desperate, mutilated, no longer able to console one another outside the shared suffering that will hold them together in the afterlife" (Feyder 1992, 7). The dramatist uses the flashback technique to interweave sex into family relationships. Miriam uses sex "as a revenge against her parents, pursuing her own destruction with an energy which is terrible to watch" (Bayley 1991, Arts 19).

Most reviewers have been favorable toward Cruz's work. Hedy Weiss wrote about the effectiveness of the use of magical realism: "Like her mentor, playwright Maria Irene Fornes, Cruz brings a distinctly urban feminist point of view to this style. And the result is unique in the way it mixes eroticism and emotional violence, while alternating sharply between the bizarrely funny and the exceptionally grim" (Weiss 1992, 2: 37). Clare Bayley, on the other hand, commenting on the London production, found fault with Janet Amsden's production, which "surrenders itself to the terrifying intensity" of Cruz's writing, "but there is more here of darkness and the smell of blood than the laughter and love that the playwright mentions in the programme. Despite compelling acting, the pace and pitch of emotion peak too soon and the production falls apart in the second half. Still, it remains a disquietingly vivid portrayal of the helplessness of grief and guilt" (Bayley 1991, Arts 19).

By February of 1991 Cruz was teaching playwriting at Princeton University, and she had won the runner-up prize of $1000 for *The Have-Little* in the 13th Annual Susan Smith Blackburn Prize competition.[4] *The Have-Little* was produced at INTAR in 1991 under the direction of Nilo Cruz. It is a sweeping story of a woman's life in the South Bronx from childhood to motherhood. Lillian Rivera's life revolves around abandonment: her father, José, who turns to drink; her best friend, Michi, whose life is carefully planned for an education and upward mobility in life; and her mother, who leaves her through death. She gets pregnant by the first young man who makes love to her, but he too abandons her, to an overdose of heroin. Yet, just as her mother had always turned to prayer and the rosary, Lillian also turns to prayer as she and her young son sit in coldness and desolation with little hope of a brighter tomorrow. Despite the lack of a solution in this all-too-familiar story, Cruz was lauded by the *New York Times* reviewer for her abilities to convey a broad range of sentiments, from sadness to frustration to an understanding and sympathy for the characters' plight. The reviewer added: "If she offers no solutions for breaking the cycle that devours so many of the nation's youth, she at least brings understanding and sympathy to their plight" (Hampton 1991, C14). Yet, some weaknesses were also mentioned, including the need for considerable work on imagery and more carefully crafted handling of the writing overall, raising themes without pursuing them adequately, and further development of the subject of blood which came up frequently without being woven adequately into the context of the play. Nevertheless, the effective performances of the three women were said to lift the characters above the level of stereotypes, and the director was complimented on his work.

Other works by Cruz include the 1992 music-theatre piece *Frida,* which opened the tenth anniversary season of the Next Wave Festival at the Brooklyn Academy of Music. Cruz co-authored this representation of the artist Frieda Kahlo which illustrates the turbulent life of the Mexican painter. In 1993 Cruz won an Artists Residency Award Grant, in a program developed and administered by the Theater Communications Group and funded through a grant from the Pew Charitable Trusts, to work at the Classic Stage Company in New York. In 1994 Cruz's *Latins in LA-LA Land* was featured in the 17th Bay Area Playwrights Festival at Mame Hunt's Magic Theater in San Francisco, along with several other new works (Anderson 1994, 82).

In recent years Cruz has premiered numerous works with the Latino Chicago Theater Company, with which she is affiliated. *Another Part of the House,* a play produced at Classic Stage Company in New York, was praised for its glimpse of a "desperate world" seething to life in this production, "enticing us as irresistibly as Pepe el Romano beckons the daughters of Bernarda Alba" in this "magic-tinged tragedy" inspired by Federico García Lorca's *La Casa de Bernarda Alba* (Solomon 1997, 11).

YALE AND ACADEMIC TRAINING: EDIT VILLAREAL

Some Latinas have gone the more traditional route of training in playwriting to develop their craft. Edit Villareal (b. ?) is one of those artists. In 1981 Villareal was one of only two women in the group of six Spanish-speaking playwrights named to participate in the four-year playwright-in-residence program sponsored by INTAR. She subsequently received her M.F.A. in playwriting at Yale, and she currently teaches playwriting at the University of California, Los Angeles.

This Los Angeles–based writer grew up in the bilingual, bicultural Texas border town of El Paso. Her most notable work is *My Visits with MGM* (*My Grandmother Marta*),[5] first presented in the 1989 Hispanic Playwrights Project at South Coast Repertory Theatre, one of the leading producers of new works by Latinas/Latinos. It was later produced at the Los Angeles Theatre Center. In this semi-autobiographical "comic fantasy" about the Texas native's Mexican grandmother, Villareal effectively wields the fluid backward-and-forward movement of time typical in the Latin American style of magical realism. The play revolves around a young Chicana's exploration of her relationship to the two women who raised her, her Mexican grandmother, Marta Grande, "a ranchera [rancher] who trekked with her reluctant sister to Texas during the Mexican Revolution of 1910," and Florinda, her grandmother's sister (Rubio 1992, F6).

Integrated into the plot is the contemporary granddaughter's relationship with "an amorous renegade priest." Described as a light-hearted comedy, this piece "demonstrates the vital place the deceased often occupy in Hispanic culture," according to one critic. The reviewer adds that "in its fond, humanizing depiction of a unique senior relative, it's more about breaking down stereotypes of handwringing, dependent Mexican women." This poignant portrayal of the grandmother, a woman who had the courage to leave her homeland and begin anew, offers an important role model of a liberated identity. The granddaughter's own "personal revolution" is her courageous act of leaving her home with its memories and past, but not without the guiding spirit of her grandmother to lead the way (F6).

In 1993 American Playhouse filmed Villareal's play *La Carpa,* in association with the Film Festival of International Cinema Students and the National Latino Communications Center. In this piece, which is influenced by Luis Valdez and El Teatro Campesino's earlier *La Carpa de los Rasquachis,* a Mexican vaudeville company, reminiscent of the tent shows of the 1930s found throughout the United States, travels through the fields of Southern California. The *carpa,* or tent, provides a forum for entertainment in the vaudeville tradition. However, the harsh reality of injustice within the entertainment industry emerges when the sheriff's deputy shoots one of the workers. The sheriff's office justifies it as an accidental death. The *carpa* provides the setting for unveiling the facts about the tragic killing through a witness who discloses the wrongful death. The reviewer in the *Chicago Sun-Times* noted that the tent theatre was used as "a symbol of freedom, a refuge of Mexican culture in a hostile land. Part vaudeville show and part carnival, La Carpa Castillo represents a liberating alternative" for the witness (Grahnke 1993, 2:51).

Villareal has been an important workshop leader and dramaturg for aspiring playwrights, and her work at UCLA has enabled other Chicanas/Chicanos/Latinas/Latinos to pursue playwriting. She has also encouraged academic training in other areas of the profession. Villareal has a firm grasp of traditional play structure, and her abilities to instruct others about character development, story line, and other elements of drama can provide more training for those interested in this area of theatre. In fact, Villareal serves as an excellent example of the type of skilled artist that Valdez had envisioned for *teatro* practitioners at the inception of Chicana/Chicano theatre.

Another aspect of *teatro* espoused first by Valdez and tested by many practitioners since then is the investigation of cultural roots, that is, going back into oneself and staging culture. The Midwest, although it is viewed by some as an unlikely source, has provided us with two performers/playwrights who have sought to perform their dual ethnicity as Chicanas/Indias—native to American soil.

FROM THE MIDWEST TO BEFORE THE CONQUEST: THE COLORADO SISTERS AND AN INDIGENOUS PAST

The "Colorado Sisters," as they have come to be known, are important voices who have reached toward an Hispanic indigenous history that took place long before the conquest. Elvira and Hortensia Colorado, the co-founders of the Coatlicue Theatre Company, were born in Blue Island, Illinois, a small town south of Chicago. These sisters were part of a large Mexican community primarily formed around areas where the jobs in the stockyards, steel mills, and railroads were (see Perkins and Uno 1996, 79–80). The Mexican Revolution pushed their mother out of México and the railroads brought their father to the Midwest, as they did countless other Mexicanos.

In many ways similar to Villareal's fountain of resources, the Colorado Sisters draw from stories they heard from their grandmother, who was the center of their lives as they were growing up. Their reason for writing reflects deeply rooted origins that go far beyond the border identity that political necessity and economic hardship could have imposed on their parents. In Perkins and Uno's interview with these artists, the two women speak about their drive to write: "We became writers out of necessity to speak in our own voices instead of being spoken for. We come from a lineage of strong Indian women who have been silenced for too long and it is through our work that we give voice to their stories, the unsung heroines" (79).

This long heritage of Native blood has been traced to Chichimec/Otomi traditions. Through the oral tradition of storytelling, these two sisters have been performing together for over ten years in New York City in such venues as the National Museum of the American Indian, the American Museum of Natural History, the American Indian Community House, the Bronx Museum, and with the Thunderbird American Indian Dance Company. They have also appeared throughout the country and abroad in museums, cultural centers, universities, and on reservations. The Coatlicue Theatre Company holds writing and theatre workshops for immigrant women in New York City community centers, and its two members have an extensive list of theatre, film, and television work to their credit. Besides being recognized as storytellers, playwrights, and performers, they are also known as community activists.[6]

The work of the Colorado Sisters confronts racism and prejudice against their indigenous blood: "Growing up with racism—the thing about color and the denial of being Indian. The denial in our family is so imbedded that we didn't know our father's side of the family—they were too Indian! We had to say we were Spanish and not Mexican. Least of all Indian" (79). The name of

Colorado Sisters in *Open Wounds on Tlalteuctli*.
Photo by Katherine Fogden.

their company, Coatlicue, comes directly from Aztec mythology. Coatlicue is the name of the deity Mother Earth, or earth/creation figure. By incorporating the Náhuatl language into their stories, they bring attention to their native culture and traditions. They weave stories of the deities within their own personal stories about their family, themselves, and themes and ideas affecting the Indian, Chicana/Chicano, and Mexican communities in which they operate. Their performance is largely educational theatre and they work with Mexican and Indian communities in New York City as well as in various other Mexican communities. In the process of educating their audiences, they effectively strive to "reaffirm their survival as urban Indian women" as they also entertain those who witness their performances.[7]

In one of their earliest works, *La Llorona—The Wailing Woman*, the central figure appears in multiple roles. The performers illustrate how strength is drawn from this complex figure about whom stories have traveled on both sides of the border from before Christianity to the present day. The sisters describe her as follows: "She is Malinche, Cortez's mistress, interpreter and mother. She is Cihuacoatl, Aztec deity, protector of women who died in childbirth and who became warriors. She is a witch/sorceress/seer, who possessed supernatural powers. She is Matlacihuatl, who appeared to men at night, dressed in white, frightened them and ate them. She is all of these women, and we draw strength from her" (Coatlicue Theatre Company Press Kit Collection). *La Llorona* was performed at The United Nations Decade for Women, New York, in 1986, the Theatre for the New City, New York, in 1989, the American Indian

Community House, Native American Women in the Arts Festival, New York, in 1989, and the Women's Caucus for Art National Conference in 1990.

1992: Blood Speaks, published in Perkins and Uno's *Contemporary Plays by Women of Color,*[8] uses humor as it chronicles the conquest through a multimedia production that includes music and song. Murals painted on scrims provide the visual images necessary to reveal the "gradual encroachment of colonization, as our people welcomed and shared." As they note in their description of this performance piece: "The conquistadors conquered with the sword and the cross, destroying our places of worship and sacred books. We are still here—not in museums! The colonization is still going on" (Coatlicue Theatre Company Press Kit Collection). It is their intent to display a way for their people to take ownership of this historical detriment: "By turning around the atrocities committed and taking a searing look at the Columbus myth and the role that religion played in the genocide of Native peoples, the action of the play goes from the sublime to the absurd, and from farce to reality." They effectively "dispel the Columbus myth," and "reclaim our voices and begin to rewrite our history" (Coatlicue Theatre Company Press Kit Collection). An interweaving of three languages, Zapotec, Spanish, and English, offers a celebratory note of survival as the performers strive to offer hope for future generations of Native women.

A Traditional Kind of Woman: Too Much Not 'Nuff (1995) has toured to reservations, health care facilities, HIV/AIDS outreach events, the Public Theatre's "Free at Three" Series in New York, and numerous Native American and women's conferences. In this work a broad range of topics brings to the fore healing and empowering stories of women "which serve to empower other native women and educate health care providers in the beliefs, values and practices of native women." The issues include domestic violence, incest, rape, HIV/AIDS, alcoholism, drugs, cancer, diabetes, nutrition, and racism (Press Kit Collection).

The New World Theatre in Amherst, Massachusetts, under the artistic direction of Roberta Uno, has been a significant site for workshops at which many new playwrights of color have been able to develop their work. In 1996, the Colorado Sisters used a New World Theatre Commissioning Grant to develop the piece "Chicomoztoc–Mimixcoa–Cloud Serpents" which was performed as a work in progress at the New World Theatre in 1996. The struggling sense of optimism in this and other works has brought their message about the wide range of mestiza experience in the United States to an attentive audience. One of the central goals of the Colorado Sisters has been to empower Mexican people with a sense of pride in their heritage and traditions: "It is a way for recognizing, reaffirming and reinforcing our indigenous culture by having indigenous people from both sides of the border dialogue and share traditions" (Perkins and Uno 1996, 81). Through each of their performance pieces, a positive "sense of sisterhood in the immediate sense as sibling and in the larger sense as women" of the Colorado Sisters stands out (John Bell, "*Huipil,*" *Theatre Week,* March 9, 1992, in Press Kit Collection).

FROM THE STAGE TO THE SCREEN: EVELINA FERNÁNDEZ

Some women have moved from working in various venues in the theatre and have begun to reach far wider audiences through their extensive work and passionate perseverance to keep a Latina voice in the forefront. Evelina Fernández (b. ?) is one of these women. Born in East Los Angeles, her career has taken her from acting in such notable roles as the female lead in Luis Valdez's *Zoot Suit* in its original stage production at the Mark Taper Forum to numerous TV and film roles, including the female lead in *American Me,* in which she starred with Edward James Olmos. It is clear that this individual's professional career has stretched far beyond her work as a playwright. Yet it is the voice of the playwright that must be singled out for our purposes here.

Fernández's writing credits include an original screenplay, *Luminarias,* recently released following its earlier life as a stage play under the auspices of the Latino Theatre Company in Los Angeles (1996). Under the direction of her husband, the highly recognized director José Luis Valenzuela, "the seamless script" by Fernández, who also stars in the film, follows four Latina friends who meet regularly at Luminarias Restaurant. *Luminarias* takes "an approving view of romances between Latinas and non-Latino men," Valenzuela told a reporter for the *Los Angeles Times.* "This is a tough proposition for our audience, because in most of our plays we're victims" (Shirley 1996, F2). In this play "one [woman] is a lawyer involved with a Jew, another a therapist attracted to a recent Mexican immigrant. An artist dates a Korean, while a trendy clothing store owner comes to grips with her gay brother and gives up sex for Lent." Fernández was quoted as saying, "It's inevitable that we're all going to fall in love with each other—all races" (O'Connell 1999, 3E).

Fernández has also written a screenplay for Columbia Pictures and a television sitcom for Disney. Driven by the lack of significant roles for Latinas in any performative venue, including film, television, and the theatre, she has tried to make strides toward creating roles that portray Chicanas as a viable and real part of life. Fernández states: "I am concerned that our stories will not be told. That they will not be passed on. That my daughter and other young Latinas will not know that their legacy is that of strong, courageous, passionate, intelligent women" (Perkins and Uno 1996, 159). Her goal is to provide positive roles for Latinas and Latinos in all performative media in order to build community self-esteem and encourage visibility for those who are otherwise invisible in today's media market.

Fernández's *How Else Am I Supposed to Know I'm Still Alive* arose from her goal of providing opportunities for Chicanas to play leading roles. The brief story revolves around two middle-aged Chicanas talking about their life and difficulties as they face the possible pregnancy of one of them. Highly humorous, the issues become serious as they each draw from their barrio life and traditions and sincere friendship. This work was first produced at La Plaza de La Raza in East Los Angeles as the winner of the Nuevo Chicano L.A. Theaterworks contest of 1989. The piece went on to be produced by El Centro Su Teatro in Denver, Colorado, and by Teatro Vision in San Jose, California. It toured nationally with El Teatro Campesino (with Josefina López's *Simply Maria*). It was adapted into an award-winning film through the Hispanic Film Project at Universal Studios under the direction of Fernández's husband, the former director of the Los Angeles Theatre Center's Latino Lab, José Luis Valenzuela.

Many Latinas shared in the experience described by Evelina Fernández, namely, having to write their own stories in order to accommodate opportunities for themselves on the stage. Fernández, who works closely with Valenzuela, has had many more opportunities than others normally find. Her scripted work has been lauded for effective staging, and she has been noted for her abilities as an actor to bring the work to life on the stage. Yet, like many others, she suffers from being pulled in too many directions and not being able to work at one aspect of her talent full time.

OTHER WOMEN PLAYWRIGHTS

There are many other Chicanas/Latinas writing plays and performance work. We must acknowledge the work of other notable pathfinders, including Lynne Alvarez and Dolores Prida, largely in New York; Denise Chávez in New Mexico; and Silviana Wood, initially in Tucson, Arizona, and now in San Antonio, Texas. There are also emerging new voices that are continuing to broaden the scope of this unique group, including Lourdes Blanco, Ana María Simo, Sylvia Morales, Lina Gallegos, Yareli Arizmendi, Sylvia González, Lisa Loomer, Nancy De Los Santos, and Amparo García. Many are breaking away from traditional models while others draw from standard forms, yet all seem to have a major goal in common. The drive to write politically seems to be at the heart of the entire body of work by this group of artists. These women are challenged to break from an invisibility that has been pervasive in their contemporary history, and they are making great strides in finding their voice across the country. The work of these women provides vital new opportunities to study the representation of women as subject on the American stage. Yet, while their contribution as playwrights and performance artists has been considerable, there are many other directions that these women and a host of others have taken that ensure a lasting presence from this group and from Latina writers as well. We now turn to performance to explore the broader role Latinas have crafted through their work in the theatre.

WOMEN IN PRODUCTION: CREATING NEW CONTEXTS

It is impossible to account for every Latina individual involved in production. The following section is not intended to provide an exhaustive list of all of those who have contributed in various areas of production. Instead, some venues, organizations, events, and individual cases serve as representative examples to indicate the type of activity that has fostered the growing involvement and presence of Chicanas/Latinas in the theatre.

THEATRE COMPANIES AND PRODUCING ORGANIZATIONS

East Coast

On the East Coast, two important community organizations were responsible for developing community cultural events. Joanne Pottlitzer founded Theatre of Latin America, Inc. (TOLA) in 1969, producing Latin American plays in English in New York, bringing Latin American touring groups to the United States, and providing a network between artists in the United States and Latin America. TOLA received Obie Awards for two productions, *Latin American Fair of Opinion* (1972) and *Chile! Chile!* (1976). Another important theatre organization was the Association of Hispanic Arts (AHA). Marta Moreno Vega, a recognized leader in Latina/Latino arts promotion, founded and directed AHA in 1975 in an attempt to strengthen ties between other Hispanic arts organizations and to strengthen advocacy of the arts (Pottlitzer 1988, 22–25).

In 1966 Miriam Colón's Puerto Rican Traveling Theatre (PRTT) brought bilingual works to the Spanish-speaking communities of New York City. By the early 1970s, this company was providing a laboratory theatre and an actors' training program. Colón, a stage, film, and television actor, was a student of Erwin Piscator and the first Puerto Rican member of the Actors Studio, the famous workshop for professional actors in New York. She joined a group of bilingual actors, which led to the founding of the PRTT.

Under her direction, this theatre has been an important site for contemporary Latina/Latino drama and for a cultural center which includes training units for young playwrights. In 1979 the PRTT moved to its present location, a former firehouse on West 47th Street, renovated in 1974 to allow for rehearsals and production facilities. Colón raised close to $3 million for the renovations, and the result was a well-equipped 196-seat theater.

Other women have been instrumental in strengthening theatrical activity in New York, including Magali Alabau, Silvia Brito, Lourdes Casals, Alba Olms, Elsa Ortiz, Ilka Tanya Payan, and Margarita Toraic. In Miami, Cuban American Olga Garay-Ahern is important for her administrative position in the Metro-Dade Cultural Affairs Council. Through Garay-Ahern's initiative, a coalition of Miami-based Cuban theatres was formed in 1984 in order to encourage and strengthen theatrical activity there. In 1972 Theresa Maria Rojas, who had received dramatic training in Havana, founded the Teatro Prometeo at Miami-Dade Community College as an alternative to commercial theatre. Teatro Prometeo gave more opportunities to Latina actors.

Other establishments founded by Latinos were important because of the experience and exposure they gave to actors. The Repertorio Español, founded by Gilberto Zaldivar and Rene Buch in 1968, continues to offer an important place for plays produced in Spanish; it offers simultaneous English translations. An award-winning nonprofit repertory company, Repertorio Español has been headquartered at New York's Gramercy Arts Theatre since 1972. The company averages 300 performances annually of various forms, including dramatic, musical productions (particularly the very popular Spanish *zarzuelas*) and dance productions.

Zaldivar and Buch were trained in theatre, and their work has largely been drawn from the classical Spanish stage. Many actors have found their work with the classics at this venue to be an important training ground. Raul Julia once commented about his experience playing Astolfo in Calderón de la Barca's *Life Is a Dream* at the Teatro Español in 1964: "*Life Is a Dream* was my first play in New York and a perfect beginning for my years of playing the classics with the New York Shakespeare Festival."[9] Buch is also an important director who has directed on numerous regional stages throughout the United States in Latina/Latino-related venues.

West Coast

On the West Coast, the Bilingual Foundation of the Arts at the Los Angeles Theatre Center (LATC) was co-founded by stage and television actor Carmen Zapata and Argentine designer Estela Scarlata. It is under the artistic direction of Margarita Galban, a Cuban-born actor, who has directed over sixty plays since the Foundation was formed in 1973. As a performer in México, Galban won that country's Best Actor Award for her performance in *The House of Bernarda Alba* before coming to the United States to study directing at Lee Strasberg's Actors Studio. Galban staged many of García Lorca's plays.

Through this producing organization, Latina/Latino actors were given many opportunities to perform, and in some instances Latina/Latino designers also found work. Estela Scarlata served as scene designer and Octavio Ramirez was the lighting designer for one project, and Scarlata generally designed scenery for this organization (Jones 1985, E6). Its more than thirty-year history allowed many productions of Latin American and Latina/Latino works by expert performers with full production elements to be seen. The productions were presented in both Spanish and English on alternate nights.

Zapata, who served as producing director from its inception, also had a recurring role on the television soap opera *Santa Barbara*. Born in New York to a Mexican father and Argentine mother, Zapata grew up speaking Spanish. "I missed the theater when I moved out here," said the actor who had trained as an opera singer. She made her Broadway debut at eighteen in the chorus of *Oklahoma*. "There wasn't a great deal of theater to speak of anyway—and whatever there was certainly wasn't ethnic. They were not hiring Carmen Zapata to play Lady Macbeth. But while I was here, I began to delve into my culture, my own roots and background. I became very involved in the Hispanic community" (Arkatov 1989, 98).

Zapata has received numerous awards. When she first met Galban, the latter had a company, Seis Actores, and was doing a Spanish-language play. Zapata has produced a series of translations from Spanish works along with her partner, Michael Dewell. She states that they chose to do everything bilingual, because that "would make us unique as a theatre." She adds: "We'd started to do it only in Spanish and found we were losing a great many young people from our community who didn't speak the language well enough to appreciate the literature. We also thought it would be nice if we reached into the non-Hispanic community, and had them enjoy the beauty of our literature" (98).

The South Coast Repertory Company in Costa Mesa, California, has been an important venue for workshopping and developing new plays. The company maintains a separate endowment for the purpose of developing new plays, and Jose Cruz Gonzales has served as director of the Hispanic Playwrights Project for many years. Because it offered Latina/Latino actors and dramaturges to aid the playwright, many works originating in this series went on to full stage life.

ACTORS, DIRECTORS, DESIGNERS, AND OTHERS

East Coast

The history of Latinas on the Broadway stage is probably much more extensive than we know. To date, Latinas have rarely been acknowledged for their enormous contributions in important roles in musicals and drama. We owe a debt of gratitude to Don B. Wilmeth and Tice L. Miller, who included more women of color than are typically found in compilations like their edition of the *Cambridge Guide to American Theatre*. More often than not we hear about chorus members and extras that may have been from an ethnic group, but the chronicles about these individuals still remain to be written. There are, however, at least two notable contemporary actors that require notice, Rita Moreno and Chita Rivera. Their names have come to light primarily through the tributes they have begun to receive from numerous Hollywood and community-based organizations that have targeted Latinas/Latinos for their contributions specifically because they have represented their ethnic communities in a wide range of the work that they do.

Rita Moreno (b. 1931), the Puerto Rican–born actor who first worked as a

Spanish dancer and in nightclub entertainment, has appeared in numerous stage plays, including *The Sign in Sidney Brustein's Window* (1964) by Lorraine Hansberry, and toured in the 1985 female version of *The Odd Couple*. She won a Tony Award for her supporting role in *The Ritz* (1975) and is the only performer of any culture to have won an Academy Award, an Emmy, a Tony, and a Grammy.

Chita Rivera (née Dolores Conchita Figueroa del Rivero, 1933), a dancer, singer, and actor, attended the American School of Ballet before starting her career as a Broadway dancer. She appeared in *Guys and Dolls* (1950) and received high critical acclaim for her performance as Anita in *West Side Story* (1957). She has also been critically recognized for her roles in such musicals as *Bye Bye Birdie* (1960), *Bajour* (1964), *Chicago* (1975), *The Rink* (1984), *Jerry's Girls* (1985), and the recent *Kiss of the Spiderwoman*.

West Coast and the Southwest

The Los Angeles Theatre Center (LATC) began as the Los Angeles Actors' Theatre (1975) under Ralph Waite and Diane White, modeled after New York's Public Theatre. Within ten years, the company had presented numerous premieres, including several produced by the Latino Theatre Lab, a special project under the direction of José Luis Valenzuela. In 1985 Bill Bushnell and Diane White saw a production by Valenzuela in a tiny theatre in East Los Angeles when they were putting together the LATC Company. Valenzuela was first hired only as an accountant, but they soon authorized him to build the Latino Lab after hours. When the Ford Foundation chipped in $200,000, the Lab began to produce a series of works on LATC's main stages. Milcha Sanchez-Scott's *Roosters* was among those new works which received full mounting.

The LATC doors closed in late 1991, but the Lab moved to the Mark Taper Forum, where Valenzuela directed the Taper's well-endowed Latino Theatre Initiative. Valenzuela remained until 1994 when he left to run his own company, the Latino Theatre Company. However, the Los Angeles Mark Taper Forum Latino Theatre Initiative, a special project devoted specifically to diversity, has been even more instrumental in new play development in Los Angeles and continues to be the most significant for Latinas in theatre. Under the artistic direction of Gordon Davidson, Diane Rodríguez was named as one of its co-directors. A thirteen-year veteran of Luis Valdez's El Teatro Campesino, she is a founding member of El Teatro de la Esperanza and the legendary comedy troupe, Latins Anonymous. The Latino Theatre Initiative has been instrumental in the development of plays by Latinas/Latinos, and Rodríguez's vast experience as a director ensures that women's voices will be heard on the stage as well as in the written work. She was recently invited to direct Luis Santiero's *Our Lady of the Tortilla* at the Phoenix Theatre in Arizona. The artistic director of the Phoenix Theatre hired Rodríguez because of the cultural perspective she could bring to the work as well as her expertise in the field (Lawson 1997, Weekend D5).

In Texas, several important figures have worked in theatre. Whether they have learned their craft through academic training, professional training, or by learning the process as amateurs, what stands out in this group is the fact that most of these women are involved in a broad range of activity. In order to have the opportunities to work professionally, they are often driven to write the work that creates those opportunities. The women listed here are excellent examples of those who have been successful in their ventures; they have claimed workable spaces in order to ensure that they will have continuing work as practitioners and artists in their field.

Ruby Nelda Pérez, one of the original members of Joe Rosenberg's Teatro Bilingue, founded in the early 1970s at Texas A & I University in Kingsville, Texas, has been acting farther and farther afield since she left that group. She has often written her own work in order to broaden her talent and keep working. Her most recent piece, "Doña Rosita's Jalapeño Kitchen" (retitled), written in collaboration with Rodrigo Duarte Clark (a veteran of Jorge Huerta's original core group, Teatro de la Esperanza), has been performed widely. Her strength lies in comedy. This work revolves around a multi-character solo play, in which Doña Rosita invites the audience into her restaurant in Salsipuedes (Getoutifyoucan) while she thinks of selling her home of twenty-three years. The comedy hinges on the idea of a cook who eventually goes to heaven in search of the perfect kitchen, but jalapeños are nowhere to be found (Welsh 1997, Entertainment 4).

Other actors on the Texas stage include three Latina artists recently profiled on the Austin scene. Myrna Cabello is a film and stage actor, singer, graphic designer, and writer. She is often cast in television commercials and film; she appeared as Maria Elena in the Zachary Scott Theatre's *Buddy Holly Story.* Irene González played the matriarch in *Our Lady of the Tortilla,* and continues to act in the region. Her background does not include training as an actor, but she has learned through experience and through plays that allow her to develop characters of the barrio that are familiar images.

Perhaps the most recognized of the Austin Latinas is Amparo García, a professional playwright, actor, and director. García teaches at the Austin Theater for Youth Conservatory. She has starred in numerous productions, most notably as Carla in "In the West," a compilation of monologues written by several Austin writers during the 1980s, a piece that was eventually made into a film, *Deep in the Heart.* García received her B.A. in drama, her M.A. in theater history and criticism, and an M.F.A. in writing at the Texas Center for Writers. She also teaches undergraduate playwriting at the University of Texas at Austin and gives private acting lessons.

García's new play, *Under a Western Sky,* received its world premiere in New York City Off-Broadway in 1997 to favorable reviews in the *New York Times.* Her work is described as disturbing, with "dreamlike qualities that have pervaded García's life. Full of high plateaus and bleak, shadowy lows, the plays are a sort of gossamer screen on which García's real-life dramas have been pro-

Costume design by Tina Cantú Navarro for the
character of Margarita, the mother, in the premiere
of Milcha Sanchez-Scott's *The Old Matador,*
Arizona Theatre Company. Directed by Peter
Brosius (1995).
Photo by Pedro C. Ramírez.

jected, from a father's murder to a young girl's loss of innocence to a mother's
sexual disgrace" (Bass 1997, E1). *Under a Western Sky* tells a story based on an
actual event, a gang rape during a cock fight in a small town in the Valley. The
play's plot is interspersed with the characters' moments of truth. One reviewer
notes: "Through the brutality, hints of poetry emerge. García's theater of the
soul, as she calls it, deals in parallel universes, which at first seem contradic-
tory." García adds: "Theater of the soul is more about, I feel that, I experience
that," because "to know something and to experience something are different
things. It's like, perception precedes awareness" (E1).

Tina Cantú Navarro (b. 1942) is the only known Chicana designer. She
began in theatre at San Antonio College and completed her B.A. degrees in art
and theater at Trinity University in San Antonio before continuing in scene
design at the Dallas Theater Center under the direction of Paul Baker. After a
year she took other paths and eventually attended the University of Texas at
Austin, where she studied creative drama and children's theatre before turning
to costume design with Paul Reinhardt. She spent a year as a special student in
the Yale Graduate Program in drama. Ming Cho Lee had been a referee in a regional competition in design and her project had received first place. He soon
took her into a design program at Yale with an emphasis on all three areas of
design: costume, scenery, and lighting.

Navarro studied with Lee and Jane Greenwood, and completed her M.F.A. at Yale in theater design in 1986. Through the New York Local, Navarro became a member of United Scenic Artists Local 829 soon after completing her degree at Yale. Navarro has been involved in numerous new play projects by Latinas. At Yale during the time that Edit Villareal was also a student there, Navarro worked on several projects by Villareal. Most often, she has worked with Milcha Sanchez-Scott, both on new plays and recent productions of earlier works. She designed costumes for the Los Angeles Theatre Center's production of *Roosters,* Berkeley Rep's production of José Rivera's *Each Day Dies with Sleep* (which moved to Circle Rep in New York), and San Francisco's Magic Theatre's production of Nilo Cruz's *A Park in Our House.* Navarro generally works with Roberta Levitow and Mary Donaldson, and demand for her work has taken her to Asolo, Arizona Theatre Company, and the Alley Theatre in Houston.

Margarita Martínez, born in 1946 in Española, has contributed to the development of Chicana/Chicano talent in New Mexico.[10] Her work in the film industry has allowed for further inclusion of such talent at the national level. She is one of only a few Latina producers and casting agents creating opportunities for Latina/Latino actors to be seen on television, film, and stage. She joined her husband in producing records with Latina/Latino musical artists. When she began looking for an opportunity for her own children to act in theatre, she discovered an acting workshop offered by the University of Albuquerque's Multicultural Department in 1977.

The workshop led to the creation of New Mexico's premiere bilingual theatre company, La Compañía de Teatro de Albuquerque. Martínez became the company's first producer, working with artistic director José Rodríguez. She secured financial backing to sustain the company in producing Spanish and bilingual plays specifically targeting the New Mexican Latina/Latino population. In Los Angeles she worked with Carmen Zapata's Bilingual Foundation for the Arts, arranging a state-wide tour of García Lorca's *Bodas de Sangre* (*Blood Wedding*). Her networking with the film industry's actors and production personnel led to work with Columbia Pictures television, where she cast the programs *Who's the Boss* and *Married with Children.* During her three-year contract with Universal Studios she produced a number of film shorts starring Latina/Latino actors in their Hispanic Film Project. Her casting company, Martínez Management, has represented some twenty film performers.

Irene Oliver-Lewis (b. 1949) is another theatre artist with more than twenty years in the field as producer, director, actor, writer, and creative dramatist. Born in Las Cruces, her Latina/Latino family has lived in the Mesilla valley for hundreds of years. She has a B.A. in journalism and theatre from New Mexico State University. Her theatre productions have appeared in the United States, México, and Asia. In 1986, she was named producing artistic director for La Compañía de Teatro de Albuquerque, making her one of only a few Latinas to serve as artistic directors in the country.

During her tenure with the company, she produced and directed a play which became part of the Joseph Papp Festival Latino in New York and the Edinburgh International Festival in Scotland, after which she returned to tour it state-wide. She secured several grants for the company, and they were able to tour extensively within the state and elsewhere. In 1988 she resigned from the company in order to start one of her own, ALMA Productions. Her co-production of *Santa Fe Spirit* received the Wrangler Award for Outstanding Musical from the National Cowboy Hall of Fame in 1989. In her view, "Theater has given me the opportunity to explore, nurture, introduce, or reinforce my culture. My greatest success is that I'm able to do the work I love and believe in and that it has proven to have positive effects on so many people."[11]

Denise Chávez (b. 1948), a playwright, fiction writer, actor, poet, performance artist, director, and teacher, was born in Las Cruces. She won a scholarship in drama to New Mexico State University, receiving her B.S. in drama in 1971. She earned two master's degrees, an M.F.A. in drama from Trinity University in 1974 and an M.A. in creative writing from the University of New Mexico in 1984. She has given numerous readings and performances throughout New Mexico and on college campuses nationwide. She often presents characters from her one-woman show, *Women in the State of Grace,* a narrative weaving scenes about nine women's lives. She has had numerous plays produced, and La Compañía de Teatro de Albuquerque has debuted many of her works. She has had plays produced at the University of Houston, the Edinburgh Festival of the Arts in Scotland, and at the Festival Latino de Nueva York, sponsored by Joseph Papp.

Silviana Wood (b. ?) of Arizona has written numerous plays. Most of her initial work was in adapting children's stories from the Chicana/Chicano tradition, and she soon began to write and stage works as well. She has directed at the Guadalupe Cultural Arts Center in San Antonio, Texas and often holds workshops in writing for the stage. Her efforts to continue Chicana/Chicano *teatro* have been difficult; funding is scarce and company members have changed often. Nevertheless, her work with Teatro Libertad since the mid-1970s and the numerous plays she has written for various venues have been important in sustaining cultural activity in Tucson for a long time. In honor of César Chávez, she recently previewed her new play-in-progress, *Surcos de Oro/ Watered with Tears,* in a play reading at the Guadalupe Cultural Arts Center. The debut of this original, bilingual work inspired by the life of the labor leader and activist is scheduled for the fall of 2000 (Vargas 1999, 1E, 8E).

STAND-UP COMEDY

Stand-up comedy is another arena which has been responsible for greater visibility among Chicanas. San Antonio was recently the site of a whole series of female actors essentially doing performance art via the comedy routine. Sponsored by the Guadalupe Cultural Arts Center, "An Evening of Latina Comedy" included sets by Mary Jo Massara, Josie Cassarez, Lynda Lynch, Sherry Coca-Candelaria, and Irene Peña. The evening featured Ruby Nelda Pérez and Paulina Sahagun, who reprised excerpts from their works, "Doña Rosita's Travelin' Jalapeño" and "Trio Las Girlfriends," respectively. As one reviewer noted, performers credit this type of arena for offering viable opportunities for performance. The current marketing for these events has shown that there is a demand for these performers, and audiences are definitely interested (Saldaña 1998, 1, 12G).

CONTEMPORARY LATINO MALE VOICES
WRITING WOMEN AS SUBJECT: NEW STAGE ROLES

Latino male voices have made great strides in their constructions of women in performance. José Rivera, Octavio Solis, and Guillermo Gómez-Peña are among those who have made the most impact. José Rivera (b. 1955) was born in Puerto Rico. His family moved to Long Island, New York, when he was four. On graduating from Denison University, he returned to New York, joining Theatre Matrix in the Bronx. In 1983, his *The House of Ramon Iglesias,* nominated by Ensemble Studio Theatre, won the FDG/CBS New Play Award. Produced under the direction of Jack Gelber, the teleplay aired nationally as part of the *American Playhouse* series in 1986. *The Promise* (1988) premiered at the Los Angeles Theatre Center, and *Each Day Dies with Sleep* premiered at Berkeley Repertory Theatre in 1990 before its Off-Broadway premiere at Circle Repertory Theatre in 1990.

Rivera's plays revolve around Puerto Rican traditions and culture; they evidence an increasing interest in magical realism (Ramírez, "José Rivera," 400). In 1989, he studied screenwriting with Nobel Prize winner Gabriel García Márquez at the Sundance Institute, and in 1990 he was in residence at the Royal Court Theatre in London. His works tend to be excessively spectacular, drawing away from the stage presence of the actors; his play *Marisol* revolves around a central character in such a way that it provides a substantial role for an actor.

Described as "an apocalyptic urban fantasy in the style of magical realism," *Marisol* won an Obie Award for best Off-Broadway play of 1993. The story revolves around a young Latina who is a copy editor for a Manhattan publisher. After narrowly escaping a physical attack on the subway, Marisol is visited by her guardian angel, who is Black. The angel informs her that she can no longer serve as Marisol's protector; the angel has been called to join in the revolution to save the world. A chaotic heavenly war spills over into New York City, and Marisol is left alone in a nightmare journey. It is a powerful piece, described in *The Village Voice* as "angry, fearsome, fantastic, and poetically frenzied, without surrendering its sanity or its mordant sense of humor. It's a cry from the

José Rivera's *Marisol*. Bonital Oliver (left) and Aleida
Sanabria, Spring 1998.
Courtesy of New World Theatre, under the artistic direction of
Roberta Uno. Photo by Edward Cohen.

poet's heart."[12] Because of the interest in this play on numerous regional stages,
Latinas have been able to garner notable success and notoriety when cast in
this particular role.[13]

Octavio Solis (b. ?), an El Paso, Texas native and former Dallas playwright,
is one of the most commissioned Latino playwrights today. In the 1996 production of *La Posada Magica*, he took the traditional Christmas story of the
search of Mary and Jesus for a place to sleep as the basis for a re-telling of this
Chicana/Chicano yearly re-enactment found in any neighborhood throughout the Southwest. Gracie, a young girl who has recently suffered the loss of
her baby brother, wants no part of the holiday. The community rallies around
her, but when she refuses them she is cast into a dark journey that culminates in
her embrace of others in the true meaning of Christmas.

Guillermo Gómez-Peña has been highly noted for his controversial performances about some of the most heated national debates today. Confronting
immigration issues, examining colonized cultures, and staging a "border" experience that cannot be explained in Western European terms, his look at "bi-

Vilma Silva as the bride and Vetza Trussel as the mother in García
Lorca's *Blood Wedding*, Oregon Shakespeare Festival, directed by Jim
Edmundson (1995). Both actors are Latinas. Silva trained at the
American Conservatory Theatre in San Francisco and has been a
member of the OSF company since 1995.
Photo by T. Charles Erickson. Courtesy of Oregon Shakespeare Festival.

cultural Latinos in the United States (be they Chicanos, Nuyoricans, or others)
and monocultural citizens of Latin American" tells us about conflict in our
society (Gómez-Peña 1994, 17–29). The term most associated with this artist,
who recently received the MacArthur "genius" award for his work, is intercultural performance, and by writing and staging his own work, he has been successful in broadening the scope of performance art to political identity.

Other contributions by Latinos in performance have been made by community agencies working directly on issues of AIDS, homophobia, and discrimination. The gay and lesbian artists Luis Alfaro and Monica Palacios are
project directors for Teatro VIVA in Los Angeles where a safe-sex program
targets the gay and lesbian population (Sandoval 1994, 54).

ASSESSMENTS

Chicanas seem to have had a more difficult time gaining recognition in theatre
than Latinas on the East Coast. The collective organizational structure of the
teatros served to support their work in theatre, but they were also hampered in
many ways by traditional lifestyles and expectations. Chicanas found the sexism
within the Chicana/Chicano Movement excessive. Many soon found various

The Nurse (Susan Corzatte, *right*) delivers the heartbreaking news to Juliet (Vilma Silva) in the Oregon Shakespeare Festival's 1996 production of William Shakespeare's *Romeo and Juliet*. Directed by René Buch, scenic design by Richard L. Hay, costume design by Susan Mickey, lighting design by Robert Peterson. Photo by Andrée Lanthier. Courtesy of Oregon Shakespeare Festival.

Diane Rodríguez in *The Ballad of Ginger Esparza* by Luis Alfaro and Diane Rodríguez. The Mark Taper Forum's New Work Festival 1995, Los Angeles, California.
Photo by Craig Schwartz Photography. Courtesy of Diane Rodríguez.

means of expression to address their issues and concerns. Joanne Pottlitzer mentions that Silviana Wood used to solve the problem of taking care of her children during rehearsals and having to stay at home with them while her company went on tour by writing children's roles into her plays so her children could be with her. While the instances in which women were integrally involved in decision-making positions and running companies were scarce, subsequent headway was made once regional stages began to broaden their offerings to include Latina/Latino plays, actors, and other members of production teams.

Although they are few, the emergence of producing organizations and the availability of more regional stages for acting, directing, and play development (among other areas of theatrical activity) have resulted in more Chicana voices in the theatre throughout the United States. In 1986 Brava, founded that year in San Francisco, California by Ellen Gavin, aimed to "help emerging and professional women artists gain greater visibility and increase audiences for their work, and to help them increase their professionalism," as Charlotte Canning notes in her important study on *Feminist Theaters in the U.S.A.* (Canning 1996, 213). The Latina project under Brava helped fund productions and sponsor workshopping of new works. In the 1990s a more effective dialogue was begun between organizations and artists, calling attention to the work of others and helping to nurture and strengthen the work itself. We see more and more training and effective writing than ever before, and venues in which to produce the works. We have also started to see increased attention to women's roles in plays by men, allowing for a broader range of parts for female actors and better opportunities for performance.

CONCLUSION
APPROACHING THE MILLENNIUM:
LEGACIES AND CHANGING TRENDS

To date, American theatre history and criticism tell us that Latinas/Latinos, the fastest-growing underrepresented ethnic group in the United States, comprise the second largest group (after African Americans) to develop ethnic theatre. However, this group, as well as all other underrepresented groups in the United States, has been largely neglected and ignored, and chronicles and scholarship of this history have been sadly lacking. This book has attempted to provide a history of the Chicana/Latina experience on the American stage in order to broaden the scope of historical inquiry.

Many forms of Spanish-language entertainment, both amateur and professional, have flourished within the United States. Dating back to the sixteenth century, Spanish-language theatre predates the first English-speaking theatre on this continent. The tradition of educating the Indians through religious drama, begun by the first friars in México, was continued by the Spanish colonists throughout the Southwest. During the nineteenth century and perhaps earlier, Spanish-language acting companies arrived in the Southwest from México and Spain, forming a lasting tradition in the U.S. Mexican American professional theatre that thrived for about fifty years in Texas, California, and other regions of the Southwest, the Midwest, and the East. With the coming of radio and film, especially during the Great Depression, Mexican American theatre died out, only to be revived again in the 1960s with the founding of El Teatro Campesino. The success of that company gave rise to a whole generation of Latina/Latino theatre groups.

The historical antecedents of Latinas/Latinos in the United States provided the roots for theatrical expression, but this heritage remained dormant for several years before Luis Valdez reawakened it on the contemporary stage. Contemporary Latina/Latino theatre represents diverse backgrounds. A 1985 survey found 101 Latina/Latino theatre groups: 29 Chicana/Chicano, 24 Cuban, 28 Puerto Rican, and 20 of other Latina/Latino backgrounds.[1] El Teatro Campesino, the best known of these groups, was founded by Luis Valdez in 1965. This Chicana/Chicano theatre company first sought to show the plight of the farm workers in California and subsequently broadened its scope to include social, political, and cultural issues revolving around the Chicana/Chicano experience in the United States.

For more than twenty-five years, the Teatro's history was one of creativity, work, and change. From the early *actos* that first demonstrated the plight of striking farm workers to its position as a leader in alternative theatre, El Teatro Campesino continued to evolve and grow as it sought to reach a mass audience. In 1978, *Zoot Suit* was an immediate success on one of the major regional stages in the United States. Luis Valdez had ventured through an odyssey that led to this culmination of his work in theatre. But by 1980, after Valdez and El Teatro had worked with the people, he came to realize that the "powerful weapon of theatre" could also reach a broader audience. Through various notable works, Valdez and his internationally known company continued to impress their audiences and critics, and by 1987 Valdez ventured farther afield as a leading Chicano filmmaker. Yet, his work and that of El Teatro Campesino began a movement that influenced the development of a Chicana/Latina presence on the American stage that came to prominence in the 1990s.

Other influences besides Valdez and El Teatro Campesino impacted on the evolution of the Chicana/Latina voice. Today, the trend in Chicana/Latina theatre is toward professionalism, with practitioners who are paid for their work in the theatre. Chicana/Latina playwrights, directors, actors, directors, designers, dramaturges, and technicians in both professional and in amateur community-based activity continue to serve their respective communities. The shift from amateur to professional took us from the period of cultural nationalism and striving for identity through political activism toward the broader inclusion of Chicanas/Chicanos/Latinas/Latinos in mainstream performance.

The venues have changed, and the topic of the urgent need to survive has shifted to the economic struggles of Chicanas/Chicanos reflected on regional stages across the United States. But the future indicates that the progress we have seen in this long history will continue. Latina/Latino theatre in the United States is highly diversified in artistic expression and cultural heritage. There is little reason to believe that the growth in the Latina/Latino population will cease. This population numbers over 18.7 million Chicanas/Chicanos, Cubans, Puerto Ricans, Dominicans, Central Americans, and South Americans in the fifty states and more than 3.3 million Puerto Ricans living in Puerto Rico. With all of its diversity, Latina/Latino expression, stemming from as far back as when the conquistadores provided the first dramatic performance on American soil, continues to make a significant, vital contribution to the theatre of the United States.

The current attempts to address multiculturalism and diversity can shed light on practical means to understand other cultures within the dominant community. For several years now, there has been concern and anxiety about multiculturalism and diversity in the United States. As we have evaluated social policies related to multicultural development, we have witnessed little success. Individuals along the entire political and economic spectrum seem to be growing impatient, a matter made especially crucial because of changing U.S. demographics. If we do not find workable solutions to the multicultural issue, "a fragmented, highly factionalized society" will result.[2] The changing demographic mix in the United States requires changing ideology and practice (Pear 1992, A1, 10).

Instead of turning the issues into "political action, protest and street theatre," demanding "equal rights and cultural recognition" for all, with each group competing, "demanding its own share of media attention, admiration, awards and foundation funding," as Robert Brustein fears, we must first find the positive value of these issues.[3] I would argue for an "intercultural" approach, or perhaps a broader cross-cultural exploration. Cherríe Moraga envisions a much more radical change in order to sustain this voice in an America that continues to be "fractured and disintegrating," as she states: "I hold a vision requiring a radical transformation of consciousness in this country, that as the people-of-color population increases, we will not be just another brown faceless mass hungrily awaiting integration into white Amerika [sic], but that we will emerge as a mass movement of people to redefine what an 'American' is."[4] Clearly, omitting or ignoring the contributions that people of color have made to the multicultural richness of theatrical history is not the answer.[5]

In the history presented here it is clear that the Chicana/Latina contribution is vast and requires its place in theatre history. As Jorge Huerta points out, if Chicana/Chicano plays are to survive in non-Chicano venues, "then it is incumbent upon those companies to educate themselves to guarantee that they are culturally competent."[6] Guillermo Gómez-Peña notes that "a whole generation of artists and intellectuals have begun the dialogue." These are artists, writers, and arts administrators, and, he adds: "From these people, the most vocal and enlightened are women. They are the true cultural leaders of our communities."[7]

For Chicanas/Chicanos/Latinas/Latinos renewal of community, of connecting and discovering history and culture, can come through performance, whereby language is heard, visual icons are presented, and reconnections with a culture that will not die ensure continual Chicana/Chicano/Latina/Latino expression. If non-Latina/Latino theatres want to produce Latina/Latino plays, they must begin by grounding themselves and educating themselves about that culture and experience before they attempt to offer that experience to others. Distinctions between Latinas/Latinos must be understood and respected, language differences and capabilities must be considered, and audience tastes and demands must be satisfied. Yet, despite changing trends and forms in theatrical discourse and practice, it seems clear that the cultural centers that have formed around Latina/Latino theatrical activity have provided continuity because of community participation and support. The fact that more and more regional stages are targeting these audiences ensures an even broader representation of the Latina/Latino voice as we enter the next millennium.

NOTES

Introduction

1. The term Latina/Latino will be used here to designate the larger population of women and men in the United States who are descended from Spanish-speaking groups. The terms Hispanic and Mexican American are used in relation to specific periods of history and tradition and are distinguished from the term Chicana/Chicano, which will be used to designate the period from the 1960s to the present. It will also be used to denote women and men residing within the United States for any length of time. Although the term has a certain ideological and political meaning connected to the Chicano Movement, research supports the view that this term is generally accepted as appropriate for this particular underrepresented group in the United States. The slash will be used where appropriate to make Spanish terms gender inclusive. See Frank de Varona, *Latino Literacy: The Complete Guide to Our Hispanic History and Culture* (New York: Henry Holt, 1996); and Earl Shorris, *Latinos: A Biography of the People* (New York: W.W. Norton, 1992).

1. Homeland/Sin Fronteras to Borderlands

1. See Francis Borgia Steck, *Motolinia's History of the Indians of New Spain* (Washington: Academy of American Franciscan History, 1959), 167; for sources of Spanish text see Jorge A. Huerta, *Chicano Theater: Themes and Forms* (Ypsilanti, Mich.: Bilingual Press, 1982), 191–192, and 237n14. For the only English translation of the Náhuatl version see Marilyn Ravicz, *Early Colonial Religious Drama in Mexico* (Washington, D.C.: Catholic University of America Press, 1970), 83–98.

2. Frances Gillmor, "Spanish Texts of Three Dance Dramas from Mexican Villages," *University of Arizona Bulletin* 13 (October 1942): 3–83. The entire text of an extant copy of *Los Moros y Los Cristianos* is available in this issue. See George C. D. Odell, *Annals of the New York Stage,* vol. 1 (New York: Columbia University Press, 1927).

3. See Jeanette Rodriguez, *Our Lady of Guadalupe: Faith and Empowerment among Mexican-American Women* (Austin: University of Texas Press, 1994).

4. Aurelio M. Espinosa, trans., "Los Comanches," *University of New Mexico Bulletin,* Language Series 1 (1907): 1–46; Gilberto Espinosa, trans., *Los Comanches,* in *New Mexico Quarterly* 1 (May 1931): 133–146; Aurelio M. Espinosa and J. Manuel Espinosa, trans., "The Texans: A New Mexican Folk Play of the Middle Nineteenth Century," *New Mexico Quarterly Review* 13 (Autumn 1943): 299–309.

5. See Edward Murguía, *Assimilation, Colonialism and the Mexican American People* (Austin, Tex.: Center for Mexican American Studies, 1975), 1–124; and Robert J. Rosenbaum, *Mexicano Resistance in the Southwest: "The Sacred Right of Self-Preservation"* (Austin: University of Texas Press, 1981).

6. My research draws primarily on rare collections of plays, playbills, and memorabilia in the Mexican American Project of the Benson Latin American Collection at the

University of Texas at Austin and on the extensive Spanish-language newspaper collection at the Eugene C. Barker Texas History Center in Austin, along with private collections and accounts.

7. See Elizabeth C. Ramírez, "Concepción Hernández," *The New Handbook of Texas*, edited by Ron Tyler, et al. (Austin: Texas Historical Association, 1996).

8. Carlos Villalongín, "Memoirs," newspaper clipping from Matamoros, México, "Por el Teatro," February 20, 1910, 95–96. A copy of a newspaper review is found in Carlos Villalongín's unpublished memoirs found in the private collection of his daughter, Sra. María Luisa Villalongín de Santos, San Antonio, Texas.

9. Ibid.

10. Concepción Hernández performed at the Teatro Aurora, the Teatro Zaragoza, and the Teatro Salón San Fernando in San Antonio and toured throughout the Rio Grande valley until her retirement in the early 1920s. Later in life she married Alberto Orozco, Jr., the properties master and an infrequent actor with the company. She remained a resident of San Antonio until her death.

11. *La Prensa* [San Antonio], November 21, 1926, 5, 7; December 28, 1926, 10; December 31, 1926, 10; January 6, 1927, 5, 6; January 13, 1927, 4; January 23, 1927, 8.

12. *La Prensa* [San Antonio], April 4, 1923; November 25 and November 28, 1926; May 2, 1928; Manuel Mañon, *Historia del Teatro Principal de México* (México: Editorial "Cultura," 1932), 152.

13. "Benavente vuelve muy satisfecho a México" [Benavente returns to México very satisfied], *La Prensa*, March 26, 1923, 1; March 28, 1923, 1; December 9, 1926, 5, 10; "'Una mujer sin importancia' de Oscar Wilde en el Teatro Nacional," November 26, 1926, 5; "'El abanico de Lady Windemere' de Oscar Wilde," December 5, 1926, 15.

2. The Critical Role of the Mexican Revolution and Its Impact on the American Stage

1. Ramón Eduardo Ruíz titles his book on the subject of the Mexican Revolution *The Great Rebellion*. See *The Great Rebellion: Mexico 1905–1924* (New York: W.W. Norton, 1980).

2. The promptbook of *La llorona* was copied by Luis Hernández in San Antonio, Texas, on August 31, 1911. Hernández was one of the members of the Compañía Hernández-Villalongín. See Promptbook #54 in the Carlos Villalongín Dramatic Company Collection.

3. Sra. María Luisa Villalongín de Santos, Sr.; Carlos Villalongín, Jr.; and Sr. Lalo Astol, San Antonio, Texas, May 1981; *El Demócrata Fronterizo*, Laredo, Texas, December 22, 1906, 2; *La Prensa*, San Antonio, Texas, April 6, 1915, 8; November 21, 1917, 7; and February 18, 1918, 2; *Evolución*, Laredo, Texas, December 14, 1918, 4; and Limón, 1990, 414–415.

4. The border patrol of the Immigration Service was not established until 1924. As Carey McWilliams tells us, "Prior to 1924 the border could be crossed, in either direction, at almost any point from Brownsville to San Diego, with the greatest of ease." See Carey McWilliams, *North from Mexico* (New York: Greenwood Press, 1968), 59–62.

5. See Ricardo Romo, *East Lost Angeles: History of a Barrio* (Austin, Tex.: University of Texas Press, 1983) and Mario T. García, "Border Culture," in *From Different Shores: Perspectives on Race and Ethnicity in America,* ed. Ronald Takaki (New York: Oxford University Press, 1994) for more about the family.

6. Acuña draws much of this information from the in-depth study by Mario T. García for his dissertation. See "Obreros: The Mexican Workers of El Paso, 1900–1920" (Ph.D. diss., University of California at San Diego, 1975).

7. *El Demócrata Fronterizo* reported a performance of *La mujer adúltera* in Laredo, Texas, on June 17, 1905, by the Compañía Dramática Solórzano, calling the drama a "beautiful" and "sensational" *joya del teatro Español* [gem of the Spanish theatre], but the advertisement attributed the work to Pérez Escrich instead of Velázquez.

8. See Elizabeth C. Ramírez, *Footlights Across the Border: A History of Spanish-Language Professional Theatre on the Texas Stage* for an extensive study of the repertory and bill of nineteenth- and twentieth-century professional theatrical troupes appearing in the United States from Spain and México.

3. Barrios, Borderlands, and Mujeres

1. For more extensive discussion of community building by Mexican Americans, see "The Building of the Southwest: Mexican Labor, 1900–1930" and "Mexican American Communities in the Making: The Depression Years," in Rodolfo Acuña, *Occupied America: A History of Chicanos*, 3rd ed. (New York: HarperCollins Publishers, 1988); David G. Gutiérrez, *Walls and Mirrors: Mexican Americans, Mexican Immigrants, and the Politics of Ethnicity* (Berkeley: University of California Press, 1995); and Ronald Takaki, *A Different Mirror: A History of Multicultural America* (Boston: Little, Brown and Company, 1993).

2. See Moisés Sandoval, *On the Move: A History of the Hispanic Church in the United States* (New York: Orbis, 1990); Joseph P. Fitzpatrick, *Puerto Rican Americans: The Meaning of Migration to the Mainland,* 2nd ed. (New York: Prentice Hall, 1987); and Denis Lynn Daly Heyck, *Barrios and Borderlands: Cultures of Latinos and Latinas in the United States* (New York: Routledge, 1994).

3. See José Llanes, *Cuban Americans: Masters of Survival* (Cambridge, Mass.: Abt Books, 1982); Sandoval, *On the Move;* Earl Shorris, *Latinos: A Biography of the People* (New York: W.W. Norton and Co., 1992); and Heyck, *Barrios and Borderlands.*

4. Upon her return from New York to their home in San Antonio, Chata Noloesca married her third husband, Ruben Escobedo, a San Antonio musician. She worked in radio and continued to do live performances, including many benefits, through the 1970s. In 1975 she was honored by the Mexican National Association of Actors in San Antonio. She died in San Antonio on April 4, 1979. Interview with Sra. Belia Camargo, Noloesca's daughter, San Antonio, Texas, July 15, 1981. Sra. Camargo performed for many years in San Antonio upon settling there and eventually married Sr. Mateo Camargo, an important figure in Spanish-language radio performance.

5. Tey Diana Rebolledo (*Women Singing in the Snow*) and Raymund A. Paredes ("Mexican-American Literature: An Overview") both include Josephina Niggli (b. 1910) in their discussions of Chicana narrative. Rebolledo, citing Gloria Treviño, views Niggli as an early Chicana writer who wrote in English. Niggli was born in México and lived there until her family fled the Mexican Revolution when she was three; they returned to live in México from 1920 to 1925, and then moved to San Antonio, Texas. Known as a playwright, she published one-act plays and essays on drama. However, her parents are Scandinavian American and, therefore, discussion of her work will not be included in this study. Niggli's work deals with identity and issues about heritage and being an outsider in both Mexican and American societies.

6. This term has been used in a variety of ways. David G. Gutiérrez provides a helpful explanation of the distinct use of this term historically and in the present: "al-

though La Raza is a term that today has come to mean the entire mestizo population of greater Latin America, in the last third of the nineteenth century Mexican Americans often employed the term to describe the Mexican 'race' on both sides of the new border" (*Walls and Mirrors*, 35). He adds that "use of group terms as La Raza varied widely from region to region, but given the historical heterogeneity of the Spanish-speaking population the use of such terminology by Mexican Americans to describe campaigns of protest and resistance in Texas, New Mexico, and California is remarkable." The term may be used in reference to the Mexican population in California or anywhere that a large population of people from that ethnic group exist, or it may refer to the Hispanic race or people, and, as Richard Griswold del Castillo tells us in *The Los Angeles Barrio, 1850–1890* (Berkeley: University of California Press, 1979), there are many ways of using this term, depending on the context. "La Raza Mexicana," "La Raza Hispano-Americana," "La Raza Española," and "La Raza Latina" were all used "to convey a sense of the racial, class, and national variety within the Spanish-speaking community," but Griswold adds, "in general the use of 'La Raza' implied membership in a cultural tradition that was separate from" that of Euroamericans (133–134).

7. See Yolanda Broyles-González, *El Teatro Campesino: Theater in the Chicano Movement* (Austin: University of Texas Press, 1994).

8. These studies include David Montejano, *Anglos and Mexicans in the Making of Texas, 1836–1989* (Austin: University of Texas Press, 1987), 257–287; Rodolfo Acuña, *Occupied America*; Juan Gómez-Quiñones, *Chicano Politics: Reality and Promise, 1940–1990* (Albuquerque: University of New Mexico Press, 1990); and David G. Gutiérrez, *Walls and Mirrors*.

9. See Broyles-González, *El Teatro Campesino*, 97.

10. Don B. Wilmeth and Tice L. Miller, *Cambridge Guide to American Theatre* (New York: Cambridge University Press, 1993), 411.

11. See Jorge A. Huerta, *Chicano Theater: Themes and Forms* (Ypsilanti, Mich.: Bilingual Press, 1982).

12. Luis Valdez, comments from Playwriting Workshop, San Juan Bautista, 1973; also see David Savran, "Border Tactics: Luis Valdez Distills the Chicano Experience on Stage and Film," *American Theatre Magazine* (January 1988): 14–21, 56–57.

13. See Oscar G. Brockett and Robert Findlay, *Century of Innovation: A History of European and American Theatre and Drama Since the Late Nineteenth Century*, 2nd ed. (Boston, Mass.: Allyn and Bacon, 1991), 139. In the chapter on "Forging a New Art of the Theatre," Brockett and Findlay point out that "the most important event in the French theatre of the time occurred in 1913 when Theatre du Vieux Columbier was founded by Jacques Copeau (1879–1949), who would dominate the French theatre between the two world wars as thoroughly as Antoine had in the years before World War I." Copeau "proclaimed that the renovation of the stage required a return to the bare stage (*le tréteau nu*), since only then could attention be focussed fully on the actor, the essence of the theatre as the 'living presence' of the author." For Copeau, as Brockett and Findlay note, "the director's ultimate task was the transformation of a written text," which the director has studied until every nuance is understood, "into a 'poetry of the theatre,' of which acting is the principal ingredient and in which decor should be reduced to absolute essentials."

14. See the chronology provided by Davis in *The San Francisco Mime Troupe: The First Ten Years* where he cites Valdez's participation in numerous events (199, 201, 208, and 211).

15. See Broyles-González, *El Teatro Campesino*, 80.

16. Broyles-González states that "the special contributions of women are among those facets that are absent in the writing of theatre history" (Broyles-González 1996, 132). Any scholar who might question Huerta's inclusion of women in his significant early work on Chicana/Chicano theatre must look closely at the numerous entries that shed light on the notable role that Chicanas played in the evolution of *teatro*. See Huerta, *Chicano Theater,* 119–127, 140–153, 161–167, and 192 for some examples. Huerta has given me sound nurturing, instilling a responsibility to pursue the study of theatre as the only Chicana with a doctoral degree in theatre; he also has been a supportive and collaborative colleague. I have had the opportunity to participate in numerous rehearsals, workshops, and presentations in which Huerta's attention to the voices of Chicanas/Latinas has led to greater contributions by this group.

17. Rodolfo Acuña describes the Brown Berets as the "counterpart of the Black Panthers and the Puerto Rican Young Lords. Formed in East Los Angeles in 1967, the Young Citizens for Community Action was a group sponsored by an interfaith church organization which evolved from a community service club into an 'alert patrol'" (Acuña 1988, 337).

18. W. B. Worthen has written about the issues involved in the uses of history in the staging of ethnic identities in his article "Staging América: The Subject of History in Chicano/a Theatre," *Theatre Journal* 49, no. 2 (May 1997): 101–120.

19. See commentary on cover of Rodolfo Gonzales, *I Am Joaquín* (New York: Bantam Books, 1972).

4. The Emergence of a Latina Stage

1. U.S. Bureau of the Census, *The Hispanic Population in the United States: March 1986 and March 1987,* Advance Report, ser. P20 #416 (Washington, D.C.: U.S. Government Printing Office, 1986), 2, 5; U.S. Bureau of the Census Estimates Reports, *Estimates Report of the Population of Puerto Rico and the Outlying Areas: 1980–1986,* #P25–1009 (Washington, D.C.: U.S. Government Printing Office, 1986), 7; Joanne Pottlitzer, *Hispanic Theater in the United States and Puerto Rico* (New York: Ford Foundation, 1988), 1–5; Juan Gómez-Quiñones, *Chicano Politics: Reality and Promise, 1940–1990* (Albuquerque: University of New Mexico Press, 1990), 73, 191–192; Robert Pear, "New Look at the U.S. in 2050: Bigger, Older, and Less White," *New York Times,* December 4, 1992, A1, 10; Tom Bower, "Hispanic Count on the Increase," *San Antonio Express-News,* September 4, 1998, Section M, B1.

2. No information was available from this group in the questionnaire responses I gathered for my master's thesis at the University of California, Los Angeles (1974) entitled "The Annals of Chicano Theater: 1965–1973."

3. This style was first introduced by Los Mascarones, a Mexican troupe that was an active member of TENAZ. See Ramírez, "The Annals," 1974.

4. Unpublished script of *Bernabé* obtained from Luis Valdez for the production I directed at California State University, Sacramento, 1975.

5. See Elizabeth Salas, *Soldaderas in the Mexican Military* (Austin, Tex.: University of Texas Press, 1990), which includes discussion about both the historical figure as well as contemporary representations within the Chicana/Chicano Movement through the 1980s; and Julia Tuñon Pablos, *Women in Mexico: A Past Unveiled,* trans. Alan Hynds (Austin, Tex.: University of Texas Press Institute of Latin American Studies, 1999), 85–91.

6. Conversations with the actors and with Luis Valdez at the 1973 *teatro* festival in

San Jose, California, and follow-up telephone conversations with Smiley Rojas and others in preparation for staging this work at California State University, Sacramento, in 1974.

7. Alfonso Caso, *The Aztecs: People of the Sun* (Norman: University of Oklahoma Press, 1958), 32–33, 53; and Miguel León-Portilla, *Pre-Columbian Literatures of Mexico* (Norman: University of Oklahoma Press, 1969), 43–48. In these texts, the legend of Tonatiuh is explained. He is the god who in the guise of Huitzilopóchtli struggles nightly against the stars to rise every day.

8. Miguel León-Portilla, *Pre-Columbian Literatures of Mexico*. The lineage of Indians from which the Chicana/Chicano stems is discussed in this text.

9. Ibid., 31–32, 38, 140–141, for descriptions of the "bloody" sacrifices; also in Caso, *The Aztecs*, 67.

10. See León-Portilla, *Pre-Columbian Literatures*, 61–62 for an explanation of the legend of the wise man who becomes a god when he dies.

11. *Dark Root of a Scream*, published in Lillian Faderman and Omar Salinas, compilers, *From the Barrio: A Chicano Anthology* (San Francisco: Canfield Press, 1973), 79–98. See Dan Sullivan, "Homecoming of a Dead GI," *Los Angeles Times*, September 25, 1971, II, 8, for a review of the production; also Huerta, *Chicano Theater*, 1982, 97–103 and 113–114 especially.

12. *La Bamba* (1987) represents Luis Valdez's most recognized work on film.

13. *Corrido* is a term used for the musical form of traditional narrative ballads. See Américo Paredes, *A Texas-Mexican "Cancionero": Folksongs of the Lower Border* (Urbana: University of Illinois Press, 1976); and *"With His Pistol in His Hand": A Border Ballad and Its Hero* (Urbana: University of Illinois Press, 1958).

14. See Sandra Messinger Cypess, *La Malinche in Mexican Literature: From History to Myth* (Austin: University of Texas Press, 1991) for further reading on the La Malinche figure.

15. See Ramírez, "The Annals of Chicano Theater," for a comprehensive listing of all known extant groups in the United States from the inception in 1965 to 1973.

16. See my review on Kent's work in *Choice* 34, no. 4 (December 1996).

17. This text is another valuable addition to an already impressive series on *Theatre: Theory/Text/Performance* under the editorship of Enoch Brater at the University of Michigan Press.

18. Personal interview with Maria Irene Fornes, Northwest Theatre Conference, Eugene, Oregon, 1996.

19. See Scott Cummings, "Seeing with Clarity: The Visions of Maria Irene Fornes," *Theater* 17, no. 1 (1985): 51–56, for more about Maria Irene Fornes and the playwriting workshops.

5. The Emerging Chicana Playwright

1. See the following articles in Hector Calderón and José David Saldívar, eds., *Criticism in the Borderlands* (Durham: Duke University Press, 1991): Ramón Saldívar, "Narrative, Ideology, and the Reconstruction of American Literary History," 11–20; Norma Alarcón, "The Theoretical Subject(s) of *This Bridge Called My Back* and Anglo-American Feminism," 28–38; and Sonia Saldívar-Hull, "Feminism on the Border: From Gender Politics to Geopolitics," 203–220.

2. Portions of this section on Estela Portillo Trambley have been published in my review of her book. See Elizabeth C. Ramírez, "Estela Portillo Trambley, 'Sor Juana'

and Other Plays," *Latin American Theatre Review* (Spring 1984): 103–104. The Estela Portillo Trambley papers dating from 1969 to 1978 are available in the Benson Latin American Collection at the University of Texas at Austin. This collection includes holograph and typescript manuscripts, working drafts, scripts, notes, notebooks, plays, short stories, essays, poems, music sheets, a novela and novel, programs, leaflets, newsclippings, letters, and eight cassette tapes.

3. *Day of the Swallows,* published in Roberto J. Garza, ed., *Contemporary Chicano Theater* (Notre Dame: University of Notre Dame Press, 1976), 206–245; Philip D. Ortego, *We Are Chicanos: An Anthology of Mexican-American Literature* (New York: Washington Square Press, 1973), 224–271; and Octavio Romano-V and Herminio Ríos, eds., *El Espejo—The Mirror: Selected Chicano Literature* (Berkeley: Quinto Sol, 1972), 149–193.

4. Interview with Estela Portillo Trambley, California State University, Sacramento, 1974.

5. See "About the Author" in the Dramatists Play Service text of Milcha Sanchez-Scott's play *Roosters* (New York: Dramatists Play Service, 1988).

6. Program notes, Martin Luther King Jr. Theater Company, *Real Women Have Curves,* Eugene, Oregon, 1992, author's private collection.

7. Jorge Huerta, "Moraga's *Heroes and Saints:* Chicano Theatre for the '90s," *Theatre Forum* 1 (Spring 1992): 49–52.

8. Moraga wrote, "I want to thank Luis Valdez for his play *The Shrunken Head of Pancho Villa,* whose head character became, for me, a point of departure. I also wish to thank El Teatro Campesino for allowing me access to their archives on the McFarland Situation." Cherríe Moraga, *Heroes and Saints and Other Plays* (Albuquerque: West End Press, 1994), 89.

9. A form drawn from the choral poetry style introduced by Los Mascarones in the 1970s and performed during the many collaborative workshops and festivals produced jointly by TENAZ and CLETA, the sister organization of Mexican teatros. Perhaps more closely associated with the work by Dorinda Moreno in the Bay Area, the form incorporated poetry, prose, dance, mime/pantomime, and the *corrido.* See Ramírez, "Annals of Chicano Theater," 59–64, 229, and 259; and Ramírez, Private Collection of TENAZ, and CLETA correspondence, brochures, and printed materials.

6. Current Trends and Practices

1. A portion of this chapter was published as "Chicanas/Latinas in Performance on the American Stage: Current Trends & Practices" in the *Journal of Dramatic Theory and Criticism* 13 (Fall 1998): 133–141.

2. Jorge Huerta points out an important concern among Chicanas/Chicanos/Latinas/Latinos in performance, namely, the prominence of Euroamerican women directing Latina/Latino and Latin American plays: "Female directors of any background are grossly underrepresented in the regional theatres, but why should non-Latinas be chosen to direct ethno-specific plays that have nothing to do with their own backgrounds?" "Looking for the Magic: Chicanos in the Mainstream," in *Negotiating Performance,* edited by Diana Taylor and Juan Villegas (Durham: Duke University Press, 1994), 41–42.

3. The full playtext is published in the anthology edited by Linda Feyder, *Shattering the Myth: Plays by Hispanic Women* (Houston, Tex.: Arte Público Press, 1992), 51–83.

4. A joint award given in 1999 to Cheryl West for *Before It Hits Home* and Rona Munro of Edinburgh for *Bold Girls*. See Wilborn Hampton, "Reviews/Theater," *New York Times*, June 21, 1988, C 16.

5. The full playtext is published in Feyder, *Shattering the Myth*, 143–208.

6. Information on this company is drawn from their Publicity and Press Kit in the author's private collection.

7. Publicity and Press Kit.

8. Interview, production history of the play, and full playtext of *1992: Blood Speaks*, published in Kathy A. Perkins and Roberta Uno, eds., *Contemporary Plays by Women of Color* (New York: Routledge, 1996), 79–89.

9. Telephone interview with Mr. Julia's publicist, Cambridge, Mass., 1989.

10. Tey Diana Rebolledo, ed., *Nuestras Mujeres: Hispanas of New Mexico* (Albuquerque, N.M.: El Norte Publications, 1992), 90–91.

11. Ibid., 91–92.

12. Marpessa Dawn Outlaw, "War of Angels," *The Village Voice*, May 25, 1993, pp. 90, 92.

13. I directed *Marisol* at the University of Oregon in 1994.

Conclusion

1. Joanne Pottlitzer, *Hispanic Theater in the United States and Puerto Rico* (New York: Ford Foundation, 1988). This is a report to the Ford Foundation.

2. Open hearing on the subject of "Diversity and Multicultural Concerns: Their Impact on the Preparation of Theatre Professionals," in "Notes and Sample Issues," presented by the National Association of Schools of Theatre (NAST) for discussion by the Task Force on Multicultural Concerns at the 1991 Annual Meeting and Retreat, Tucson, Arizona. Members of the Task Force included Winona Fletcher, Oscar G. Brockett, and Elizabeth C. Ramírez.

3. Robert Brustein, "A House Divided," *American Theatre Magazine* 8, no. 7 (October 1991): 45.

4. See Cherríe Moraga, "Art in America con Acento," in *Negotiating Performance: Gender, Sexuality, and Theatricality in Latin/o America*, ed. Diana Taylor and Juan Villegas (Durham: Duke University Press, 1994).

5. Citing Guillermo Gómez-Peña's work as "among the most powerful examples of intercultural performance," Richard Schechner argues for an "intercultural" approach, which he describes as the following: "Where multiculturalism falters, where fusion does not occur, interculturalism happens. Just as mountains rise where continents collide, and deep ocean basins form where they pull apart, so new arts, behaviors, and human interactions are negotiated at the interfaces and faults connecting and separating cultures." See Richard Schechner, "An Intercultural Primer," *American Theatre Magazine* 8, no. 7 (October 1991): 30, 135.

6. See Jorge Huerta, "Looking for the Magic: Chicanos in the Mainstream," in *Negotiating Performance: Gender, Sexuality, and Theatricality in Latin/o America*, ed. Diana Taylor and Juan Villegas, 37–48.

7. See Guillermo Gómez-Peña, "The Multicultural Paradigm: An Open Letter to the National Arts Community," in *Negotiating Performance: Gender, Sexuality, and Theatricality in Latin/o America*, ed. Diana Taylor and Juan Villegas, 17–29.

WORKS CITED

SPECIAL COLLECTIONS

Astol, Lalo. Promptbooks. Benson Latin American Collection, University of Texas at Austin.

Coatlicue Theatre Company Press Kit. Collection of the author.

López, Josefina. *Real Women Have Curves.* Unpublished ms. Courtesy Tina E. Cantú Navarro, Costume Designer for Asolo Production, Florida.

Neve, Francisco. *La Llorona.* Date unknown. Promptbook #54, copy dated August 31, 1911, in the Carlos Villalongín Dramatic Company Collection. Benson Latin American Collection, University of Texas at Austin.

Ramírez, Elizabeth C. Personal archives of the author. Includes photographs, programs, and other materials; and TENAZ and CLETA correspondence, brochures, and printed materials. San Antonio, Texas.

Sanchez-Scott, Milcha. *The Old Matador.* Unpublished ms. Elizabeth C. Ramírez, Dramaturg, Arizona Theatre Company Production, Tucson, Arizona.

Santos, Sra. María Luisa Villalongín de. Private Collection. Includes numerous photographs, promptbooks, and unpublished memoirs of Carlos Villalongín. San Antonio, Texas.

El Teatro Campesino Archives. San Juan Bautista, California.

TENAZ Collection. San Juan Bautista, California.

Trambley, Estela Portillo. Literary productions, personal and biographical materials, plays, prose fiction, essays, and poetry. Benson Latin American Collection, University of Texas at Austin.

Valdez, Luis. *Dark Root of a Scream* and *Bernabé.* Unpublished mss. Collection of the author.

Velásquez, Juan P. *La mujer adúltera.* Date unknown. Promptbook #162, copy dated 1907, in the Carlos Villalongín Dramatic Company Collection. Benson Latin American Collection, University of Texas at Austin.

Villalongín, Carlos. Carlos Villalongín Dramatic Company Collection. Benson Latin American Collection, University of Texas at Austin.

INTERVIEWS AND CORRESPONDENCE

Sr. Lalo Astol and Sra. Susie Astol. Personal interviews and telephone interviews, San Antonio, Texas, 1981–1990.

Sra. Belia Camargo. Personal interview and telephone interviews, San Antonio, Texas, 1981–1982.

Maria Irene Fornes. Telephone interviews, Cambridge, Massachusetts, 1988; Personal interview, Northwest Theatre Conference, Eugene, Oregon, 1996.

Sra. Otila Garza. Telephone and personal interviews, Austin, Texas, 1981–82.

Jorge A. Huerta and Ginger Huerta. Correspondence, electronic mail, telephone, and personal interviews, 1971–1976 and 1998–1999.

Raul Julia. Telephone interview with Mr. Julia's publicist, Cambridge, Massachusetts, 1989.

Dorinda Moreno. Telephone interview, Los Angeles, California, 1973–1974.

Diane Rodríguez. Electronic mail and correspondence, San Antonio, Texas, 1998–1999.

Ruben Sierra. Correspondence, electronic mail, telephone interviews, and personal interviews, San Antonio, Texas, Los Angeles, California, and Eugene, Oregon, 1970–1998.

Estela Portillo Trambley. Personal interviews and correspondence, Sacramento, California, 1974–1976.

Luis Valdez and Lupe Valdez. Correspondence and telephone interviews, 1972–1982, 1992.

Sra. María Luisa Villalongín de Santos. Telephone interviews and personal interviews. San Antonio, Texas, 1981–1992.

BOOKS, ARTICLES, AND OTHER WORKS

Acuña, Rodolfo. *Occupied America: A History of Chicanos.* 3rd ed. New York: Harper-Collins Publishers, 1988.

Adorno, Theodor. *Negative Dialectics.* Trans. E. B. Ashton. New York: Seabury Press, 1973.

Alarcón, Norma. "The Theoretical Subject(s) of *This Bridge Called My Back* and Anglo-American Feminism." In *Criticism in the Borderlands,* ed. Hector Calderón and José Saldívar. Durham: Duke University Press, 1991. 28–38.

Alarcón, Norma, et al., ed. *Chicana Critical Issues.* Berkeley, Calif.: Third Woman Press, 1993.

Alatorre, Angeles Mendieta. *La mujer en la Revolución Mexicana.* Mexico City: Biblioteca Nacional de Estudios Históricos de la Revolución Mexicana, 1961, No. 25.

Antush, John V., ed. *Nuestro New York: An Anthology.* New York: Mentor, 1994.

Asi fue la Revolución Mexicana. Vol 5: *El Triunfo de la Revolución.* México: Consejo Nacional de Fomento Educativo, 1985.

Austin, Gayle. *Feminist Theories for Dramatic Criticism.* Ann Arbor: University of Michigan Press, 1990.

Austin, Mary. "Folkplays of the Southwest." *Theatre Arts Monthly* (August 1933): 599–606.

Bell, John. "*Huipil.*" *Theatre Week* (March 9, 1992). In Coatlicue Theatre Company Press Kit.

Bhabha, Homi. *Location of Culture.* New York: Routledge, 1994.

Blau, Herbert. *The Impossible Theater: A Manifesto.* New York: Collier Books, 1964.

Blauner, Robert. "Colonized and Immigrant Minorities." In *From Different Shores: Perspectives on Race and Ethnicity in America,* ed. Ronald Takaki. 2nd ed. New York: Oxford University Press, 1994.

Blea, Irene I. *La Chicana and the Intersection of Race, Class, and Gender.* New York: Praeger, 1992.

Brockett, Oscar G. *History of the Theatre.* 6th ed. Boston: Allyn & Bacon, 1991.

———. *History of the Theatre.* 7th ed. Boston: Allyn & Bacon, 1995.

Brockett, Oscar G., and Robert Findlay. *Century of Innovation: A History of European and American Theatre and Drama Since the Late Nineteenth Century.* 2nd ed. Boston: Allyn & Bacon, 1991.

Brokaw, John W. "A Mexican-American Acting Company, 1849–1924." *Educational Theatre Journal* 17 (March 1975): 23–29.

———. "Teatro Chicano: Some Reflections." *Educational Theatre Journal* 29 (December 1977): 535–544.

Broyles-González, Yolanda. *El Teatro Campesino: Theater in the Chicano Movement.* Austin: University of Texas Press, 1994.

Buck-Morss, Susan. *The Dialectics of Seeing: Walter Benjamin and the Arcades Project.* Cambridge, Mass.: MIT Press, 1989.

Candelaria, Cordelia. "La Malinche, Feminist Prototype." *Frontiers* 5, no. 2 (1980): 1–6.

Canning, Charlotte. *Feminist Theaters in the U.S.A.* New York: Routledge, 1996.

Cantú, Norma E. "Los Matachines de La Santa Cruz de la Ladrillera." In *Feasts & Celebrations in North American Ethnic Communities,* ed. Ramón A. Gutiérrez and Genevieve Fabre. Albuquerque: University of New Mexico Press, 1995. 57–67.

———. "Women, Then and Now: An Analysis of the Adelita Image versus the Chicana as Political Writer and Philosopher." In *Chicana Voices: Intersections of Class, Race, and Gender,* ed. Teresa Córdova, et al. Austin, Tex.: Center for Mexican American Studies, 1996. 8–10.

Case, Sue Ellen. *Feminism and Theatre.* New York: Methuen, 1988.

———. "Seduced and Abandoned: Chicanas and Lesbians in Representation." In *Negotiating Performance: Gender, Sexuality, and Theatricality in Latin/o America,* ed. Diana Taylor and Juan Villegas. Durham: Duke University Press, 1994. 88–101.

Caso, Alfonso. *The Aztecs: People of the Sun.* Norman: University of Oklahoma Press, 1958.

Castañeda, Antonia I. "The Political Economy of Nineteenth Century Stereotypes of Californianas." In *Between Borders: Essays on Mexicana/Chicana History,* ed. Adelaida R. Del Castillo. Encino, Calif.: Floricanto Press, 1990. 213–236.

———. "Presidarias y Pobladoras: The Journey North and Life in Frontier California." In *Chicana Critical Issues,* ed. Norma Alarcón, et al. Berkeley: Third Woman Press, 1993. 73–94.

Castañeda García, Carmen. "Fuentes para la historia de la mujer en los archivos de Guadalajara." In *Between Borders: Essays on Mexicana/Chicana History,* ed. Adelaida R. Del Castillo. Encino, Calif.: Floricanto Press, 1990. 101–112.

"Chicano Theatre." *Tenaz* 8, no. 5 (Spring 1972): 7–8.

Chipman, Donald E., and Harriett Denise Joseph. *Notable Men and Women of Spanish Texas.* Austin: University of Texas Press, 1999.

Córdova, Teresa, et al. *Chicana Voices: Intersections of Class, Race, and Gender.* Austin: Tex.: Center for Mexican American Studies, 1986.

Crónica de Madrid. Spain: Plaza & Janes Editores, S.A. 1990.

Cummings, Scott. "Seeing with Clarity: The Visions of Maria Irene Fornes." *Theater* 17, no. 1 (1985): 51–56.

Cypess, Sandra Messinger. *La Malinche in Mexican Literature: From History to Myth.* Austin: University of Texas Press, 1991.

Dahl, Mary Karen. *Political Violence in Drama: Classical Models, Contemporary Variations.* Ann Arbor, Mich.: UMI Research Press, 1987.

Davis, R. G. *The San Francisco Mime Troupe: The First Ten Years.* Palo Alto, Calif.: Ramparts Press, 1975.

Del Castillo, Adelaida R., ed. *Between Borders: Essays on Mexicana/Chicana History.* Encino, Calif.: Floricanto Press, 1990.

Dewey, Janice. "Doña Josefa: Blood-pulse of Transition and Change." In *Breaking Boundaries: Latina Writing and Critical Readings,* ed. Asuncion Horno Delgado, Eliana Ortega, Nina M. Scott, and Nancy Saporta Sternback. Amherst: University of Massachusetts Press, 1989.

Díez Borque, José María. *Historia del Teatro en España.* 3 vols. Madrid: Taurus, 1988.

Dolan, Jill. *The Feminist Spectator as Critic.* Ann Arbor: University of Michigan Press, 1988.

Driscoll, Barbara A. "Chicana Historiography: A Research Note Regarding Mexican Archival Sources." In *Chicana Voices: Intersections of Class, Race, and Gender,* ed. Teresa Córdova, et al. Austin, Tex.: Center for Mexican American Studies Publications, 1986. 136–145.

DuBois, Ellen Carol, and Vicki L. Ruíz, eds. *Unequal Sisters: A Multicultural Reader in U.S. Women's History.* New York: Routledge, 1990 and 1994.

Dworkin y Méndez, Kenya C. "The Tradition of Hispanic Theater and the WPA Federal Theatre Project in Tampa-Ybor City, Florida." In *Recovering the U.S. Hispanic Literary Heritage,* ed. Ramón Gutiérrez and Genevieve Fabre. Vol. 2. Houston, Tex.: Arte Público Press, 1996. 279–294.

Dysart, Jane. "Mexican Women in San Antonio, 1830–1860: The Assimilation Process." *Western Historical Quarterly* (October 1976): 366.

Espinosa, Mary Lou. "La Madre de Aztlan." In *Aztlan: An Anthology of Mexican American Literature,* ed. Luis Valdez and Stan Steiner. New York: Alfred A. Knopf, 1972. 279–280.

Estés, Clarissa Pinkola. *Women Who Run with the Wolves.* New York: Ballantine Books, 1992.

Feyder, Linda, ed. *Shattering the Myth: Plays by Hispanic Women.* Houston, Tex.: Arte Público Press, 1992. 113–141.

Fitzpatrick, Joseph P. *Puerto Rican Americans: The Meaning of Migration to the Mainland.* 2nd ed. New York: Prentice Hall, 1987.

Flores, Richard R. *Los Pastores: History and Performance in the Mexican Shepherd's Play of South Texas.* Washington, D.C.: Smithsonian Institution Press, 1995.

Fornes, Maria Irene. *The Conduct of Life.* In *Maria Irene Fornes: Plays.* New York: PAJ Publications, 1986. Also in M. Lizabeth Osborn, ed., *On New Ground: Contemporary Hispanic-American Plays.* New York: Theatre Communications Group, 1987.

Franco, Jean. *Plotting Women: Gender and Representation in Mexico.* New York: Columbia University Press, 1989.

Funes, Concepción Ruíz, and Enriqueta Tuñón. "Panorama de las Luchas de la Mujer Mexicana en el Siglo XX." In *Between Borders: Essays on Mexicana/Chicana History,* ed. Adelaida R. Del Castillo. Encino, Calif.: Floricanto Press, 1990. 336–357.

Gamio, Manuel. *Mexican Immigration in the United States.* Chicago: University of Chicago Press, 1930.

García, Alma M. "The Development of Chicana Feminist Discourse, 1970–1980." In *From Different Shores: Perspectives on Race and Ethnicity in America,* ed. Ronald Takaki. 2nd ed. New York: Oxford University Press, 1994. 175–183. Also in *Unequal Sisters: A Multicultural Reader in U.S. Women's History,* ed. Vicki L. Ruíz and Ellen Carol Dubois. 2nd ed. New York: Routledge, 1994. 531–544.

————. "Studying Chicanas: Bringing Women into the Frame of Chicano Studies." In *Chicana Voices: Intersections of Class, Race, and Gender*, ed. Teresa Córdova, et al. Austin, Tex.: Center for Mexican American Studies, 1986. 19–29.

García, Mario T. "Border Culture." In *From Different Shores: Perspectives on Race and Ethnicity in America*, ed. Ronald Takaki. New York: Oxford University Press, 1994. 72–81.

————. "La Familia: The Mexican Immigrant Family, 1900–1930." In *Work, Family, Sex Roles, Language*, ed. Mario Barrera, Albert Camarillo, and Francisco Hernandez. Berkeley: Tonatiuh-Quinto Sol, 1980. 117–139.

————. "Obreros: The Mexican Workers of El Paso, 1900–1920." Ph.D. diss., University of California, San Diego, 1975.

Garibay, Angel María. *Historia de la literatura náhuatl.* 2 vols. México: Editorial Porrúa, 1987.

Garza, Roberto J. *Contemporary Chicano Theatre.* Notre Dame, Ind.: University of Notre Dame Press, 1976.

Gillmor, Frances. "Spanish Texts of Three Dance Dramas from Mexican Villages." *University of Arizona Bulletin* 13 (October 1, 1942): 3–83.

Gómez-Peña, Guillermo. "The Multicultural Paradigm: An Open Letter to the National Arts Community." In *Negotiating Performance: Gender, Sexuality, and Theatricality in Latin/o America*, ed. Diana Taylor and Juan Villegas. Durham: Duke University Press, 1994. 17–29.

Gómez-Quiñones, Juan. *Chicano Politics: Reality and Promise 1940–1990.* Albuquerque: University of New Mexico Press, 1990.

————. *Development of the Mexican Working Class North of the Rio Bravo.* Popular Series No. 2, Chicano Studies Research Center Publications. Los Angeles: University of California, Los Angeles, 1982.

————. "Questions within Women's Historiography." In *Between Borders: Essays on Mexicana/Chicana History,* ed. Adelaida R. Del Castillo. Encino, Calif.: Floricanto Press, 1990.

Gonzalez, Maria. "Love and Conflict: Mexican American Women Writers as Daughters." In *Women of Color: Mother-Daughter Relationships in 20th-Century Literature*, ed. Elizabeth Brown-Guillory. Austin, Tex.: University of Texas Press, 1996. 153–169.

González, María R. "El embrión nacionalista visto a través de la obra de Sor Juana Inés de la Cruz." In *Between Borders: Essays on Mexicana/Chicana History,* ed. Adelaida R. Del Castillo. Encino, Calif.: Floricanto Press, 1990. 237–253.

Gutiérrez, David. *Walls and Mirrors: Mexican Americans, Mexican Immigrants, and the Politics of Ethnicity.* Berkeley: University of California Press, 1995.

Gutiérrez, Ramón. "Marriage and Seduction in Colonial New Mexico." In *Between Borders: Essays on Mexicana/Chicana History,* ed. Adelaida R. Del Castillo. Encino, Calif.: Floricanto Press, 1990. 447–457.

Gutiérrez, Ramón A., and Genevieve Fabre, eds. *Feasts & Celebrations in North American Ethnic Communities.* Albuquerque: University of New Mexico Press, 1995.

Gutiérrez, Ramón, and Genaro Padilla, eds. *Recovering the U.S. Hispanic Literary Heritage.* Houston, Tex.: Arte Público Press, 1993.

Herrera-Sobek, Maria. "The Mexican/Chicano Pastorela." In *Feasts & Celebrations in North American Ethnic Communities,* ed. Ramón A. Gutiérrez and Genevieve Fabre. Albuquerque: University of New Mexico Press, 1995. 47–56.

Heyck, Denis Lynn Daly. *Barrios and Borderlands: Cultures of Latinos and Latinas in the United States.* New York: Routledge, 1994.

Huerta, Jorge A. *Chicano Theater: Themes and Forms.* Ypsilanti, Mich.: Bilingual Press, 1982.

———. "The Evolution of Chicano Theater." Ph.D. diss., University of California, Santa Barbara, 1974.

———. "Looking for the Magic: Chicanos in the Mainstream." In *Negotiating Performance: Gender, Sexuality, and Theatricality in Latin/o America,* ed. Diana Taylor and Juan Villegas. Durham: Duke University Press, 1994.

———. "Moraga's *Heroes and Saints*: Chicano Theatre for the '90s'." *TheatreForum* 1 (Spring 1992): 49–52.

———. *Necessary Theater: Six Plays about the Chicano Experience.* Houston, Tex.: Arte Público Press, 1989.

Jameson, Fredric. *The Political Unconscious: Narrative as a Socially Symbolic Act.* Ithaca, N.Y.: Cornell University Press, 1991.

Jay, Julia De Foor. "(Re)claiming the Race of the Mother." In *Women of Color: Mother-Daughter Relationships in 20th-Century Literature,* ed. Elizabeth Brown-Guillory. Austin: University of Texas Press, 1996. 95–111.

Jones, Willis Knapp. *Behind Spanish American Footlights.* Austin: University of Texas Press, 1966.

Kanellos, Nicholas. *A History of Hispanic Theatre in the United States: Origins to 1940.* Austin: University of Texas Press, 1990.

Kent, Assunta Bartolomucci. *Maria Irene Fornes and Her Critics.* Westport, Conn.: Greenwood Press, 1996.

La Independencia de México. México: Instituto Nacional de Estadística, Geografía e Informática, 1985.

Leinaweaver, Richard E., trans. *"Rabinal Achí."* *Latin American Theatre Review* 1 (Spring 1969): 3–53.

León-Portilla, Miguel. *Pre-Columbian Literatures of Mexico.* Norman: University of Oklahoma Press, 1969.

Limón, Jóse E. "La Llorona, The Third Legend of Greater Mexico: Cultural Symbols, Women, and the Political Unconscious." In *Between Borders: Essays on Mexicana/Chicana History,* ed. Adelaida R. Del Castillo. Encino, Calif.: Floricanto Press, 1990. 399–432.

Longauez y Vasquez, Enriqueta. "The Woman of La Raza." In *Aztlan: An Anthology of Mexican American Literature.* ed. Luis Valdez and Stan Steiner. New York: Alfred A. Knopf, 1972. 272–278.

López, Josefina. *Simply María; or, The American Dream.* In *Shattering the Myth: Plays by Hispanic Women,* ed. Linda Feyder. Houston, Tex.: Arte Público Press, 1992.

Magaña-Esquivel, Antonio. *Breve Historia del Teatro Mexicano.* Mexico City: Ediciones de Andrea, 1958.

Malvido, Elsa. "El Uso del Cuerpo Feminino en la Epoca Colonial Mexicana a Través de los Estudios de Demografía Histórica." In *Between Borders: Essays on Mexicana/Chicana History,* ed. Adelaida R. Del Castillo. Encino, Calif.: Floricanto Press, 1990. 113–130.

Mañon, Manuel. *Historia del Teatro Principal de México.* México: Editorial "Cultura," 1932.

Marrero, María Teresa. "Chicano and Latino Self-Representation in Theater and Performance Art." Ph.D. diss., University of California, Irvine, 1992.

McWilliams, Carey. *North from Mexico: The Spanish-Speaking People of the United States.* New York: Greenwood Press, 1968.

Montejano, David. *Anglos and Mexicans in the Making of Texas, 1836–1989.* Austin: University of Texas Press, 1987.

Monterde, Francisco. *Bibliografía del teatro en México.* New York: Burt Franklin, 1970.

Moraga, Cherríe. *Heroes and Saints and Other Plays.* Albuquerque: West End Press, 1994.

———. *Heroes and Saints.* In *Contemporary Plays by Women of Color,* ed. Kathy A. Perkins and Roberta Uno. New York: Routledge, 1996. 230–261.

Moroff, Diane Lynn. *Fornes: Theater in the Present Tense.* Ann Arbor: University of Michigan Press, 1996.

Mulvey, Laura. "Visual Pleasure and Narrative Cinema." In *Modern Feminisms: Political, Literary, Cultural,* ed. Maggie Humm. New York: Columbia University Press, 1992.

Murguia, Edward. *Assimilation, Colonialism and the Mexican American People.* Austin, Tex.: Center for Mexican American Studies, 1975. 1–124.

Odell, George C. D. *Annals of the New York Stage.* Vol. 1. New York: Columbia University Press, 1927.

Olavarría y Ferrari, Enrique de. *Reseña historical del teatro en México: 1538–1911.* 5 vols. Mexico City: Editorial Porrua, S.A., 1961.

Orozco, Cynthia E. "The Origins of the League of United Latin American Citizens (LULAC) and the Mexican American Civil Rights Movement in Texas with an Analysis of Women's Political Participation in a Gendered Context, 1910–1929." Ph.D. diss., University of California, Los Angeles, 1993.

Ortego, Philip D. "The Chicano Renaissance." In *Introduction to Chicano Studies: A Reader,* ed. Livie Isauro Duran and H. Russell Bernard. New York: Macmillan, 1973. 331–335.

Osborn, M. Lizabeth, ed. *On New Ground: Contemporary Hispanic-American Plays.* New York: Theatre Communications Group, 1987.

Pablos, Julia Tuñon. *Women in Mexico: A Past Unveiled.* Trans. Alan Hynds. Austin: University of Texas Press, 1999.

Paredes, Américo. *A Texas-Mexican "Cancionero": Folksongs of the Lower Border.* Urbana: University of Illinois Press, 1976.

———. *"With His Pistol in His Hand": A Border Ballad and Its Hero.* Urbana: University of Illinois Press, 1958.

Paredes, Raymund. "Mexican-American Literature: An Overview." In *Recovering the U.S. Hispanic Literary Heritage,* ed. Ramón Gutiérrez and Genaro Padilla. Houston, Tex.: Arte Público Press, 1993. 31–51.

Pérez, Emma M. "'A La Mujer': A Critique of the Partido Liberal Mexicano's Gender Ideology on Women." In *Between Borders: Essays on Mexicana/Chicana History,* ed. Adelaida R. Del Castillo. Encino, Calif.: Floricanto Press, 1990. 459–482.

Perkins, Kathy A., and Roberta Uno, eds. *Contemporary Plays by Women of Color.* New York: Routledge, 1996.

Pesquera, Beatriz M., and Denise M. Segura. "There is No Going Back: Chicanas and Feminism." In *Chicana Critical Issues,* ed. Norma Alarcón et al. Berkeley, Calif.: Third Woman Press, 1993.

Poggi, Jack. *Theatre in America: The Impact of Economic Forces, 1870–1967.* Ithaca, N.Y.: Cornell University Press, 1968.

Portillo, Estela. *The Day of the Swallows.* In *El Espejo—The Mirror: Selected Chicano Literature,* ed. Octavio Ignacio Romano-V and Herminio Rios C. Berkeley, Calif.: Quinto Sol Publications, Inc., 1972. 151–193. Also in *Contemporary Chicano The-*

atre, ed. Robert J. Garza. Notre Dame, Ind.: University of Notre Dame Press, 1976. 205–245.

Portillo Trambley, Estela. *"Sor Juana" and Other Plays.* Ypsilanti, Mich.: Bilingual Press, 1983.

Pottlitzer, Joanne. *Hispanic Theatre in the United States and Puerto Rico.* New York: Ford Foundation, 1988.

Quirk, Robert E. *Mexico.* Englewood Cliffs, N.J.: Prentice Hall, 1971.

Ramírez, Elizabeth C. "The Annals of Chicano Theater: 1965–1973." M.A. thesis, University of California, Los Angeles, 1974.

———. "Combination Companies on the American Stage: Organization & Practice in Texas." *Theatre History Studies* (1989): 77–91.

———. "[Compañía Juan B.] Padilla" and "[Compañía] Villalongín." In *American Theatre Companies, 1888–1930,* ed. Weldon Durham. Westport, Conn.: Greenwood Press, 1986.

———. "Contextualizing Chicanas: The Emerging Female as Subject on the American Stage during the Mexican Revolution." Forthcoming in *Latinas on Stage: Criticism and Practice,* ed. Lilliana Mansor and Alicia Arrizón. Berkeley, Calif.: Third World Press. 360–390.

———. "Estela Portillo Trambley." *Latin American Theatre Review* (Spring 1984): 103–104.

———. *Footlights across the Border: A History of Spanish-Language Professional Theatre on the Texas Stage.* New York: Peter Lang Publishing, 1990.

———. "Hispanic American Women on the Texas Stage." In *Women in Texas History: Selected Essays,* ed. Fane Downs and Nancy Baker Jones. Austin: Texas Historical Association, 1993a. 34–41.

———. "José Rivera." *Cambridge Guide to American Theatre,* ed. Don B. Wilmeth and Tice L. Miller. Cambridge: Cambridge University Press, 1993b, 399–400.

———. "Maria Irene Fornes and Her Critics." *Choice* 34, no. 4 (December 1996), p. 624.

Ravicz, Marilyn Ekdahl, trans. *Early Colonial Religious Drama in Mexico: From Tzompantli to Golgotha.* Washington, D.C.: Catholic University of America Press, 1970.

Rebolledo, Tey Diana. *Women Singing in the Snow.* Tucson: University of Arizona Press, 1995.

———, ed. *Nuestras Mujeres Hispanas of New Mexico.* Albuquerque, N.M.: El Norte Publications, 1992.

Rebolledo, Tey Diana, and Eliana S. Rivero. *Infinite Divisions: An Anthology of Chicana Literature.* Tucson: University of Arizona Press, 1993.

Reyes de la Maza, Luis. *El teatro en México.* México: U.N.A.M., 1953–1970.

Romano-V, Octavio Ignacio, and Herminio Rios C., eds. *El Espejo—The Mirror: Selected Chicano Literature.* Berkeley, Calif.: Quinto Sol Publications, Inc., 1972.

Romo, Ricardo. *History of a Barrio: East Los Angeles.* Austin, Tex.: University of Texas Press, 1983.

———. "The Urbanization of Southwestern Chicanos in the Early Twentieth Century." *New Scholar* 6 (1977): 183–207.

Rosenbaum, Robert J. *Mexicano Resistance in the Southwest: "The Sacred Right of Self-Preservation."* Austin: University of Texas Press, 1981.

Ruíz, Ramón Eduardo. *The Great Rebellion: Mexico 1905–1924.* New York: W.W. Norton and Company, 1980.

Ruíz, Vicki L. *From Out of the Shadows: Mexican Women in Twentieth-Century America.* New York: Oxford University Press, 1998.

————. "Obreras y Madres: Labor Activism among Mexican Women and Its Impact on the Family." In *La Mexicana/Chicana,* Renato Rosaldo Lecture Series, vol. I, Series 1983–84, Summer 1985: 19–38. Tucson: Mexican American Studies and Research Center, University of Arizona.

Said, Edward. *Orientalism.* New York: Vintage Books, 1979.

Salas, Elizabeth. *Soldaderas in the Mexican Military: Myth and History.* Austin: University of Texas Press, 1990.

Saldaña, Hector. "Latina Comic Ready for Liftoff." *San Antonio Express-News,* February 4, 1998, S.A. Life 1G, 126.

Saldívar, José David. *Border Matters.* Berkeley: University of California Press, 1997.

————. "Chicano Border Narratives as Cultural Critique." In *Criticism in the Borderlands: Studies in Chicano Literature, Culture, and Ideology,* ed. Hector Calderón and José David Saldívar. Durham: Duke University Press, 1991. 167–180.

Saldívar, Ramón. *Chicano Narrative: The Dialectics of Difference.* Madison: University of Wisconsin Press, 1990.

————. "Narrative, Ideology, and the Reconstruction of American Literary History." In *Criticism in the Borderlands: Studies in Chicano Literature, Culture, and Ideology,* ed. Hector Calderón and José David Saldívar. Durham: Duke University Press, 1991. 11–20.

Saldívar-Hull, Sonia. "Feminism on the Border: From Gender Politics to Geopolitics." In *Criticism in the Borderlands: Studies in Chicano Literature, Culture, and Ideology,* ed. Hector Calderón and José David Saldívar. Durham: Duke University Press, 1991. 203–220.

Sánchez, Rosaura. "The History of Chicanas: Proposal for a Materialist Perspective." In *Between Borders: Essays on Mexicana/Chicana History,* ed. Adelaida R. Del Castillo. Encino, Calif.: Floricanto Press, 1990. 1–29.

Sanchez-Scott, Milcha. *Dog Lady* and *The Cuban Swimmer.* New York: Dramatists Play Service, 1988.

————. *Roosters.* New York: Dramatists Play Service, 1988. Also in *On New Ground: Contemporary Hispanic-American Plays,* ed. M. Lizabeth Osborn. New York: Theatre Communications Group, 1987.

Sandoval, Alberto. "Staging AIDS: What's Latino Got to Do With It?" In *Negotiating Performance: Gender, Sexuality, and Theatricality in Latin/o America,* ed. Diana Taylor and Juan Villegas. Durham: Duke University Press, 1994. 49–66.

Sandoval, Moisés. *On the Move: A History of the Hispanic Church in the United States.* New York: Orbis, 1990.

Savran, David. "Border Tactics: Luis Valdez Distills the Chicano Experience on Stage and Film." *American Theatre Magazine* (January 1988): 14–21, 56–57.

Schechner, Richard. "An Intercultural Primer." *American Theatre Magazine* (October 1991): 28–31, 135–136.

Schlissel, Lillian, Vicki L. Ruíz, and Janice Monk. *Western Women: Their Land, Their Lives.* Albuquerque: University of New Mexico Press, 1988.

Shergold, N. D. *A History of the Spanish Stage: From Medieval Times until the End of the Seventeenth Century.* Oxford: Clarendon Press, 1967.

Shorris, Earl. *Latinos: A Biography of the People.* New York: Avon Books, 1992.

Showalter, Elaine. *Sexual Anarchy: Gender and Culture at the Fin de Siècle.* New York: Penguin Books, 1990.

Smith, Pamela A., and Elizabeth C. Ramírez. "Beatriz Escalona Pérez." In *The New Handbook of Texas.* Austin: Texas Historical Association, 1996. 888–889.

Solomon, Alisa. "House and Home." *The Village Voice,* March 25, 1997, Theater, 101.

Soto, Shirlene. *The Emergence of the Modern Mexican Woman: Her Participation in Revolution and Struggle for Equality 1910–1940.* Denver: Arden, 1990.

———. "The Women's Movement in Mexico: The First and Second Feminist Congresses in Yucatan, 1916." In *Between Borders: Essays on Mexicana/Chicana History,* ed. Adelaida R. Del Castillo. Encino, Calif.: Floricanto Press, 1990. 483–491.

Spivak, Gayatri Chakravorty. "Imperialism and Sexual Difference." In *Contemporary Literary Criticism,* ed. Robert Con Davis and Ronald Schleifer. 2nd ed. New York: Longman, 1989.

Steck, Francis Borgia. *Motolinia's History of the Indians of New Spain.* Washington: Academy of American Franciscan History, 1959.

Steiner, Stan. *La Raza: The Mexican Americans.* New York: Harper Colophon, 1970.

Stolcke, Verena. "Invaded Women: Gender, Race, and Class in the Formation of Colonial Society." In *Women, "Race," and Writing in the Early Modern Period,* ed. Margo Hendricks and Patricia Parker. New York: Routledge, 1994.

Suleiman, Susan Rubin. *Subversive Intent: Gender, Politics, and the Avant-Garde.* Cambridge, Mass.: Harvard University Press, 1990.

Takaki, Ronald. *A Different Mirror: A History of Multicultural America.* Boston: Little, Brown and Company, 1993.

Taylor, Diana. *Theatre of Crisis: Drama and Politics in Latin America.* Lexington: University Press of Kentucky, 1991.

Tyler, Ron, et al., eds. *The New Texas Handbook.* 6 vols. Austin: Texas State Historical Association, 1996.

U.S. Bureau of the Census. *Fifteenth Census of the United States: 1930. Abstract of the Census.* Table 94. Washington, D.C.: Government Printing Office, 1931. 179.

U.S. Bureau of the Census. *The Hispanic Population in the United States: March 1986 and March 1987.* Advance Report, ser. P20 #416. Washington, D.C.: Government Printing Office, 1986. 2, 5.

U.S. Bureau of the Census Estimates Reports. *Estimates Report of the Population of Puerto Rico and the Outlying Areas: 1980–1986.* #P25–1009. Washington, D.C.: U.S. Government Printing Office, 1986. 7.

Usigli, Rodolfo. *Mexico in the Theatre.* Trans. Wilder E. Scott. University, Miss: University of Mississippi Romance Monographs, 1975.

Valdez, Luis. *Actos.* San Juan Bautista, Calif.: Menyah Productions, 1971.

———. *Dark Root of a Scream.* In *From the Barrio: A Chicano Anthology,* compiled by Lillian Faderman and Omar Salinas. San Francisco: Canfield, 1973. 79–98.

Valdez, Luis, and Stan Steiner, eds. *Aztlan: An Anthology of Mexican American Literature.* New York: Alfred A. Knopf, 1972.

Varona, Frank de. *Latino Literacy: The Complete Guide to Our Hispanic History and Culture.* New York: Henry Holt and Company, 1996.

Veyna, Angelina F. "Women in Early New Mexico: A Preliminary View." In *Chicana Voices: Intersections of Class, Race, and Gender,* ed. Teresa Córdova, et al. Austin: Center for Mexican American Studies, University of Texas at Austin, 1986. 120–135.

Villegas, Juan. "Closing Remarks." In *Negotiating Performance,* ed. Diana Taylor and Juan Villegas. Durham, N.C.: Duke University Press, 1994. 306–320.

Waite, Rachel Chipman. "Milcha Sanchez-Scott: An Emerging Latina Voice." M.A. thesis, University of Oregon, 1993.

Waller, Marguerite. "*Border* Boda or *Divorce* Fronterizo." In *Negotiating Performance: Gender, Sexuality, and Theatricality in Latin/o America,* ed. Diana Taylor and Juan Villegas. Durham, N.C.: Duke University Press, 1994. 67–87.

Wilmeth, Don B., and Tice L. Miller. *Cambridge Guide to American Theatre*. New York: Cambridge University Press, 1993.

Worthen, W. B. *Modern Drama: Plays, Criticism, Theory*. New York: Harcourt Brace and Company, 1995.

———. "Staging América: The Subject of History in Chicano/a Theatre." *Theatre Journal* 49, no. 2 (May 1997): 101–120.

Yarbro-Bejarano, Yvonne. "The Female Subject in Chicano Theatre: Sexuality, 'Race,' and Class." In *Performing Feminisms: Feminist Critical Theory and Theatre*, ed. Sue Ellen Case. Baltimore: Johns Hopkins University Press, 1990. 131–149.

Zoraida Vasquez, Josefina. "Educación y Papel de la Mujer en México." In *Between Borders: Essays on Mexicana/Chicana History*, ed. Adelaida R. Del Castillo. Encino, Calif.: Floricanto Press, 1990. 375–398.

NEWSPAPERS

"2 Plays, $5, A Bargain." *New York Times*, March 16, 1990, C 19.

Anderson, Porter. "Teasers & Tormentors: Bay Area Play Area." *The Village Voice*, August 30, 1994, 82.

Arkatov, Janice. "Big Mix: Theater." *Los Angeles Times*, February 5, 1989, Calendar 98.

Bass, Shermakaye. "Latinos at Center Stage." *Austin American-Statesman*, June 20, 1997, Lifestyle, E1.

Bayley, Clare. "Theatre." *The Independent*, October 16, 1991, Arts 19.

Bommer, Lawrence. "'Flowers' Explores Aftermath of a Tragedy." *Chicago Tribune*, August 30, 1991, CN 6.

Bower, Tom. "Hispanic Count on the Increase." *San Antonio Express-News*, September 4, 1998, Section M, B1.

Brennan, Mary. "Life in Abundance Underneath the Arches." *The Herald* (Glasgow), October 25, 1994, 21.

Churnin, Nancy. "Hodgepodge on Gays, Lesbians." *Los Angeles Times*, November 23, 1991, F1.

El Demócrata Fronterizo, Laredo, Tex., December 22, 1906, 2.

Evans, Greg. "Artist Residence Awards Granted." *Variety*, November 22, 1993, Legit 77.

Evolución, Laredo, Tex., December 14, 1918, 4.

Goldman, Saundra. "Face to Face with Mythology." *Austin American-Statesman*, June 4, 1994, 13.

Graham, Renee. "Gay and Lesbian Latinos Come Out with Humor." *The Boston Globe*, April 14, 1994, 58.

Grahnke, Lon. "Expanding Horizons: PBS 'Playhouse' Reaches Out With Hispanic Drama." *Chicago Sun-Times*, June 16, 1993, Sec. 2, 51.

Hampton, Wilborn. "Theater in Review." *New York Times*, June 12, 1991, C 14.

Jones, Welton. "'Blood Wedding' Slowed by Several Shortcomings." *The San Diego Union-Tribune*, October 21, 1985, Lifestyle E6.

La Prensa, San Antonio, Tex., April 6, 1915, 8; November 21, 1917, 7; February 18, 1918, 2; "Benavente vuelve muy satisfecho a México," March 26, 1923, 1; December 9, 1926, 5, 10; "'Una mujer sin importancia' de Oscar Wilde en el Teatro Nacional," November 26, 1926, 5; "'El abanico de Lady Windemere' de Oscar Wilde," December 5, 1926, 15; May 2, 1928, 6, 9.

Lawson, Kyle. "'Our Lady' Grants Wish for Comedy." *The Arizona Republic*, May 9, 1997, Weekend D5.

Martinez, Al. "Always Leave 'Em Thinking." *Los Angeles Times,* February 26, 1991, B2.

McKenna, Kristine. "An Artist Is Uncaged." *Los Angeles Times,* September 14, 1993, F1.

Obejas, Achy. "A Dynamic Duo Fits Into One Performer." *Chicago Tribune,* October 25, 1996, 34.

O'Connell, Joseph. "Pair of Latino Films Shine at SXSW Film Fest." *San Antonio Express-News,* March 23, 1999, 3E.

Pear, Robert. "New Look at the U.S. in 2050: Bigger, Older and Less White." *New York Times,* December 4, 1992, A1, 10.

Pincus, Robert L. "Substantial Slapstick." *San Diego Union-Tribune,* September 19, 1993, E1.

Powell, Stewart M. "Hispanics Gain Explosive Clout in Voting Booth." *San Antonio Express-News,* October 11, 1998, 1A.

Rubio, Jeff. "Theatre Review: 'My Visits' Counters Hispanic Stereotypes with Comedic Charm." *The Orange County Register,* June 3, 1992, Show F6.

Shirley, Don. "Setting the Latino Theatre Company Stage: Theater." *Los Angeles Times,* May 4, 1996, Calendar F2.

Stamets, Bill. "Fest Spotlights Women Directors." *Chicago Sun-Times,* March 15, 1994, 2:33.

Sullivan, Dan. "Homecoming of a Dead GI." *Los Angeles Times,* September 25, 1971, Section II, 8.

Vargas, Daniel J. "Honoring César Chávez: Play, March to Celebrate Life of Labor Leader, Activist." *San Antonio Express-News,* March 23, 1999, 1E, 8E.

Weiss, Hedy. "Excellent Performances Lift 'Lucy Loves Me.'" *Chicago Sun-Times,* March 11, 1992, 2:37.

Welsh, Anne Marie. "Sushi Festival Celebrates Female Performance Art." *The San Diego Union-Tribune,* March 6, 1997, Entertainment, Night & Day 4.

INDEX

Italicized page numbers refer to illustrations.

García Lorca, Federico, 90, 106, 134, 142, 147

García Márquez, Gabriel, 149

Garza, Dolores, *21*

Gavin, Ellen, 120, 153

Gelber, Jack, 149

gender politics, 125; La Malinche and, 35–36; Moraga and, 119; in *Roosters*, 112; Spanish-language theatre and, 42–48

Giving Up the Ghost (Moraga), 119

godmothering (*comadrazgo*), 83

Gold Rush, California, 74

Gomez, Marga, 126–27

Gómez-Peña, Guillermo, 130, 149, 150–51, 156, 164n5(2)

Gómez-Quiñones, Juan, 58–59, 80, 83

González, Irene, 145

Gonzalez, Maria, 28

González, Rodolfo "Corky," 78

González, Sylvia, 140

Gotanda, Philip Kan, 132

Gramercy Arts Theatre, New York, N.Y., Repertorio Español, 142

Great Depression, 51, 56

Great Theatre of the World, The (El gran teatro del mundo), 4

Greenwood, Jane, 146

Greenwood, Lee, 146

Greetings From a Queer Señorita (Palacios), 127

Griswold del Castillo, Richard, 159–60n6

Guadalupe Cultural Arts Center, San Antonio, Tex., 148–49

Guerrero, María, 16

"guerrilla" theatre, 60

Guild of Catholic Women, St. Paul, Minn., 52

Guimerá, Ángel, 13

Gutiérrez, Andrés Valenzuela, *84*

Gutiérrez, David G., 49–50, 58, 159–60n6

Guys and Dolls, 144

Hansberry, Lorraine, 144

"happening" form, 64

Have-Little, The (Cruz), 132, 133

Hernández, Antonia Pineda de, *11,* 11–12

Hernández, Concepción, 12–15, *13,* 158n10

Hernández, Encarnación, 11

Hernández, Herlinda, 12

Hernández, Luis, 12, 158n2

Hernández-Villalongín Company, 12

Heroes and Saints (Moraga), 119, 120–24

Hispanic, defined, 157n1(1)

Hispanic American Dramatic Club, Las Vegas, N.M., 52

Hispanic Playwrights-in-Residence Laboratory, New York, N.Y., 101

Historia de la Nueva México (History of New Mexico), 7

History of a Barrio: East Los Angeles (Romo), 50

homophobia, 105, 126

homosexuality, 105–106, 123

House of Bernarda Alba, The (García Lorca), 106, 142

House of Ramon Iglesias, The (Rivera), 149

How Else Am I Supposed to Know I'm Still Alive (Fernández), 116, 139–40

huelga (strike), 70–72

Huerta, Dolores, 121

Huerta, Ginger, 94

Huerta, Jorge, 61; on Chicana/Chicano theatre, 69, 125, 156, 161n16; and El Teatro de la Esperanza, 86, 94; on ethnospecific theatre, 106; on Euroamerican women directors, 163n2; on *Los vendidos,* 74; on Moraga, 118, 120, 123–24; on use of masks, 66–67; on use of serpents in *auto sacramentales,* 6

Huitzilopóchtli, 2, 162n7

I Don't Have to Show You No Stinking Badges! (Valdez), 125

I Get Nothing Out of School (No saco nada de la escuela), 77

identity politics, 103–104, 128–31, 135; in *Heroes and Saints,* 122–23; Margo Gomez and, 126–27; in *Milk of Amnesia,* 127–28; in *Real Women Have Curves,* 116–18

immigration: Latina/Latino, 50–51; Mexican, 18, 22, 24–26, 38–39, 49–50

Impossible Theater: A Manifesto, The (Blau), 62

improvisation, 63–65

indigenous mythology, 1–4; in plays by Portillo Trambley, 107–108; in plays by Valdez, 87–91; in productions by Colorado Sisters, 136–39

INTAR (International Arts Relations), 101–102, 110–11, 119; playwright-in-residence program, 134; and playwriting workshops by Fornes, 132

interculturalism, 104, 129–30, 156, 164n5(2)

Irving, Jules, 62, 65

It Can't Happen Here, 56

ELIZABETH C. RAMÍREZ is Director of Theatre and the Fine Arts Department at St. Philip's College. She is author of *Footlights Across the Border: A History of Spanish-Language Professional Theatre* and numerous articles and reviews on Chicana/Chicano/Latina/Latino theatre and multiculturalism and diversity in performance and in higher education. She has also served as dramaturg for Anne Bogart, Andrei Serban, David Wheeler, Ed Call, and Gary Gisselman, and most recently Jim Edmundson for the Oregon Shakespeare Festival's production of *Blood Wedding*.